100 THINGS STEELERS FANS
SHOULD KNOW & DO
BEFORE THEY DIE

Matt Loede

TRIUMPH
BOOKS

The Library of Congress has catalogued the previous edition as follows:

Loede, Matt.
 100 things Steelers fans should know and do before they die / Matt Loede.
 p. cm.
 ISBN 978-1-60078-384-5
 1. Pittsburgh Steelers (Football team)—Miscellanea. I. Title. II. Title: One hundred things Steelers fan should know and do before they die.
 GV956.P57L64 2010
 796.3329640974886—dc22

                                                              2010009732

This book is available in quantity at special discounts for your group or organization. For further information, contact:
 Triumph Books LLC
 814 North Franklin Street
 Chicago, Illinois 60610
 (312) 337-0747
 www.triumphbooks.com

Printed in U.S.A.
ISBN: 978-1-60078-871-0
Design by Patricia Frey
Photos courtesy of AP Images unless otherwise indicated

To my two heroes in life, my mom and dad, and to Steelers fans everywhere

Contents

1 "The Chief," Art Rooney

Hall of Fame Steelers quarterback Terry Bradshaw called him "the greatest man who ever walked." He was the face of the Pittsburgh Steelers and still is to this day, two decades after his passing. He was known as "the Chief," and even today it's hard to find any aspect of the Steelers that Art Rooney's fingerprints are not on. Why are the Steelers arguably the most successful franchise in the history of the game? Rooney. It was not only the way the franchise was run, starting at the top, it was his approach to treating people—both on and off the field.

"From day one my father set the tone on how the Steelers operate," Dan Rooney said of his dad. "He has always said that what the people think is important, and that we have to think that way. He very much felt that everyone was his equal. You must treat people with respect."

Respect was something that Rooney and the Steelers didn't have for decades after they were formed in July 1933 as part of the Eastern Division of the 10-team NFL. The franchise started as the Pirates and underwent a few name changes before they finally became the Steelers before the 1940 season. The names changed, but the losing for Rooney continued, that is, until 30 years later, as the team finally turned the corner.

And once it turned that corner, Rooney and his franchise took off like a freight train. There was the move to the new Three Rivers Stadium, the hiring of Chuck Noll as head coach, the drafting of Hall of Fame players like "Mean" Joe Greene, Bradshaw, Mike Webster, Lynn Swann, Jack Ham, Jack Lambert, and many more.

It seemed only fitting that it would finally pay off for Rooney and the club. In the 1970s the Steelers won seven AFC Central titles, four conference championships, and four Super Bowls (1974, '75, '78, and '79). It was commonplace in the '70s to see Rooney standing with a cigar, hugging yet another Lombardi Trophy after another Super Bowl victory.

What made Rooney so special, though, wasn't the winning, it was the way he dealt with the club and the people who were involved with it. In today's cutthroat world of business, where only the strong survive, Rooney never treated anyone with anything less than respect—from a despised opponent on the field to an 11-year-old ballboy at practice during training camp.

"He always had good things to say, encouraging words, and a pat on the back," Steelers Hall of Fame running back Franco Harris said of Rooney. "It was really wonderful because leadership is everything. You can tell an organization by how the people conduct themselves at the top."

While Rooney turned over most of the operations of the Steelers to son Dan in the mid-1960s, he still was there on a daily basis, talking to players, people involved with the team, and attended every game, enjoying the fruits of his labor with the winning the team did after years of futility.

When Rooney passed away on August 25, 1988, following a stroke at the age of 87, the NFL world, the Steelers, and the city of

Tribute to the Chief

Two years after owner Art Rooney's death, a statue to honor his legacy was erected. The bronze statue, which was built by Raymond Kaskey, is a figure of Rooney sitting down with his trademark cigar in hand. The statue was the idea of John Howel, a Pittsburgh native, who did the fund-raising for the cost. More than 7,000 individuals contributed to the project. The statue was unveiled in October 1990 and remains a favorite fan photo op outside Heinz Field to this day.

Legendary Steelers owner Art Rooney, left, and son Dan plan for the addition of quarterback Terry Bradshaw, their No. 1 pick in the draft, on January 27, 1970.

Pittsburgh mourned. While the NFL lost one of its great pioneers, and the Steelers lost its founder and driving force, the legacy of Art Rooney will remain as the lifeblood of the Pittsburgh Steelers forever.

2 The Emperor Takes Over the Steelers

When Charles Henry Noll took over the Steelers as their head coach in 1969, owner Art Rooney was hopeful that this new voice for his team could eventually guide it into being a force in the NFL. Never did even he expect that Noll would become the legendary coach to lead the Steelers to four Super Bowl victories. But in the end, that is exactly what Noll did.

Pittsburgh Mayor Pete Flaherty looks on as coach Chuck Noll shows off the Lombardi Trophy to the crowd at the Pittsburgh Airport on Monday, January 19, 1976, as he and the team retuned from Miami. Noll is the only coach in NFL history to lead a team to four Super Bowl titles.

He is the only coach in NFL history to lead a team to four Super Bowl titles, as the Steelers won Super Bowls IX, X, XIII, and XIV. He did it by getting the most out of his players by paying attention to detail, as well as picking players who fit the Steelers' system of superior defense and offensive running.

Noll was never a rah-rah type of coach, as was his successor, Bill Cowher, who took over after Noll retired in 1991. But the one thing that most of his players always said about him was that they never wanted to let him down. Players were prepared under Noll, and it showed in the way they systematically dominated teams year in and year out. From 1972 to 1984 Noll's teams never suffered a losing season. In that stretch, the coach led the Steelers to a run that most NFL franchises have never seen: four Super Bowls, four AFC conference titles, nine AFC Central titles, and a record of 130–58 in the regular season and 15–7 in the postseason. Then, of course, was the fact that under Noll the Steelers had a legendary defense that struck fear in the hearts of opponents.

Noll's coaching credentials began as a player for the Cleveland Browns. After he left the game as a player in 1959, he became an assistant coach for the Los Angeles and San Diego Chargers and then the Baltimore Colts. While with the Colts, Noll took over the defense, and in 1968 he helped them set an NFL record for fewest points allowed in a season, with 144. The following season, he was ready to take over the Steelers.

When Noll came in, the Steelers had had only four winning seasons in 19 years, and had won only 18 games in the previous five. The one thing that Noll did was commit to the draft. He started with the drafting of Joe Greene, and from there he brought in big-name talent to build his dynasty.

After a 1–13 season Noll's first year came Terry Bradshaw, then Franco Harris. The 1974 draft continues to go down as one the greatest in NFL history. Lynn Swann, John Stallworth, Jack Lambert, and Mike Webster all joined the team, four Hall of Famers in one draft year, which has never been done before, and almost surely will never happen again.

Noll was the brains behind the teams that won four titles, as he was able to make smart decisions and motivate his players with his wit and game-planning. As a coach, Noll never got the attention and media coverage he deserved. It wasn't until he led an over-achieving team in 1989 to the playoffs, going 9–7, and then helped them pull off an upset of coaching rival Jerry Glanville and the

Another Famous Coach Nearly Takes Over in '69
When Chuck Noll took the Steelers' coaching position in January 1969, he wasn't the only candidate for the job. Truth be told, Noll was the Steelers' second choice. The first was current Penn State and legendary head coach Joe Paterno. At the time the position was offered, Paterno was 42 years old. Word was Paterno considered the job, but once he turned it down, the team moved quickly to hire Noll, who was the Colts' defensive coordinator at the time. The rest, as they say, is history.

Oilers on New Year's Eve in the AFC wild-card game that he garnered any amount of media accolade. It was Noll's last playoff win.

Two years later he left the Steelers. With the same quiet demeanor and charm that he used in coaching the team for 23 seasons, Noll left his post as "the Emperor" and rode off into the sunset with a coaching mark of 209–156–1, including the postseason.

He was elected to the Pro Football Hall of Fame in 1993, his first year on the ballot. He still holds the ceremonial title of administration adviser in the Steelers' front office but does not have a role in the team's operations—just the way you would think Noll would want it after a career that put rings on players' fingers and trophies in the front office of the organization.

3 The Immaculate Reception

Usually it's a coach, owner, season, or player that defines a franchise. While many say that Art Rooney is that to the Steelers, there has never been a play that has defined a team more than that of the Steelers' winning touchdown in their 1972 playoff game. That play of course is otherwise known as the "Immaculate Reception." Every

Steelers fan and pretty much any fan of the NFL knows of the play, its controversy, and the impact it had on the team. It's still NFL Films' "greatest single play of all-time."

The play is so famous that the turf from Three Rivers Stadium where running back Franco Harris made the catch and eventual touchdown was cut out from the field and is in the Pro Football Hall of Fame. The play has been revisited and replayed so many times, it is clearly one of the most famous plays in NFL history, and Steelers play-by-play man Jack Fleming's call of the play remains the most famous in Steelers history.

To relive the play still gives goose bumps to Steelers fans everywhere. The club trailed the Oakland Raiders 7–6 with 22 seconds left in the AFC divisional playoff game, December 23, 1972. It had been a hard-fought game, and Raiders quarterback Ken Stabler's late touchdown that gave the Raiders a one-point lead seemed like it was going to be the difference in the game.

The play took place on fourth down, with the Steelers needing 10 yards for a first down standing on their own 40-yard line. So desperate was the situation, owner Art Rooney had already headed downstairs to be with his club following the tough loss. The beloved owner never even saw the play.

Quarterback Terry Bradshaw took the snap and headed back to pass. He was pressured and began to run for his life. Running to his right, trying to avoid the pressure, he fired a pass, looking for running back John "Frenchy" Fuqua at the Raiders' 35-yard line. When the ball arrived, Raiders safety Jack Tatum arrived as well, and the ball hit off his shoulder pad.

The ball, still in the air, traveled back a few yards on the rebound after it hit Tatum. The Raiders, thinking the ball was about to be called incomplete, began to celebrate. They missed Harris, who was trailing the play in case Bradshaw needed another receiving option. Harris, being alert and seeing the ball heading toward the turf, scooped it up and began racing toward the end zone.

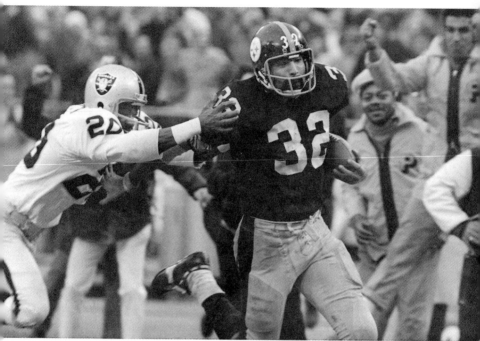

*Franco Harris (32) eludes a tackle attempt by the Oakland Raiders'
Jimmy Warren on the way to scoring the go-ahead touchdown in the AFC
Championship Game in Pittsburgh. Pittsburgh won 13–7. The play was the
Immaculate Reception, a desperation pass by Terry Bradshaw that deflected off
either Oakland's Jack Tatum or Pittsburgh's Frenchy Fuqua before Harris made
a shoestring catch.*

He ran past Raiders linebacker Gerald Irons and then laid a
stiff arm on Oakland defensive back Jimmy Warren at about the
Raiders' 10-yard line. Keeping himself in bounds, Harris went in
for the touchdown. The crowd at Three Rivers went into a wild
celebration, and fans jumped onto the field to mob Harris and the
rest of the team. The extra point was kicked, and the Steelers went
on for the 13–7 win to advance to the AFC Championship Game.

The controversy over the call came from the Raiders, who
stated that the ball bounced off Fuqua, which, if true, would have
meant it was an illegal play and therefore nullified the touchdown.
Tatum at first said there was no way that the ball hit him, but then

later admitted in his memoirs that he couldn't honestly say if the ball hit him or not.

Fuqua remains silent on what really happened, saying he knows what happened, but will never tell. The back and forth about the play went on for years, though during halftime of the 1998 AFC Championship Game, NBC showed the play from the original broadcast. The footage showed a different angle, where it seemed more than ever the ball hit only one player—Tatum.

The aftermath of the play was legendary. The Steelers lost the next week to the eventual undefeated Super Bowl–champion Miami Dolphins 21–17. But they rebounded after losing to Oakland in the playoffs the following season, winning the Super Bowl after the 1974 season, their first. They went on to win three more after that, while the Raiders won just one Super Bowl in the same time frame.

The Immaculate Reception, a play that means almost as much to the Steelers franchise as anything else, kicked off a dynasty of winning and made stars of eventual Hall of Famers Bradshaw and Harris.

4 Terry Bradshaw

While the Steelers of the 1970s were ruled by defense, there is no doubt that their success in winning four Super Bowls and becoming the team of the decade would not have happened without the leadership of quarterback Terry Bradshaw. While Bradshaw's fame and success didn't happen overnight, the 1970 No. 1 overall draft choice matured into a tough-as-nails winner.

Bradshaw also was at his best when it mattered most. He went 4–0 in Super Bowls, and in those four games he threw for 932 yards and nine touchdowns, Super Bowl records when he retired in 1983 due to elbow issues. Overall, in 19 playoff games, Bradshaw threw for 3,833 yards and completed 261 passes.

The Steelers won the right to select Bradshaw in a coin flip with the Chicago Bears. The season before, coach Chuck Noll had addressed the defensive side of the ball in the first round, taking Joe Greene, but he knew deep down that the offense would need to be upgraded to reach the next level. This was not hard to see after the team went 1–13 in Noll's first year.

The relationship between Noll and Bradshaw started out rocky, to say the least. Noll couldn't handle the mistakes that the quarterback made, and he was quick to come down on Bradshaw. The QB in his rookie season threw an unreal 24 interceptions and just six touchdowns as the Steelers went 5–9. In his first four seasons, as players came aboard to help the club, Bradshaw still struggled, throwing 73 interceptions and 41 touchdowns, hardly what the team had in mind for their franchise quarterback.

Then in 1974 Noll had seen enough. He decided to sit his first overall pick and give the starting QB job to then-backup Joe Gilliam. The team was ready to make a run at a title, and Gilliam started

An Unlikely Source Gives Noll Advice

When Steelers coach Chuck Noll had the quandary as to whom to start at QB between Terry Bradshaw and Joe Gilliam, an unlikely source told him he should go with Bradshaw: Oakland Raiders owner Al Davis. The rival owner told NFL Films that he was the one who sparked the Steelers' run. Davis said Bradshaw came to him after the quarterback had been benched, asking that he trade for Bradshaw. "I said to him [Bradshaw], 'I love ya, but I got enough problems,'" Davis said. "'I can't get ya, but let me put in a good word for ya.' Chuck Noll had been a close friend, and one of the dumbest things I ever did, I says to him, 'Why don't you start playin' Bradshaw and stop playing Gilliam? He [Bradshaw] can win for you.'" True or not, it's yet another interesting sidebar to the Steelers-Raiders history.

the year red hot, leading them to a 4–1–1 mark through six games. Gilliam's bright star faded, though, as he threw for just 78 yards in a 20–16 win over Cleveland. The decision was made to go back to Bradshaw.

It was then that the future Hall of Famer finally started to make his mark. He went 5–2 as a starter, and the team went 10–3–1 for the season. Bradshaw wrapped up the year throwing seven touchdowns and eight picks. In the playoffs, he played well, keeping mistakes down and making sure to lean on the defense and run game to lead the team to their first Super Bowl win, a 16–6 victory over Minnesota on January 12. Finally, at the age of 27 in 1975, Bradshaw had arrived.

He lived up to the billing, throwing for 18 touchdowns and just nine interceptions as the club dominated the NFL, going 12–2 in what was their best regular season ever. They rolled through the playoffs, and in Super Bowl X against the Dallas Cowboys, Bradshaw threw for 209 yards with two touchdowns and no interceptions.

As Bradshaw grew up and got better, so did the Steelers' offense. In Super Bowl XIII, the Steelers won 35–31 over the Cowboys. Bradshaw won the MVP as he threw for 318 yards with four touchdowns and one interception. The following season, against the Los Angeles Rams, he shined and won the Super Bowl MVP again, throwing for 309 yards with two more touchdowns and three interceptions as the Steelers rallied for a 31–19 win. He also shared *Sports Illustrated*'s "Sportsmen of the Year" honors with Pittsburgh Pirates legend Willie Stargell.

Of course, what also made Bradshaw turn into an elite quarterback was the fact he had plenty of weapons around him. Players like Franco Harris, Rocky Bleier, Lynn Swann, and John Stallworth gave the Steelers one heck of an offense for those Super Bowl seasons. They also made the sometimes-not-on-target Bradshaw look very good.

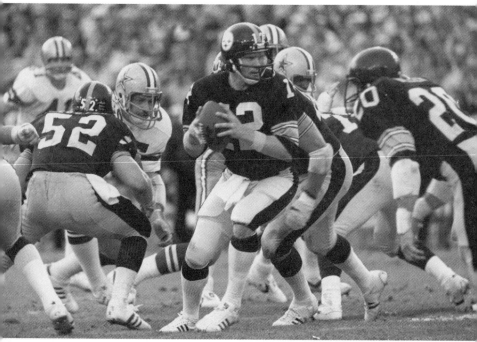

Quarterback Terry Bradshaw (12) leads the Steelers to a 35–31 victory over the Dallas Cowboys in Super Bowl XIII in Miami, on January 21, 1979. Bradshaw was elected to the Pro Football Hall of Fame in 1989.

Four years after the two back-to-back Super Bowl seasons, it was over for Bradshaw. The quarterback had off-season elbow surgery following the strike-shortened 1982 season, and it was clear that the reins at the quarterback spot were being turned over to the likes of Cliff Stoudt and Mark Malone. The final season for Bradshaw saw the team go 9–2 without him, but then three straight losses put the season in doubt.

In a final heroic effort, with his elbow still in pain, Bradshaw started the team's 15th game of the season at Shea Stadium against the New York Jets. Playing just a half before his elbow gave out, he threw two touchdowns and led the Steelers to a 34–7 win, one that helped the team make the postseason. He left the game at the end of the year, but for sure didn't leave the public eye.

In 1984 he joined CBS as a color commentator, and then six years later joined the studio as a cohost of *NFL Today*. He won an Emmy for best performance by a studio analyst in 2001 working for Fox. He was elected to the Pro Football Hall of Fame in 1989, the first season he was eligible to be placed into football immortality.

In his 14-season career, Bradshaw completed 2,025 of 3,901 passes for 27,989 yards and 212 touchdowns. "When I look at my statistics compared to the truly great players, I'm almost embarrassed," Bradshaw wrote in his autobiography, *It's Only a Game*. "That's probably the reason I have some difficulty when people define me by my playing career."

He's still a huge fan favorite in the Steel City, and when you talk about quarterback play in Pittsburgh, it starts and ends with Terry Bradshaw.

5 "Mean" Joe Greene

When the Steelers drafted "Mean" Joe Greene with the fourth overall pick of the 1969 draft, they felt they were going to be getting a very good player who could lead their defense. What they didn't know is they were getting a player who would eventually be a Hall of Famer and change the fortunes of the Steelers for years to come.

To this very day, Charles Edward Greene is still considered one of—if not the greatest—defensive tackles in NFL history. He was the cornerstone of the Steel Curtain, and without Greene, the unit would likely have never existed...at least not with the same success that they had with Greene getting double- and sometimes even triple-teamed.

By the time defensive linemen Joe Greene (left) and L.C. Greenwood reported to training camp at Latrobe, Pennsylvania, in 1978, they had been part of the same defensive line, the famed Steel Curtain, for 10 years.

He came from a little college called North Texas State, and when the Steelers and Chuck Noll took him in 1969, a newspaper printed a story on Greene that showed just how much people didn't know about the Hall of Famer they were getting. The headline: "Who's Joe Greene?" Of course, Greene wasn't thrilled about going to the losing organization the Steelers were back in those days.

He held out at first for a larger contract, and when things got settled, he showed up at training camp out of shape and overweight. Greene did start to assert himself, and in those early years showed potential, but he also showed how "mean" he could be, allowing his emotions to get the best of him.

Incidents with Greene included throwing his helmet at the goal post so hard it broke. Then there's the story of Greene coming off the sideline of a beating by Chicago to spit into the face of legendary linebacker Dick Butkus. He also was known for throwing kicks, punches, and after-the-play hits that would result in penalties.

Despite his early problems, Greene was named the NFL Defensive Rookie of the Year. It was four years before the team finally started winning, and Greene was at the forefront of a defense that helped win four Super Bowls in six seasons. The Steel Curtain dominated offenses week in and week out and flexed their muscles with Greene running the show.

Greene hated losing, and usually if the team didn't play well, he would show it with outbursts and anger toward anyone who got in his way. But he also was a good teacher, showing the likes of fellow players like L.C. Greenwood, Ernie Holmes, and even Jack Lambert how to be better players.

By the time Greene stepped away from his playing days, he racked up some impressive numbers. He was a 10-time Pro Bowl selection, five-time All-Pro selection, three-time second-team All-Pro selection, two-time AP NFL Defensive Player of the Year, and four-time Super Bowl champion.

Greene's final stats included 181 games, 78.5 sacks (unofficially, as sacks were not an official statistic until 1982), and 16 fumble recoveries. No one has ever been able to fill the shoes of Joe Greene on the Steelers' defense, and the team didn't take long after

Not Only "Mean" but Durable

For being as physical as he was, "Mean" Joe Greene was as durable as they come. While it seems like in today's NFL it's almost commonplace for even the best players to suffer an injury here and there, *hurt* was not in Greene's vocabulary. The big man was out there every week—Greene started his career playing in 91 straight games, a streak that was only stopped by injury in 1975. By the time the Hall of Famer's career was over, he played in an amazing 181 of 190 regular-season games, missing just nine regular-season games in his stellar career.

the retirement of Greene to move from a 4-3 to a 3-4 defense, a type of defense they have run ever since.

Once he left the game, Greene continued as a teacher. He was an assistant coach for Noll starting in 1987 and even was a candidate for the vacancy that was eventually filled by Bill Cowher in 1992. Overall, Greene spent 16 years as an assistant with the Steelers, Miami Dolphins, and Arizona Cardinals.

Gaining Super Bowl rings didn't end with retirement, though. Greene returned to the Steelers as a special assistant for player personnel under GM Kevin Colbert and earned two more rings, one in 2006 against the Seahawks and another in 2009 versus the Cardinals. In early May of 2013, he retired from the Steelers for the final time.

6 Bill Cowher—"Cowher Power"

It's never easy replacing a legend, but if there's one coach who pulled it off, it was former Steelers head coach Bill Cowher. "The Jaw" stepped in for Chuck Noll in 1992 and lit a fire under the Steelers that burned for most of his 15 seasons as the face of the franchise. His dream was to bring a fifth Super Bowl to Pittsburgh, and while it took quite a while to do it, he finally delivered on his promise on February 5, 2006, when the Steelers beat the Seattle Seahawks 21–10 in Super Bowl XL.

Cowher was a hometown boy, born and raised in Crafton, Pennsylvania. He was a very good football, basketball, and track competitor in high school. At North Carolina State, he was a starting linebacker and the team captain and MVP in his senior season. His playing career saw him make the Philadelphia

Cowher Shines against Browns, Bengals—Not So Good against 'Niners

During his 15 seasons as Steelers head coach, Bill Cowher went undefeated against just one team: the Washington Redskins. Cowher's Steelers beat the Redskins three times in his tenure as coach, never losing to them. Cowher also made mincemeat of two AFC Central/North teams while coach—the Cleveland Browns and the Cincinnati Bengals. In 54 games the Steelers played against the Browns and Bengals, Cowher's club won 40 and lost just 14. The teams Cowher had the most issues with were the San Francisco 49ers (1–3), Denver Broncos (1–3), and Jacksonville Jaguars, who beat Cowher's Steelers 10 of 18 times.

Eagles as a free agent in 1979. The following season he moved to Cleveland, where he played for the Browns for three seasons, from 1980 to 1982.

He then went back to Philly, finishing his career playing two more seasons with the Eagles in 1983 and 1984. While not the most talented player, Cowher played hard every play, just like he coached. After his career ended, he joined the Browns and their head coach Marty Schottenheimer as the special-teams coach. His energy and fire could be seen as the Browns made it to the AFC Championship Game in 1986. Cowher was on the fast track to greatness—serving as the Browns' secondary coach and then moving with Schottenheimer to Kansas City as the Chiefs' defensive coordinator in 1989.

By the end of the 1991 season, Noll had decided it was time to retire. The Steelers had become a very average to below-average team in Noll's final decade, making the playoffs just once in his last seven seasons as coach. The team needed a fresh start, and Cowher was the perfect fit.

When he was hired on January 21, 1992, he spoke right away of winning, saying that he was determined to light a fire under a group of young, talented players. Problem was, not many in the media agreed with him. The Steelers had been hampered by poor drafts and players who never lived up to their billing. Plus, some just never responded to Noll's old-school style. Enter Cowher.

He was not afraid to put players on notice right away, cutting high draft choices like linebacker Huey Richardson, a linebacker who was simply too soft to garner the first-round pick the team had used on him. He also proclaimed that the Steelers would be a team built on the running game, turning running back Barry Foster into a star by feeding him the ball 20 to 25 times a game.

He also went away from gunslinging quarterback Bubby Brister and went with a safer, less flashy quarterback in Neil O'Donnell. Cowher's fingerprints were all over this team right away—they went 3–0 to start his coaching tenure, and were instant contenders, going 11–5 in 1992 as Cowher was named the AP NFL Coach of the Year.

In each of his first six seasons, Cowher got his team to the playoffs, but only once, 1995, were they able to go the distance, reaching Super Bowl XXX before falling to the Cowboys 27–17. He was able to endure high-profile players leaving year after year via free agency and never lost that fire or push to want to make his team better.

Cowher fired up his players with emotion, something the city had not seen in years. When you talked about the Steelers in the '90s and early 2000s, it was Cowher's team, no questions asked. He suffered the hard losses right along with the team, and nothing hurt more than when the team fell in home AFC Championship Games in '94, '97, '01, and '04. The media labeled the coach and the team chokers, not able to win the big game.

That all changed in 2005, when the club turned a 7–5 record into a 11–5 mark and a sixth seed in the playoffs. They took to the road, winning in Cincinnati, upsetting the first-seed Colts in Indy, and then dominating the Broncos in Cowher's first road AFC

Championship Game in Denver. Ten years after a tough 10-point loss to Dallas in Super Bowl XXX, Cowher and his road warriors finally brought the Lombardi Trophy back to the Steel City with a hard-fought 11-point win over the Seahawks.

Questions abounded about Cowher's future after the Super Bowl. It was not a secret that he and his family were moving to North Carolina, and many took that as a sure sign that he was going to step down as Steelers coach no matter what happened after the 2006 campaign.

Those who thought that were right. Cowher's club had a bad post–Super Bowl hangover, starting the '06 season 2–6. But just like their coach, they fought to the end, going 6–2 down the stretch and finishing the season 8–8. In his final game as coach, Cowher's team knocked the Bengals out of the playoffs with a 23–17 overtime win.

Five days after the win, Cowher announced he was stepping down, saying his desire to spend more time with his family had finally gotten the best of him. He wrapped up his career with an overall record of 161–99–1 (.619) including a 149–90–1 (.623) mark in the regular season. His record with the team ranks second only to Noll's overall (209–156–1, .572) and regular season (193–148–1, .566) records. Cowher's .623 regular season and .619 overall winning percentages are the highest in Steelers history.

Many felt that his walking away from the Steelers was just the start, and he would be back on an NFL sideline the following season. Instead, about a month after he walked away, he inked a deal to be a studio analyst with CBS' *The NFL Today*. His name still pops up when there's a vacancy in the league, but for now, Cowher seems content talking about football each Sunday instead of coaching it.

7 Dan Rooney

While Art Rooney was the man behind the family that still runs the Steelers, there's another Rooney who, for the past five-plus decades, has kept them as the best organization in pro football—Dan Rooney. Art Rooney's son, Dan, has been a force in the National Football League as not only an owner but a leader in the NFL community.

Dan started his run as Steelers president in 1975 but has been involved in capacities with the team for the past 50-plus seasons. Once he became team president, Dan was given quite a bit of power by his father, who trusted him to make decisions that would help the Steelers reach the next level. His management style was that of being practical and efficient, meaning that you wouldn't see the Steelers making the outlandish out-of-the-box moves a lot of other teams made.

It wasn't that the Steelers under Dan's control were not willing to help their players to the highest degree or allow second chances, but Dan made sure they would not make decisions they would later regret. Efficiency was the key to the Steelers' success, and it never fails that, when the Steelers win, it's Rooney who gets a lot of credit for the style and moves his team makes as the reasons behind it.

Dan Rooney's hard work has paid off with six Super Bowl titles, and in 2000 he was enshrined in the Pro Football Hall of Fame in Canton, Ohio. Always humble, very much like his father, Dan has always been there as a huge part of the franchise, but at the same time has always allowed his coaches to coach, players to play, and has for the most part stayed in the background of all the winning.

Rooney was born on July 20, 1932, to be a winner. He's shown it not only with six Super Bowl rings, but also with a large role in the league overall. While Rooney has always had the team at the

Head-Coaching Consistency

No franchise in the NFL has been as solid when it comes to head coaches as the Pittsburgh Steelers. While clubs seem to hire and fire head coaches as often as they change their underwear, the Steelers are a different animal, and have set the standard when it comes to keeping coaches for an extended period of time.

When the team hired Chuck Noll in 1969, he lasted an extraordinary 23 seasons before walking away in 1991 with four Super Bowl rings. Bill Cowher could have stayed longer but stepped down with a ring and 15 seasons under his belt. Mike Tomlin came in and after just three seasons has a Super Bowl ring and was the Motorola NFL Coach of the Year in 2008. That's three coaches in 40 seasons—just unheard of in the NFL. Considering the rival Cleveland Browns have had 14 coaches in the same time, you understand how rare it is to have the successful run with head coaches like the Steelers have had.

front of his heart, he's always put the league first, never allowing the Steelers to be given any sort of unfair advantage that would put the league in a difficult position. He's served on the board of directors for the NFL Trust Fund, NFL Films, and the scheduling committee. He was chairman of the committee that in 1974 added the Seattle Seahawks and Tampa Bay Buccaneers, and he was named the chairman of the negotiating committee in 1976.

The Rooney Rule, installed in 2003, requires all NFL teams to interview minority candidates for head-coaching and senior football operation positions. Since it came into effect, several NFL franchises have hired minority head coaches, including the Steelers themselves, who in 2007 turned their head-coaching job over to former Vikings defensive coordinator Mike Tomlin. At the start of the 2006 season, the Rooney Rule had seen the overall percentage of African American coaches jump from 6 percent to 22 percent.

Dan Rooney's journey to being one of the, if not the most respected, owners in the NFL is much the same that his father took. His traits are much like that of Art—humble, respectful, and caring for not only the players, but for each and every member of the organization. It's what made the Steelers the most respected organization in the NFL and at the top of the list in just about every pro sport.

Dan Rooney's life has taken a different path than what most expected. For years, Rooney has supported Irish American charitable causes. The nomination paid off, and on March 17, 2009, he was nominated by President Barack Obama to become the next U.S. ambassador to Ireland. He was sworn in the following July 1.

In 2012, Rooney traded in his ambassadorship and returned to the Steelers as the team's chairman. He shows no signs of slowing down or losing his desire to lead the Steelers into the next generation. His and his family's legacy continues to be the driving force behind why the Steelers are the most successful franchise in the NFL.

8 Three Rivers Stadium

It was the home that saw the Steelers march to four Super Bowls in the 1970s. Three Rivers Stadium saw amazing Steelers football over the years, as the team played their home games there from 1970 to 2000. It was the place where Steelers football became a nationwide sensation, where fans far and wide came to see the Steelers win five AFC titles, and in the end, where four Super Bowl trophies were won.

The stadium was often known as a "cookie-cutter stadium," as many types of stadiums in that time frame were similarly built. Places like Veterans Stadium in Philadelphia, Riverfront Stadium in Cincinnati, and even Giants Stadium in New Jersey come to mind as stadiums that looked almost like Three Rivers.

It was a multipurpose stadium that was home to the Steelers, the Pittsburgh Pirates, the Pittsburgh Maulers of the USFL, and

No Luck at Three Rivers

The Steelers made life tough on opposing teams at Three Rivers Stadium during much of the 1970s, but a lot of teams notched wins there in the 1980s and some in the early 1990s until the team started winning division titles again. With that though, in the stadium's history, there were six teams that never won a game at Three Rivers, including the Baltimore/Indianapolis Colts, who went 0–11, including three playoff losses. Also on the list of never winning at Three Rivers included the Atlanta Falcons (0–5), New York Jets (0–4), Detroit Lions (0–4), Tampa Bay Bucs (0–2), and Carolina Panthers (0–1).

even the University of Pitt for one season. But no team had quite the home-field advantage at Three Rivers that the Steelers did. In 31 seasons at Three Rivers, the Steelers went 182–72, a full 110 games over .500 at home. They also were 13–5 in the playoffs, which included winning five AFC Championship Games there, hosting eight overall.

The team sold out Three Rivers Stadium for every home game from 1972 on, and many who sat on the waiting list didn't get their shot at season tickets until Heinz Field opened in 2001. The Steelers' first game at Three Rivers ended with a 19–7 loss to the Houston Oilers on September 20, 1970. They quickly set their mark at the stadium when on December 23, 1972, the most famous play in NFL history occurred there. During their first-ever playoff game at Three Rivers, the famed Immaculate Reception took place. The play, a staple to this day in NFL history, saw the Steelers convert a wild fourth-down pass on a deflected ball to running back Franco Harris, who went 60 yards for a score and saw them pull out a 13–7 win against the Oakland Raiders.

In the 1975 season Pittsburgh beat Oakland again, this time 16–10 in the AFC Championship Game for the right to play the Cowboys in Super Bowl X. That game also is remembered for the ice that built up on the field in what may have been the worst weather day in Three Rivers history. For years the Raiders contended that the grounds crew at Three Rivers allowed water to build up on the field and freeze, giving the Steelers the advantage in the matchup, which they eventually won by six.

In the 1978 and '79 seasons the Steelers also won AFC Championship Games at home, topping the Houston Oilers both times. The first was a runaway 34–5 win, and the following year they pulled away for a 27–13 victory, which eventually lead to a 31–19 win over the Los Angeles Rams in Super Bowl XIV. In 1982 the team lost Chuck Noll's last playoff game at Three Rivers, falling to the Chargers 31–28.

It took the team a full 10 seasons to host another playoff game, when under Bill Cowher the team took home the No. 1 seed in the AFC in the 1992 season. They eventually lost to the AFC-champion Buffalo Bills 24–3 in Cowher's first playoff game. Two seasons later Three Rivers was more packed than any other game in the stadium's history. On January 15, 1995, 61,545 crowded into the stadium as the Steelers, again the top seed in the AFC, were upset by San Diego 17–13, stopping their Super Bowl run.

The following season the team finally got back to the Super Bowl, winning the AFC Championship Game at home, having come back from a fourth-quarter 16–13 deficit to beat the Indianapolis Colts 20–16. It was the last AFC title the Steelers won at Three Rivers Stadium. The last AFC Championship Game there on January 11, 1998, saw Kordell Stewart and the Steelers lose to the Denver Broncos 24–21 on January 11, 1998.

After two down seasons, the team did go 9–7 in 2000, their final year at Three Rivers, but went just 4–4 at home. They won their final game in the stadium, on a day when a lot of the legendary Steelers returned, beating the Washington Redskins 24–3.

The stadium was imploded on February 11, 2001, at 8:00 AM. The implosion took just 19 seconds, but the memories of the stadium where the Steelers won plenty of games and built a dynasty still remain.

9 Steel Curtain

When you think about the great memories of a Steelers dynasty in the 1970s, there is a term that comes to mind that still gives Steelers fans chills—*Steel Curtain*. It was a defensive front four that changed NFL history, started a run of Super Bowls for the Steel City, and eventually landed one of its own into the Pro Football Hall of Fame.

It started simply enough with the drafting of a little-known defensive tackle from North Texas State in 1969 by the name of Joe Greene. He dominated games and became the backbone of the line. In the same draft the team added a quality defensive end named L.C. Greenwood. Two years later along came another end, Dwight White, and then in 1972 the team added its final piece to the Steel Curtain puzzle—Ernie Holmes.

Each had his own qualities that made him great, but combined they were not only great, they were the greatest. It started with Greene, who was the superstar of the group. He came up with the stunt in the 4-3, and it usually took two or three linemen to block him. Even with that, Greene seemed to always be around the ball carrier or quarterback.

Greenwood was built more like a strong safety—he was tall, lean, and had amazing speed. Quarterbacks would always need to keep an eye on Greenwood, and that's while also trying to keep track of the other three. Then there was White, nicknamed "Mad Dog," a player who had a mean streak and showed up crunching quarterbacks and running backs. His aggressive style was a welcome sight to the unit every Sunday.

Holmes was the unsung hero of the bunch. He was called by Steelers linebacker Andy Russell the strongest of the group, and

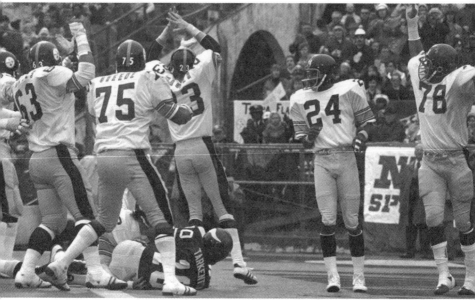

Pittsburgh's Steel Curtain defense is synonymous with the teams of the 1970s, which won four Super Bowls in six years. Here, the Steelers' defense, including Ernie Holmes (63) and Joe Greene (75), react as Vikings quarterback Fran Tarkenton (10) recovers his own fumble in the end zone for a safety in the second quarter of Super Bowl IX. The Steelers won 16–6.

Hall of Fame offensive guard Gene Upshaw said he was the best defensive tackle he had ever played against. Guards week in and week out were not able to match the strength, nor the play-in, play-out intensity that Holmes would bring.

The unit was named by a ninth grader at a local high school in 1971, Gregory Kronz. It came as a play on the phrase "Iron Curtain," which was popularized by former British Prime Minister Winston Churchill. Radio station WTAE put out a contest looking for a name for the unit, 17 people submitted "Steel Curtain," and Kronz's name was picked as the winner of that group.

The name didn't matter—these four linemen were simply the best at what they did. They picked up the offense when they couldn't score or didn't play all that well, and took it upon themselves to take over games. They held the vaunted Minnesota Vikings offense to six points in Super Bowl IX, and that actually came on a blocked punt, meaning the unit never allowed a score.

The following season they got even better. The club went 12–2 as the offense, led by Terry Bradshaw, matured. The defense, led by the front four, allowed just 11.6 points per game, good for second in the league that season. They held their opponents to under 10 points in seven of their 14 regular-season games, and then in the playoffs held Baltimore and Oakland to just 10 points each before allowing 17 to Dallas in the team's second Super Bowl win in Super Bowl X.

It was hard to believe that the best of this defense was yet to come, but in 1976 they ran a streak that no team in modern-day pro football has ever been able to duplicate. The team struggled early, losing four of their first five games, and also losing Bradshaw to injury. What happened next was astounding. The defense helped the team run off a 10-game win streak. They did not allow a touchdown in 22 straight quarters and by, the end of the regular season, shut out five of its last eight opponents.

That team was handcuffed on its way to a third Super Bowl as both 1,000-plus-yard running backs Franco Harris and Rocky Bleier were hurt in the Steelers' playoff thrashing of the Colts and were unable to play the following week in the AFC Championship Game at Oakland. Nevertheless, the curtain fell to the tune of allowing just 9.9 points per game and an unreal 22 points in their last eight games.

Two more Super Bowls would come the club's way after the 1977 season, and again the D-line was at the forefront, helping the club put two more Lombardi Trophies in the front office. By the 1980 season, the curtain had basically closed. Holmes was traded due to ongoing weight problems in 1978, and he played in three games the rest of his career. White walked away in '80, then both Greene and Greenwood retired in '81.

While there were the Purple People Eaters of the Vikings, the Orange Crush of the Denver Broncos, and the No-Name Defense of the Miami Dolphins, no unit in the annals of NFL history has ever been held in as high regard as the Steelers' front four—otherwise known as the Steel Curtain.

10 Super Bowl IX

The years of losing and agony for the Steelers had finally started to turn around once Chuck Noll came aboard in 1969. It didn't happen right away, of course, going 1–13 record in his first season, but just three years later the team went 11–3 and lost to an undefeated Dolphins team at home in the AFC Championship Game. The following season was another building block, with the Raiders stopping them cold in the playoffs 33–14.

Finally, as the Steelers continued to add players in the draft, things began to look up in 1974. With players like Joe Greene, Franco Harris, Terry Bradshaw, and others aboard, the team was poised to make a run at the title, and the '74 season finally showed the fruits of the team's labor paying off.

They raced through the regular season at 10–3–1 and then took care of the Bills in the AFC divisional playoffs 32–14. The Raiders were the final test. Noll used some words from the Raiders, who said that their divisional playoff win over Miami the week before was the real Super Bowl. The team responded, shutting the Raiders up in Oakland and beating them 24–13 to earn their first trip to the Super Bowl, ready to take on the NFC-champion Minnesota Vikings.

On January 12, 1975, the Steelers were ready to take their rightful place as one of the NFL's elite. With a defense that was up

"Mad Dog" White's Super Bowl IX Saga

The story of Dwight White and Super Bowl IX is one that shows just how tough the former member of the Steel Curtain really is. The week of the Steelers' first Super Bowl against the Minnesota Vikings, White was diagnosed with pneumonia and pleurisy. He tried to practice during the week, but was too weak to do so. He wasn't even in the team picture for the Super Bowl.

White spent part of the week in the hospital only to show up at Tulane Stadium the day of the game, ready to play. He couldn't eat much of the pregame meal, and sat covered in blankets shaking when the Steelers' offense was on the field. All White did was play just about every defensive play, and even downed Vikings quarterback Fran Tarkenton for the first points of the game, a safety to make it 2–0 Steelers. "God takes cares of fools and babies," White said about playing that day. "The bottom line, it was too big a game to miss."

to the task of stopping Fran Tarkenton and the Vikings' offense, Pittsburgh was ready to hoist its first Lombardi Trophy.

The location of the game didn't exactly fit that of a Super Bowl, as the game was played at Tulane Stadium, outdoors in New Orleans. The game was set for the brand new Superdome, but it was not finished, and the location was moved outdoors. With a high temp of just 58 degrees and a low of 34, the game seemed to suit these two cold-weather teams just fine.

This Super Bowl was low-scoring and filled with plenty of defense. Neither team was able to score a touchdown or field goal until the third quarter—up to that point the only score came via the Steelers' defense. In the second quarter the Vikings attempted a pitch handoff, and when fullback Dave Osborn fumbled, the only thing Tarkenton could do was fall on it in the end zone, and Dwight White was there to down him, giving the Steelers a safety and a 2–0 lead.

Minnesota had another shot late in the half, but a big hit by Steelers safety Glen Edwards popped an attempted pass for John

Gilliam into the air, and Mel Blount came down with it, ending the final threat of a physical and near-scoreless first half. It was the lowest halftime score in Super Bowl history to that point.

The second half saw the Steelers recover a fumble on the opening kickoff, and the team quickly took advantage of it. Harris went for 24 yards to the 6 and then two plays later went the final yards for a touchdown to give the team a 9–0 lead. With the Steelers' defense playing lights out, nine points might as well have been 100.

Minnesota finally broke through, but mostly it was due to a Steelers miscue. They blocked a Steelers punt, and Terry Brown recovered it in the end zone. The Vikings were back in the game. They missed the extra point, but the Steelers' lead was down to 9–6. The Vikings had more chances, but the Steelers came up with a big play every time. Once, the Vikings had the ball at the Steelers' 45, but another pick ended that chance.

The fourth quarter saw the Steelers finally put the game away, as they put together an impressive 66-yard, 11-play drive that clinched the team's first title. The big play in the series was a 30-yard pass play from Bradshaw to tight end Larry Brown. The drive was wrapped up as Bradshaw found Brown for a four-yard score to give the team a 16–6 lead with just 3:31 left.

Another pick by the Steelers—this time by Mike Wagner on the first play of the next drive—stopped any possible chance the Vikings had. A few minutes later, the Steelers celebrated as they lifted Noll off the field. Forty years of losing was finally over. Art Rooney lifted the Lombardi Trophy, Harris took home the MVP with 158 yards and a score, and the Steelers' legacy of winning had officially begun.

11 The 1974 Draft

When it comes to the draft, the Steelers still have what is considered to be the greatest draft class in the history of the league: the Class of 1974. It was five years into the Chuck Noll coaching regime, and the Steelers had slowly started to build a championship dynasty. Noll had already added a few players who would go on to be legends—among them Joe Greene, Terry Bradshaw, and Franco Harris. But no one, not even Noll, could have expected the success that the '74 draft brought them.

The team had success in the 1973 season, going 10–4 in the regular season, but were dispatched rather easily by the Oakland Raiders in the playoffs, 33–14. The team needed just a few more pieces, and in that famous '74 draft, they got that and a whole lot more.

With the Steelers holding the 21st pick, they went with a playmaking wide receiver in the first round, taking Lynn Swann from USC. They wanted a player with whom Bradshaw could develop a 1-2 punch, since the previous season Ron Shanklin was the team's leading receiver with 30 catches for 711 yards, though he did have 10 scores.

Over Swann's career, he was a Super Bowl MVP and put together some of the most memorable catches in NFL history. Needless to say, the pick was a success. He also played hurt, as seen after he took a vicious hit in the 1975 AFC Championship Game against the Raiders. He came back, concussion and all, to have a huge game against Dallas and take home the MVP in the Super Bowl X 21–17 win.

Round two saw the team get an undersized linebacker with attitude from Kent State by the name of Jack Lambert. As a rookie, Lambert was just 204 pounds, but he used his heart and desire to become in some experts' eyes the best middle linebacker in NFL history. He had quick feet and always seemed to be in the right place at the right time.

Lambert was the NFL Defensive Rookie of the Year and helped the team win Super Bowl IX with a dominating defensive outing, topping the Vikings 16–6. Better known as "Count Dracula in Cleats" after he lost his four upper teeth taking an elbow in high school, Lambert was a menace to running backs and quarterbacks. He went on to win four Super Bowls, attend nine straight Pro Bowls, and was the 1976 NFL Defensive Player of the Year. He went into the Hall of Fame in 1990.

The following round saw Noll and the club take Alabama A&M wide receiver John Stallworth. Another Hall of Famer, Stallworth and Swann combined to be an incredible 1-2 combo at wide receiver for the Steelers. Stallworth was not as flashy as Swann, but he set franchise records at the time with 537 grabs for 8,723 yards and 63 touchdowns. He played in four Pro Bowls and was a two-time team MVP. He went into the Hall of Fame in 2002.

The only player who never received a lot of attention from that Steelers draft was their fourth-round pick, UCLA cornerback Jimmy Allen. The 100th overall pick did play on two Super Bowl teams and even held Raiders wide receiver Cliff Branch to just one catch in three critical possessions in the 1974 AFC Championship Game in Oakland. He was a contributor on special teams, making two tackles in Super Bowl IX against Minnesota. Allen stuck around until he was traded to the Lions before the 1978 season.

The fifth and final Hall of Famer from the 1974 draft was the team's fifth-round pick, center Mike Webster. "Iron" Mike was the anchor of the Steelers' offensive line from 1976 to 1988. He started 150 straight games, was a seven-time All-Pro, and played in nine Pro Bowls. He started his career learning from Ray Mansfield and ended it teaching Dermontti Dawson. He was a great influence and a great friend with his quarterback, Terry Bradshaw, both on and off the field.

Webster was the last active player in the NFL to play on all four Steelers Super Bowl teams. The jersey he wore, No. 52, never has been reissued by the team, showing the respect they had for their late center who sadly passed away in 2002, just five seasons after he was inducted in the Pro Football Hall of Fame.

"It's nice to be lucky," Noll said of that '74 draft. "You never know how it's going to turn out, fortunately we got some guys who wanted to produce that year."

You can say that again. Five players, four Hall of Famers, and four Super Bowl trophies later, no draft class in NFL history has been held in such high regard. And for good reason.

12 Franco Harris

When the Steelers were looking for a running back early in the 1972 draft, many scouts and experts thought they were going to nab Penn State's Lydell Mitchell. Much to the shock of everyone, the Steelers instead decided to take his teammate, Franco Harris. The Nittany Lion was mostly the blocking back in his college career for Mitchell, but it didn't take long for the Steelers to show why Harris was the right fit for their system.

The son of an African American who served in World War II and a "war bride" from Italy, Harris was a fan favorite from the word go. He quickly fit into the Steelers' offense, becoming only the fourth rookie in NFL annals to rush for 1,000 yards his first season. He was named as the league's Rookie of the Year by both the *Sporting News* and UPI. He put up an impressive 5.6 yards per carry with 10 touchdowns on 1,055 yards.

It was that 1972 season when Harris gained national attention as the receiver of the most famous play in NFL history—the

Franco Harris, shown here in his 36th 100-yard game, against Minnesota in 1980, rushed for more than 1,000 yards in eight different seasons. He was inducted into the Pro Football Hall of Fame in 1990.

Immaculate Reception. The pass play earned the Steelers their first ever playoff win and made him even more of a hero to Steeler Nation.

Harris went for more than 1,000 yards in 1974 and helped the team win their first Super Bowl in a 16–6 victory over the Minnesota Vikings. He took home the MVP award in the game, rushing for a then-record 158 yards and one touchdown on 34 carries.

The back went to nine straight Pro Bowls from 1972 to 1980 and also was an All-Pro in 1977. He also snapped Jim Brown's record when he rushed for more than 1,000 yards in eight seasons. Harris always seemed to be in the right place at the right time and was in on a number of big plays in his career. "I always looked for something big," Harris said. "Make the big play. Play the situation. Have fun with it. That's why I enjoyed it for so long. I had fun."

Harris and fellow running back Rocky Bleier had a lot of fun in their Steelers careers. They combined to help the club win four Super Bowls and, along with a legendary defense, pounded a lot of teams into submission. Harris saved his best for the biggest days of the year—in four Super Bowl games he ran for 354 yards on 101 carries and had four touchdowns.

Some laid into Harris for saving himself from unnecessary hits by running out of bounds. The back stood up to those naysayers by stating he was simply trying to prolong his career, which he did—he played 13 seasons, 12 of them with the Steelers. In those 13 years, he ran for 12,120 yards, putting up 4.1 yards per carry with 91 rushing touchdowns. He also caught 307 passes for 2,287 yards and nine scores.

It was tough to see Harris and the team not able to come to terms after that 1983 season. Harris asked for a pay raise, and at 34 years old, ownership felt that his best seasons were behind him and refused to give him what he wanted. The Steelers let him go in training camp in 1984, and Harris ended his career with a very uneventful eight games playing for the Seattle Seahawks.

In 1990 Harris' stellar career landed him a place in the Pro Football Hall of Fame. Nine years later he was honored as the 83rd best all-time player on the *Sporting News'* list of the 100 Greatest Football Players. His strong connection to the glory teams of the '70s and his remarkable career continue to make him a huge fan favorite among old and young Steelers fans.

13 Count Dracula in Cleats

While the Steelers have long been known for linebackers, there is no question that when fans begin that conversation, it starts with one man—Jack Lambert. The Steelers' middle linebacker, who wore No. 58, was a force for a dynasty in the 1970s, which is remarkable considering he was deemed too small and was recruited to play quarterback in college at Kent State. Lambert was part of the historic 1974 draft class that produced four Hall of Famers, and it didn't take long after his arrival to make an impact for a team that was ready to start a string of title runs.

As a rookie, Lambert was reported to be about 6'3", 203 pounds—hardly an imposing sight to most offensive linemen or running backs that would gun for him early in his career. But make no mistake about it, Lambert never let his size, or what was perceived to be a lack of it, get in his way of being the greatest linebacker in Steelers history.

The chance for Lambert to be a force came right away in his rookie season, as he took over for injured linebacker Henry Davis. That injury paved the way for Lambert to stay as the team's middle linebacker for 11 seasons, nine of which were Pro Bowl seasons for No. 58. He was the NFL Defensive Rookie of the Year, and he was the missing piece for the Steelers to make and win their first Super Bowl over the Minnesota Vikings 16–6.

What made Lambert so special was his ability against both the run and pass. He was equally dangerous on both sides, punishing running backs when they hit the hole and hitting quarterbacks when he rushed—even showing great hands in picking off 28 passes in his career. It was as if, no matter what came Lambert's way, he was great at it.

The Missing Teeth

Many people think that Jack Lambert's missing teeth were the result of him making a vicious tackle in a game or taking a violent hit. Well, that is partially true, as the teeth being knocked out did come from a hit, but it was from a hit in high school basketball practice—not in a football game. Lambert's four front teeth were knocked out after his mouth hit the head of Steve Poling, a high school basketball teammate. Lambert had a removable partial denture, but instead of wearing it in games, he ditched it, hence his Dracula-like appearance, making him known as "Count Dracula in Cleats" in his playing days.

The Steelers already had players like Joe Greene, L.C. Greenwood, Andy Russell, Ernie Holmes, and Jack Ham, yet at the end of the day, Lambert seemed to be the one who teams wanted little or nothing to do with on Sunday. "If I was ever in a barroom brawl and needed one man to go back-to-back with me, I'd want Jack Lambert to be the man," Greene said of his teammate. "This is one rough, tough guy…someone who'll never give up."

The legend of Lambert and the Steelers defense of the '70s grew. Lambert going through offensive players with a vampire-like look was a sight to behold during the Steelers' dynasty of that era. He was not shy about his dislike of quarterbacks and felt the league did too much to protect them. He stated once that quarterbacks should "all wear dresses."

It was pretty easy to see why Lambert was so successful as the leader of the Steelers' intimating defense. He was in on just about every play. Lambert made it his duty, so it seemed, to hit someone on each and every play on each and every Sunday. It was his after-the-play throwdown of Cowboys safety Cliff Harris in Super Bowl X that seemed to turn the spirit of the game around. It came after Steelers kicker Roy Gerela missed a field goal, and Harris tapped him on the helmet. Not allowing anyone to get the better of his team, Lambert flung Harris down, almost getting himself thrown out of the championship game.

Jack Lambert (58) brings down Cincinnati Bengals running back Archie Griffin in the fourth quarter of a game in Cincinnati, in December 1977. Lambert ended his career with 1,479 tackles.

His coach, Chuck Noll, even defended the move. "Jack Lambert is a defender of what is right," Noll said after the game. Noll always came to the defense of his middle linebacker, even as those around the NFL, including commissioner Pete Rozelle, questioned if he was a dirty player. It was after what was classified as three late hits on Browns quarterback Brian Sipe that Rozelle had a meeting with Lambert over his play.

Nevertheless, no one could deny that Lambert was a game-changer and a player who always defended himself and his hard-nosed style of play. "All that stuff upsets me, because I'm not a dirty football player. I don't sit in front of my locker thinking of fighting or hurting somebody," Lambert said in a 1984 *Sports Illustrated* interview. "All I want to do is be able to play football hard and aggressively, the way it's meant to be played. But when someone deliberately clips me or someone comes off the bench and tries to bait me, I'm not going to stand for it. I will be no man's punching bag."

And he never was.

His Hall of Fame career ended with 1,479 tackles, 1,049 of which were solo, and 23.5 sacks. He was named to nine straight Pro Bowls, and even was the 1976 NFL Defensive Player of the Year. Known as "Count Dracula in Cleats," Lambert is still considered by many as the greatest middle linebacker in NFL history.

Lambert's career came to a halt in 1984 due to a severe case of turf toe, which took away his speed and ability to close in on ball carriers like he did earlier in his career. He hung the cleats up for good in '84 and leads a very private life with his wife and children away from the NFL spotlight.

14 The Terrible Towel

It has its own entry in Wikipedia. It is the symbol of a football team and, in the minds of some out there, is the ultimate good-luck tool. Yes, the Terrible Towel indeed could be described as all those things—and more. Never has an item been so associated with a team and a city as the towel, and its history and tradition are legendary.

The towel, as it came to be, began just two weeks before the Steelers' first playoff game in 1975. The story goes that the GM of Steelers flagship radio station WTAE told sportscaster Myron Cope that he needed a gimmick to attract sponsors to his talk show. Cope didn't think he needed a gimmick and wanted no part in it, but in the end the two came up with the idea for a towel with the words "The Terrible Towel" printed on it. "I said we need something that everybody already has, so it doesn't cost a dime," Cope said. "So I says, 'We'll urge people to bring out to the game gold or black towels,' then I'll tell people if you don't have a yellow, black, or gold towel, buy one. And if you don't want to buy one, dye one. We'll call this the Terrible Towel." The rest, as they say, is history.

Cope went on the radio and TV telling fans to bring a yellow dish towel to the game, and as the team took the field against the Colts in a playoff game on December 27, 1975, there were some 30,000 fans waving towels in support of their team. The Steelers went on to win 28–10, beat the Raiders the following week at home in the AFC Championship Game, and then topped Dallas in Super Bowl X. It was a gimmick, but one that would still be around some three decades later.

It's a rite of passage now for a Steelers fan to own a Terrible Towel, and they're easy to spot just about anywhere. The towel has found its way to six Super Bowls, countless playoff games, and even more regular-season games not only in Pittsburgh, but all over the country. After the last two Super Bowl wins, there have been special edition towels to help Steelers fans celebrate.

The official Terrible Towel didn't make its debut until the 1976 season, as Gimbels department store came out with "The Official Myron Cope Terrible Towel." While Gimbels is gone, today the towel is made by McArthur Towel and Sports Co. Most of the time you can find the towel online or through the official Steelers site for about $7.

While Cope is gone, his legacy with the towel remains. In 1996 he gave the rights to the Terrible Towel to the Allegheny Valley School in Coraopolis, Pennsylvania. The school provides care for people with mental and physical disabilities, including Cope's son, who is autistic. To date, towel sales have raised more than $2.2 million for the school.

The towel is also a part of the Pro Football Hall of Fame. After Cope retired from 35 years of broadcasting, he served as cocaptain for the Steelers in their 2005 home game against the Ravens. He led the fans in a towel wave at halftime (the Steelers won that game 20–19), and that towel now stands in the Hall as a signature of pride to the Steelers and their fans.

Other teams have tried to stomp on it, and the widespread belief is that it brings bad luck. Just ask the Cleveland Browns about a playoff game in 1994, or the Tennessee Titans, who jumped on the towel in a game back in 2008, then as the No. 1 seed in the AFC entering the playoffs, were one and done. Cope always said the towel was "positive force" for the Steelers, but quite a few Black and Gold fans think otherwise.

The Steelers' official website has a page dedicated to the towel and other "terrible" stuff that you can purchase—such as totes, ties, hats, shirts, bibs, and gloves. At the top of the page are Cope's words, which describe the towel best:

> Is not an instrument of witchcraft....It is not a hex upon the enemy. The towel is a positive force that lifts the Steelers to magnificent heights—and poses mysterious difficulties for the Steelers' opponents only if need be. Many have told me that the Terrible Towel brought them good fortune, but I can't guarantee that sort of thing because the Steelers, after all, are the towel's primary concern. Still, at the least, the symbol of the Terrible Towel will serve as a memento of your having been part of the Steelers' Dynasty, and if it causes good things to happen to you, so much the better.

15 Mel Blount

When it comes to great defensive backs in Steelers history, there is no denying that Mel Blount has to be at the top of the list. The AP Defensive Player of the Year in the NFL in 1975, Blount was hands down the most physical cornerback in the history of the NFL. So physical, in fact, that the NFL changed its rules about the way corners had to play wide receivers. Yes, when a rule is named after you, as the Mel Blount Rule was in '78, you know you're pretty good.

Just how good was Blount? He was a five-time Pro Bowler, four-time first-team All-Pro, and four-time Super Bowl champion. He was named to the NFL 75th Anniversary All-Time team and 1976 Pro Bowl MVP. And, of course, Blount was inducted into the Pro Football Hall of Fame in 1989.

Blount came from humble beginnings, growing up in poverty on a Georgia farm. But what an athlete he was. He was a star in four sports growing up—baseball, football, basketball, and track. He was offered a scholarship to Southern University in Baton Rouge, Louisiana, and was an All-American as both a corner and safety.

As the Steelers and coach Chuck Noll continued to build what would be considered the best defense of all time, they took Blount as their cornerstone defensive back in the third round of the 1970 draft, the 53rd pick overall. By 1972, he was a starter on the unit mostly known for its front four and played mostly the top wideouts in the league on the right side.

Blount's greatness could not be measured for what he did as the team's best corner. He was fast, had size, and could overpower most receivers, big or small. Plus, until '78, he could harass receivers to the point where quarterbacks would forget about throwing to Blount's side of the field most of the day.

He racked up interceptions as well as honors throughout his career. He finally walked away in 1983, leaving the game as the Steelers' all-time career leader in interceptions, with 57. He returned those picks for 736 yards and a pair of touchdowns. Maybe even more impressive was the fact he picked off at least one pass in every season he played—14 in all.

"I was a different kind of cornerback," Blount said in an interview. "As far as my height, size, speed, and strength, it was just unique at the time for a guy like me to be a corner. And I guess I do get credit for that bump-and-run rule change. But football is a team sport, and because of guys like Joe Greene, L.C., Dwight White, Lambert, Donnie Shell—and I could go on and on—we as a defense forced the NFL to take a hard look at the rules. But I was a physical corner, though, for sure."

As long as Blount was on the field, there was no denying that quarterbacks not only had to worry about the Steel Curtain closing down on them, but also Blount's covering or physically dominating their teams' best receivers. In other words, with Blount, the Steelers' defense was even more dangerous.

After his playing days, Blount served as the director of player relations from 1983 to 1990. He founded and runs the Mel Blount Youth Home, a shelter and Christian mission for kids who have been abused and neglected. The first home Blount opened was in his hometown of Vidalia, Georgia. The second home was opened near Pittsburgh in the town of Claysville.

16 Super Bowl X

Following the Steelers' first title in Super Bowl IX, the team seemed to be poised and ready for their dynasty to truly begin. Their defense was rounding into form, their offense was getting better, and many of their best players were starting to hit their strides. So, when the team took the field at the Orange Bowl on January 18, 1976, against the Dallas Cowboys, it was no surprise that it was the best of the first 10 Super Bowls.

The Steelers were a solid seven-point favorite entering the game, but Dallas was no slouch. Super Bowl X was already their third time to the dance, and their offense was built around comeback-kid quarterback Roger Staubach, who had thrown for 17 touchdowns and had run for 316 yards. The Steelers were 12–2, the No. 1 seed in the AFC, and dominated teams with their defense and running game.

There was an interesting storyline leading up to the game concerning Steelers wideout Lynn Swann, who had suffered a nasty concussion in the AFC Championship Game against Oakland. Many felt he wouldn't play, but by the time it was over, Swann had cemented his legacy as one of the all-time greats.

Dallas sent a message early. After a botched Steelers punt, Staubach threw a 29-yard touchdown to Drew Pearson to give the Cowboys a 7–0 lead. It was the first touchdown allowed by the Steelers in the first quarter all season, and it showed that the Cowboys could not be taken lightly.

The Steelers used Swann to put the game back to even. The Hall of Famer made a circus-like, toe-tapping, sideline catch of 32 yards to put the ball at the Cowboys' 16, and then from the 7-yard line Terry Bradshaw found tight end Randy Grossman all alone for a score to tie the game 7–7.

Cope a Writer First

What most people don't remember or even realize about broadcaster Myron Cope was his talent as one of the best sportswriters in America. Cope's career started with the *Daily Times* in Erie, Pennsylvania, and then he moved on to write for publications such as *Sports Illustrated*, the *Saturday Evening Post*, and the *Pittsburgh Post-Gazette*.

Cope's writing led him to win the E.P. Dutton Prize for Best Magazine Sportswriting in the Nation in 1963 for his portrayal of Cassius Clay. He also wrote a profile on Howard Cosell, which was selected as one of the 50 all-time classic articles in *Sports Illustrated* in 2004.

The Cowboys went up 10–7 after a field goal, and that score held at halftime as Steelers kicker Roy Gerela, who was injured on the opening kickoff, missed a 36-yard field goal late in the second quarter that could have tied the game. It was that drive where Swann, though, made the famous catch some have called the "Levitating Leap," as he went high into the air and made a falling catch for a 53-yard gain.

Despite having a 10–7 lead, it was just a matter of time until the game changed, and that happened after yet another missed kick. After Gerela missed a 33-yard field goal, Cowboys safety Cliff Harris patted Gerela on the helmet to mock the missed kick, and Steelers linebacker Jack Lambert grabbed Harris and flipped him to the ground in anger. The play changed the atmosphere of the game, and the Steel Curtain began to flex its muscles for the rest of the contest.

The Steelers' special teams also made a big play in the early stages of the fourth quarter, as running back Reggie Harrison blocked a Cowboys punt, resulting in a Steelers safety to make it a 10–9 game. Gerela then nailed a 36-yard field goal to give the Steelers their first lead at 12–10 following the free kick after the safety.

Mike Wagner picked off a Staubach pass and took it back to the Cowboys' 7-yard line, and then another Gerela field goal gave the Steelers a 15–10 advantage. The Black and Gold needed one more big play to put the game away, and again it was Swann who made it. On a third-and-4 from their 36-yard line, Bradshaw went deep for Swann, who made the grab at the 5 and went in for the score, 21–10 Steelers.

Gerela missed the extra point, but the Steelers were still up with just 3:02 left. Dallas quickly marched down the field and scored to make it 21–17 with 1:48 left. Bradshaw, who was hurt on the TD throw to Swann, was out, and the team ran four straight run plays, falling well short of a first down with time left for Dallas. It was up to the defense.

The Cowboys got to the Steelers' 38, but a couple Hail Marys fell short, then Glen Edwards picked off the final pass as time expired, clinching the 21–17 win. The win established Pittsburgh and Green Bay as the only two teams at the time to win back-to-back titles. Swann was the MVP with four grabs for 161 yards, including three catches that live on in Steelers history as some of the best ever.

17 Double Yoi!

He was one of the most beloved members of the Steelers franchise for more than 30 years, yet he never played a down, Myron Sidney Kopelman, better known as Myron Cope, was a staple whom fans grew to love and adore throughout his tenure as the team's color commentator, taking fans through some of the highest highs and lowest lows.

Cope, who passed away at the age of 79 in February 2008, will always be known as "the voice of the Steelers." His distinct style was heavy with a Pittsburgh accent as well as catch phrases such as "yoi" and "double yoi." His signature phrase has found its way onto T-shirts and into the vocabulary of Pittsburgh natives all over the country.

Everything about Cope was Pittsburgh. He was born there and graduated from the University of Pittsburgh. He started as a print journalist before he finally got behind a microphone, earning many awards working as a freelancer for national publications.

In 1968 Cope started a talk show on WTAE-AM radio in Pittsburgh and, within two years, started as a member of the Steelers' radio team. Every Sunday Cope and play-by-play man Jack Fleming filled the airwaves describing Steelers action like no other commentary duo in the NFL. It was more than a game with Fleming and Cope, it was an event listening to them call games as the Steelers evolved into a dynasty.

Cope's career took an unexpected turn in 1975, when he implored Steelers fans to bring a yellow towel to the team's playoff game against the Baltimore Colts. The towels, now of course known as the Terrible Towel, became the signature of Steelers fans across the world, to the point where they are waved at every game, home and away. Not only that, but Cope gave the rights to the Terrible Towel to the Allegheny Valley School in Coraopolis, Pennsylvania. Proceeds from the towel have raised millions for the school, which provides care for children with mental and physical disabilities.

Cope was there for the first four Steelers Super Bowls, and throughout the years no matter how good or bad the team may have been, he always made the games entertaining. He left the broadcast booth in 2005 as his health began to deteriorate. He was honored on October 31, 2005, for his lifetime accomplishments at halftime of the team's Monday night win over the Baltimore Ravens.

The beloved Cope passed away on February 27, 2008. Papers all over the country paid tribute to Cope, and a ceremony outside City Hall in Pittsburgh two days after his death honored him. There was even a one-minute silent waving of the Terrible Towel. Cope will always be remembered for the years he gave to the Steelers franchise, and his style will never be forgotten among the Steelers faithful.

18 The Bus

From 1996 to 2005 no player was the face of the Pittsburgh Steelers franchise more than Jerome Bettis. Nicknamed "the Bus" for his keen ability to carry defenders, Bettis remains today as one of the most popular players in the history of the franchise.

Bettis' career in the NFL started in Los Angeles. He was drafted by the Rams in the first round (10th overall pick) in 1993 and started having success right away. He even left an impact on the Steelers in just the second game of his pro career—playing for Los Angeles, Bettis ran over the Steelers for 76 yards on 16 carries, including a 29-yard score in a Rams 27–0 whitewash of the Black and Gold.

But after three seasons with the Rams, Bettis, for whatever reason, fell out of favor with the Rams, who were going from a running game coached by Chuck Knox to a passing-heavy attack with new coach Rich Brooks at the helm. Bettis, despite two 1,000-plus-yard seasons in his first three, was on the trade block. Much to the delight of the Steelers.

It was draft day of 1996, and the Steelers were looking to make a deal. With the future of then-feature back Bam Morris in

One Weird Line Score for the Bus

It was one of the strangest line scores in NFL history, but if you had him in your fantasy football league, you liked what you saw from Jerome Bettis on opening day 2004. The Steelers took on the Oakland Raiders at Heinz Field on September 12, 2004, and pulled out a hard-fought 24–21 win. Bettis scored all three Steelers touchdowns—all on one-yard runs. His day concluded with three touchdowns on five carries, but after losing yards on the other two carries, he ended with just one yard rushing. Five carries, one yard, three touchdowns.

question due to an arrest for marijuana possession, the Steelers targeted Bettis. The two clubs came to a deal, and the Steelers acquired Bettis for a second-round pick in 1996 and a fourth-round pick in 1997. It didn't take long for "the Bus" to quickly start rolling over teams while wearing black and gold.

He was simply amazing, using his quick moves and bruising power to gain chunks of yards. Seeing No. 36 Bettis jerseys all over Three Rivers Stadium and then Heinz Field became commonplace for Steelers faithful. His smile and energy were on display each week for the fans, and they soaked it up.

The famous nickname that Bettis carried for his career started at Notre Dame, where he played his college ball, but it was legendary Steelers radio color commentator Myron Cope who started calling Bettis "the Bus" during Steelers games, and Steelers fans everywhere quickly picked up on it. From T-shirts to cardboard cutouts of a bus, you didn't have to look hard to find avid fans.

On the field he delivered like no Steelers back since Hall of Famer Franco Harris. Bettis rushed for more than 1,000 yards in each of his first six seasons with the Black and Gold, from 1996 to 2001. He also put up three seasons in those years of more than 1,300 yards and in 1997 ran for a career-high 1,665 yards, as the Steelers ran their way to the AFC Championship Game before falling to the eventual Super Bowl–champion Broncos.

Injuries took their toll on Bettis, as he missed parts of the 2001 and 2002 seasons and then was put in a backup role to start 2003, but it didn't last very long. He took over the starting role as the Steelers struggled to a 6–10 season and then quickly found himself as a backup to Duce Staley to start the 2004 season. Again though, Bettis fans got their wish—after Staley went down due to injury, it was Bettis who came in and carried the load.

Bettis was looking at that season as a possible swan song. He knew that his time as a top back was closing, and he wanted to go out on top. Thanks to an amazing season from rookie QB Ben Roethlisberger and a defense that was top-notch, the Steelers had an incredible 15–1 regular season and a great shot to finally get their future Hall of Fame running back to the Super Bowl.

It didn't happen.

The team suffered a serious letdown in the AFC Championship Game at home versus the Patriots, losing badly, 41–27. Bettis walked off Heinz Field that day thinking that the loss could have been it, and that he was going to walk away one game short of his ultimate goal. But, after a few weeks and some prodding from teammates, he decided to return. His decision paid off—he and the team rebounded from a three-game losing streak that left them at 7–5 in November, and they won their final four games to reach the playoffs as a wild-card.

The Bus was a major part of the team's three playoff wins, putting Bettis in the position to play Super Bowl XL in his home-town of Detroit. He played a part in helping the Steelers walk away with their fifth Super Bowl title, following a 21–10 victory. On the podium after the contest, one of the Steelers' all-time greats announced he was walking away. "It's been an incredible ride," Bettis said. "I played this game to win a championship. I'm a champion [now], and I think the Bus' last stop is here in Detroit."

Bettis jerseys can still be seen at Steelers games, and for good reason. He finished his 13 NFL seasons as the league's fifth all-time leading rusher with 13,662 yards and 91 touchdowns. In 2013, Bettis was denied a bust in the Hall of Fame in Canton, Ohio, at the Pro Football Hall of Fame. There's no doubt that he will eventually gain admittance, and among Steelers fans, Bettis is still regarded as one of the most popular players on and off the field.

19 Rod Woodson

Rod Woodson was a playmaker throughout his 10 seasons with the Steelers, known for making a habit of intercepting returns for touchdowns, as well as being one of the best all-around cover corners in NFL history. The Steelers and Chuck Noll used their first-round draft pick in 1987 on Woodson, this after a successful college career at Purdue. Not only could Woodson shut down opposing receivers in college, he also played on offense and even was a great track-and-field athlete.

There wasn't much that Woodson didn't do in his decade with the Steelers. It was mostly those 10 seasons that put him in his rightful place in the Pro Football Hall of Fame in August 2009. "He, in my opinion, might be the greatest athlete that Chuck Noll ever drafted," said Mel Blount about Woodson. "And that's saying a lot when you think of all the Hall of Famers. This guy was special."

Woodson was 6'2", 200 pounds, and ran like a deer. He ran a 4.3 40, and was one of the best man-to-man cover corners in the game throughout his career. Then there was the added dimension that he was also a dangerous punt returner and kick returner—the Steelers knew early on that any way to get the ball in his hands was only going to help the team. And it did.

Woodson a Star in More than Just Football

While Rod Woodson's exploits on the football field are well documented, many are unaware of just how good Woodson was when it came to another field—track and field. While at Purdue, Woodson was twice awarded All-America honors in track and field, and as of 2010 holds the Purdue records for both the 60- and 110-meter hurdles.

In 1984 Woodson qualified for the Olympic trials in the 100-meter hurdles, and while he would have made a great run at it, he decided to continue his football career, which at the end of the day paid off not only for him but for the Steelers after they drafted him in the first round in 1987.

No. 26 ended his career, which lasted a total of 17 seasons playing with the Steelers, 49ers, Ravens, and Raiders, with 71 career interceptions, good currently for third in NFL history. His 1,483 return yards and 12 touchdowns on interceptions are the best in NFL history. He also was on the NFL's 75th Anniversary Team in 1994, one of only five active players to make the squad.

Woodson was a staple at the Pro Bowl, playing in a total of 11, and was the only player to ever make it as a cornerback, safety, and return specialist. The 1993 season was arguably one of Woodson's best—he played out of his mind all season, making big plays week after week. By the time it was said and done, he had earned the NFL Defensive Player of the Year award, joining Joe Greene, Mel Bount, and Jack Lambert as previous Steelers to win the award.

"If you tell me Rod Woodson is your top defensive back of all time," said longtime Steelers defensive coordinator Dick LeBeau, "you will get no argument from me because he certainly merits that." Two year after winning the Defensive Player of the Year award, disaster struck both Woodson and the Steelers in 1995. In an opening day win over the Lions, Woodson's foot got stuck in the Three Rivers turf as he tried to make a tackle on Hall of Fame running back Barry Sanders. "My foot stayed there, but my knee kept going," Woodson later said.

He tore his ACL, an injury that put him on the shelf for the remainder of the regular season. But there was a slight hope that he could somehow make it back if the team made it deep into the playoffs, though it was a long shot. Steelers coach Bill Cowher wasn't quick to pull the trigger and put his best player on injured reserve and kept Woodson on the active roster. It paid off. Woodson became the first player to ever come back from such an injury and play in the same season. He took part in Super Bowl XXX in Arizona against the Cowboys and made a memorable moment when he knocked away a pass from Cowboys Hall of Famer wide receiver Michael Irvin.

"He was making progress, and it was Rod Woodson. It meant so much to us. We put Carnell Lake at corner, and Willie Williams started," Cowher said about keeping Woodson on the active roster. "Rod was coaching those corners, and it kept him alive and ready. He had given so much of himself to our team, I thought it was a small thing to give him an opportunity to play in a Super Bowl."

Woodson played another season in Pittsburgh in 1996, but after that the team decided to go in a different direction, and being a free agent after the season concluded, he signed a deal with the San Francisco 49ers. He lasted just one season there before moving on to the rival Baltimore Ravens. Woodson played as a member of the Ravens in Super Bowl XXXV, finally getting his due and earning a ring. A sign hung in Three Rivers Stadium for years that said, "Rod is God." When it came to being a playmaker in the Steelers' defense as well as an emotional leader, the phrase was dead on for a Hall of Fame player who played his best seasons in black and gold.

20 Lynn Swann

As the dynasty of the '70s began to mature for the Steelers, they needed a big-play receiver on offense, and in 1974 with their first-round draft pick, they found it. It was with that pick the team selected USC wide receiver and All-American Lynn Swann. Known for his graceful moves, high-flying catches, and toughness when it counted the most, Swann was a vital part of the team's four Super Bowls.

Even one of the greatest wideouts in NFL history admired what Swann meant to the game and being ahead of his time. "Lynn Swann was an idol," Jerry Rice said. "It would amaze me how he could fly through the air and make those catches. I'll never forget the one versus Dallas. It was the greatest catch I've ever seen."

Of course the catch Rice is talking about is better known as the "Levitating Leap," the play in Super Bowl X when Swann leaped in the air and tumbled to the turf, keeping his eyes on the ball at all times, and eventually landing on top of Cowboys cornerback Mark Washington. Swann made the grab for a 53-yard gain, and the play gets replayed over and over by NFL Films.

Swann was part of the most successful draft class in Steelers and NFL history, as he, along with three other Hall of Famers—wide receiver John Stallworth, center Mike Webster, and linebacker Jack Lambert all joined the team for the 1974 campaign. In that year, the rookie class led by Swann made an immediate impact. He led the NFL with 577 punt-return yards, a franchise record at the time. Swann made just 11 catches that season for 208 yards and two scores, but stepped up in the playoffs, catching the game-winning score in the AFC Championship Game in Oakland.

At the time, the Steelers' offense was a grind-it-out, physical offense that relied more on running backs Franco Harris and

Lynn Swann (88) catches a touchdown pass despite the best efforts of two Los Angeles Rams defenders in Super Bowl XIV in Pasadena, California. Swann's playing career ended with 336 catches for 5,462 yards and 51 touchdowns.

Rocky Bleier. Swann and fellow receiver Stallworth didn't get many chances to touch the ball—in the team's Super Bowl IX win over Minnesota, Swann didn't even catch a pass. That would change the following year when the team repeated as champions.

The Steelers' offense opened up, and Swann benefited the most. He caught 49 passes in 14 regular-season games, pulling in 781 yards and 11 touchdowns, the same number of catches he had the season before. The playoffs saw Swann's career reach another level. In the AFC Championship Game at icy Three Rivers Stadium against Oakland, Swann was laid out on a pass over the middle by the Raiders' George Atkinson.

He was carried off the field by Joe Greene, suffering a nasty concussion that would leave him doubtful for Super Bowl X against the Cowboys. While many thought he wouldn't play or would have

just a small impact on the game, Swann dominated. He made a
toe-tapping catch on the sideline for his first catch, the leap over
Washington later on, and then a 64-yard catch and run for a score
that gave the Steelers a 21–10 lead.

The receiver who wasn't even supposed to play was named the
MVP. He had four catches for 161 yards and the clinching score.
Quarterback Terry Bradshaw had just nine completions for 209
yards in the entire game, showing just how big of an impact Swann
had. Swann's toughness wouldn't be questioned again, and he was
well on his way to a Hall of Fame career.

After a bit of a down season the following year, where he had
just 28 catches and played in 12 games, he rebounded in 1977 with
a 50-catch season for 789 yards and seven scores. Again, though, as
the Steelers reloaded for another big title run in 1978, Swann was
at the forefront as the team's featured wide receiver. He had his best
season that year, playing in all 16 games, making 61 catches for 880
yards and 11 scores.

Again, Swann was ready to have a major impact in a Super Bowl
win, the team's third. Playing against the Cowboys, Swann made
seven catches for 124 yards and a touchdown. Swann's 18-yard
touchdown in the fourth quarter was the team's last of the game, and
it put them ahead 35–17. The Steelers held on to win 35–31.

The following season the team made its final title run of the
decade, and Swann played in 13 regular-season games, making 41
catches for 808 yards with five touchdowns. In Super Bowl XIV
against the Los Angeles Rams, Swann made five catches for 79
yards and a touchdown before leaving the game with an injury.
Overall, he had 364 yards receiving and 398 all-purpose yards in
the team's four Super Bowl wins, both records at the time.

Swann played three more seasons before retiring after the 1982
season, wrapping up his stellar career with 336 catches for 5,462
yards and 51 touchdowns. He was named to the Pro Bowl three
times (1975, '77, and '78), and was named to the NFL's All-Decade

Team in the '70s and to the Super Bowl Silver Anniversary Team.

After his playing days ended, Swann went on to a successful broadcasting career with ABC, calling football and participating in broadcasts of the Olympics, the Kentucky Derby, dog sledding, and ABC'S *Wide World of Sports.* He left the company in 2006 to run for governor of Pennsylvania.

As a player, he is lauded for his acrobatic catches, graceful moves, and big-play ability. He was bestowed with football's highest honor in 2001, when he was elected to the Pro Football Hall of Fame.

21 Jack Ham

The Steelers have always been known for their linebackers, but no outside linebacker has been as revered in Steelers history as Hall of Famer Jack Ham. Blessed with speed to close in on any running back coming out of the backfield—or wideout trying to catch a pass in the flat—Ham also read plays as well as any linebacker ever.

Ham came aboard the Steelers' roster as a second-round draft choice (34th overall) in 1971. He came to the team after a stellar career at Penn State, where he was an All-American. His college career was so good that in 1990 he was inducted into the College Football Hall of Fame. He ended his college career with 251 tackles, 143 of them unassisted.

He quickly jumped into what the Steelers were forming on defense and became the starting left linebacker in his rookie season. His quick rise to fame was a huge reason why the Steelers were able to let loose the famed Steel Curtain, and while the front four still receive a lot of credit, Ham was a major part of that legendary defense, as well.

While Ham was not quite as colorful as the likes of "Mean" Joe Greene, Ernie Holmes, L.C. Greenwood, or Jack Lambert, one thing that his teammates knew week in and week out was that Ham was almost always mistake-free. His play on the field resulted in being named an All-Pro for nine straight seasons, and he was the only unanimous defensive choice for the 1970s NFL Team of the Decade. He made the Pro Bowl eight years in a row, setting a record for linebackers.

Ham's speed and ability were remarkable, making him a great threat when it came to intercepting passes. For his career, Ham picked off 32 passes, which currently is third among NFL linebackers. He also added five postseason picks, a Steelers record. Two came in the 1974 AFC Championship Game in Oakland, a game that put the Steelers into their first Super Bowl.

For many of the great Steelers years of the '70s, Ham was also very durable. He played in 178 of 190 possible games. One setback was Super Bowl XIV, which he missed because of a dislocated bone in his left foot, suffered during the 15th game of the 1979 season. That injury was the start of the end for Ham. His play in 1980, after surgery, showed he was less than 100 percent.

He came back ready to go in 1981, but again had a major setback, breaking his arm in the preseason against the rival Browns,

Only One Jersey Number Never to Be Officially Worn Again

While other teams have jersey retirement ceremonies and "Rings of Honor," the Steelers have neither, though they have one jersey number that appears it will never be worn again. That is No. 70, which was worn last by Ernie Stautner from 1951 to 1963. Only one other player ever wore that number, and that was Darwin Horn in 1951.

While they don't officially retire numbers, the following numbers are not worn by current players: No. 12 Terry Bradshaw, No. 32 Franco Harris, No. 52 Mike Webster, No. 58 Jack Lambert, No. 59 Jack Ham, and No. 75 Joe Greene.

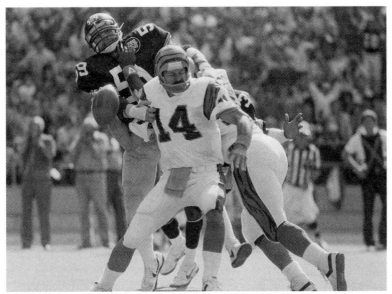

Linebacker Jack Ham (59) grabs the arm of Cincinnati's Kenny Anderson, causing Anderson to throw an interception in overtime at Pittsburgh in 1982. Ham picked off 32 passes in his career, which ranks him third in NFL history among linebackers. He was inducted into the Pro Football Hall of Fame in 1988.

and later tearing a muscle in his left knee. He continued to fight through the pain and played as hard as he could until he finally walked away from the Steelers and the NFL in 1983.

As would have been expected, five years later Ham took his rightful place in the Pro Football Hall of Fame in Canton. He was a first-ballot Hall of Famer and took his place beside many of the other great Steelers of those 1970s Super Bowl years.

That would not be the only awards coming Ham's way once his career ended. He made the NFL 75th Anniversary Team in 1994, *Sports Illustrated*'s All Century Team in 1999, and the Pro Football Hall of Fame All-Time Team in 2000.

Ham stayed involved in the game after his retirement. He has been a color analyst for the Penn State Radio Network and also has worked on several TV preseason games for the Steelers. In addition, he has worked NFL games for Westwood One Radio.

22 Super Bowl XIII: Beating the Boys Again

Many things about the Steelers had changed when the team took the field for Super Bowl XIII, a rematch with the Dallas Cowboys. No longer were they simply a smashmouth football team that relied on its defense to keep them in games. Now with a more mature Terry Bradshaw and two future Hall of Fame receivers in Lynn Swann and John Stallworth, the Steelers were able to beat teams with defense and offense, something different from years past.

So it didn't surprise many when the Steelers took the field on January 21, 1979, against the Cowboys and turned the game into a shootout, one that would go down as one of the most entertaining Super Bowls in NFL history.

Pittsburgh entered the game overall at 16–2, and were riding high on the memory of a 21–17 win over Dallas three years earlier in Super Bowl X. They knew they could outmuscle the Cowboys, and now with the NFL MVP in quarterback Terry Bradshaw playing at a high level, they felt they could put up more than enough points to win their third title.

It wasn't as easy as it sounds. Despite ending the night as the game's MVP, Bradshaw spent a good portion of the day keeping Dallas in the game. He threw one pick, lost two fumbles, and even allowed himself to be mugged on one play by Cowboys linebackers Mike Hegman and Thomas "Hollywood" Henderson, which saw them take the ball away from him for a 37-yard score.

Through it all, though, Bradshaw hung in there and finally was able to turn the game in his favor in the second quarter. Down 14–7 after Dallas had beaten him up for a score, Bradshaw found Stallworth on a beautiful 75-yard touchdown pass that showed the

Steelers' big-strike ability. The game was tied 14–14. Then right before halftime Bradshaw hit Swann for two big pass plays, and with 26 seconds left before the half, he hit running back Rocky Bleier for a seven-yard score as Bleier went high in the air for the catch to make it 21–14 Steelers.

The third quarter saw the Steelers begin to assert themselves even more on defense, and Dallas was unable to get much going until late in the quarter, when they drove to the Steelers' 10, but a famous drop by Hall of Fame tight end Jackie Smith forced Dallas to settle for a field goal to make it 21–17.

The fourth quarter saw Swann draw a pass-interference penalty to give the Steelers the ball at the Dallas 23, and a few plays later Franco Harris burst through a big hole and ran 22 yards to give the Steelers an 11-point lead at 28–17. The following kickoff was muffed by the Cowboys' Randy White, and the Steelers recovered, looking for the final knockout blow.

They went for the kill on the very next play. Bradshaw hit Swann, who made a leaping catch to give the Steelers a 35–17 lead with just 6:51 left. Dallas didn't go quietly, and quarterback Roger Staubach took them 89 yards on eight plays to draw closer on a touchdown pass to tight end Billy Joe Dupree, making it 35–24. They got an onside kick, and again Staubach drove the team quickly to the goal line, completing the drive with a four-yard touchdown pass to Butch Johnson with 22 seconds left.

The Steelers may have given up two scores, but time was on their side, and when Bleier recovered the next onside kick, the Black and Gold were one kneel-down away from their third Super Bowl title. The wide-out combo of Swann and Stallworth keyed the win—they went for 10 catches, 239 yards, and three scores. Bradshaw ended with an MVP, posting 318 yards passing on 17-for-30 with four touchdowns and a pick.

The game cemented the Steelers as the team of the '70s. They had proven once again to be the real "America's Team," topping

Tom Landry and the Cowboys for the second time on the game's biggest stage.

23 John Stallworth

When it came to the Steelers' wide-receiving corps during their dynasty run of four Super Bowls, there was an understanding when it came to Lynn Swann and John Stallworth. That understanding was that Swann was the sizzle, but Stallworth was the steak. Stallworth, a native of Tuscaloosa, Alabama, was one of those players drafted in the famous 1974 Steelers draft class. Swann was the club's first-round pick, and Stallworth was the Steelers' fourth-round pick, 82nd overall.

Stallworth was quiet but always was ready. With a season under his belt as an understudy, he was ready to step in and make an impact. He was a starter in his second season and combined with Swann to become the best wide-out tandem in the league. He had just 20 catches that 1975 season but started to show the talents that would make him one of the better receivers in the league. He also had four touchdowns that second season and averaged 21.2 yards per catch.

Injury, though, was always something Stallworth had to battle. In his 14-year Hall of Fame career, he missed 44 regular-season games due to fibula, foot, ankle, knee, and hamstring injuries. In 1976 he played in just eight games, making just nine catches. He returned to health in 1977, in time to see the team go 9–5 and get bounced from the playoffs by the Broncos. He caught 44 passes, a career high, for 784 yards and seven touchdowns, also career highs.

Finally the team came back to form in 1978, going 14–2, and rolling to an AFC title. Stallworth once again put up career numbers. He played in all 16 games, making 41 catches for 798 yards and nine touchdowns. In Super Bowl XIII Stallworth and Swann were the dynamic duo, grabbing 10 catches for 239 yards and three touchdowns. Stallworth had three catches, but he caught two touchdowns, one a 75-yard score that would be instrumental in the team's 35–31 title win over Dallas.

By 1979, Stallworth was a playmaker who actually overtook Swann as the team's best receiver. The players were getting older but had one more Super Bowl run in them, going 12–4 and facing the upstart Los Angeles Rams in the Super Bowl.

During the season Stallworth became Terry Bradshaw's go-to guy, catching 70 passes for 1,183 yards and eight scores. He shined on the big stage, once again making the big play. With the team trailing 19–17 early in the fourth quarter, Bradshaw let one fly, and Stallworth was able to run under it, make the catch, and go 73 yards to give the Steelers the lead for good in the eventual 31–19 win. Stallworth made just three catches in the game, but had 121 yards, including the game-winning score.

He played eight more seasons after the Steelers' fourth Super Bowl in 1979. He had an even better season catching passes from Mark Malone in 1984, the year the team reached the AFC Championship Game. That season Stallworth made 80 catches for 1,395 yards and 11 scores, his best season as a Steeler. He made 75 catches the following year, showing that he still had it.

By 1987, Stallworth was still a quality receiver, making 41 catches for 521 yards with two scores. He ended his stellar career with 537 receptions for 8,723 yards and 63 touchdowns.

He also was named the team's MVP twice and played in six conference championship games and four Super Bowl victories.

Another stat about Stallworth that gets overlooked is the 67-game pass-receiving streak from 1977 to 1982 that showed just how consistent he was. The quiet, always-reserved Stallworth finally got his due in 2002, when he was named to the Pro Football Hall of Fame.

Seven years later, Stallworth, a successful business owner who founded of Madison Research Corporation in 1986, became part-owner of the Steelers as part of the club's restructuring plan.

24 Big Ben Shines in the Steel City

It had been 24 years since the Steelers had spent a first-round draft pick on a quarterback when the 2004 draft approached. The club had just wrapped up a 6–10 season and was sitting with Tommy Maddox as their starter, having ended the Kordell Stewart reign at quarterback a season before. Maddox was merely a stopgap—despite having good stats for the season, he wasn't the long-term answer.

So as draft day arrived, the team had a plan. They wanted a big quarterback out of Miami, Ohio, by the name of Ben Roethlisberger. In some draft boards, Roethlisberger, who was coming off a great college career, was the best QB in the draft. Others felt that playing at a small MAC school was going to be the 22-year-old's downfall. The Steelers felt the risk was well worth it.

With the 11th overall pick, the team took Roethlisberger, thinking within a season or two he'd be ready to take over as the team's signal-caller. Boy, were they wrong. Starting with the second week of his rookie season, Roethlisberger has been the team's leader, and never did anyone think that following six seasons he would already be wearing two Super Bowl rings and own the record for most passing yards in a season by a Steelers quarterback.

His career started as fast as any quarterback in NFL history, winning his first 14 games and going 13–0 in the regular season. He did not lose a game until being a step away from the Super

A City Turns on Its Franchise QB

Steelers fans across the country stood behind Ben Roethlisberger after a motorcycle accident that could have claimed his life in June 2006. And they also backed him up after a woman came forth claiming assault, but appeared to be looking for a sizeable payday in 2009. But it seemed like the city and fans had enough after a 20-year-old college student came out and claimed assault against the QB in a nightclub in Georgia in March 2010.

As events of the allegations came out, Steelers fans quickly began letting the franchise know they had seen enough. They got rid of jerseys, ripped up bumper stickers, and put signs on storefronts saying things like "Let Ben Go."

Numerous sources say the club was active in talking to other teams about a deal that could have sent Roethlisberger to another team for a top 10 draft choice. Despite the more than $50 million the team has spent on the former first-round quarterback, the club knows its fan base, and made it known they wanted to make sure they took the allegations of the case seriously. For now, though, Roethlisberger remains a Steeler, hoping to rebuild his image and hoping the fans will once again embrace him as the leader of the team.

Bowl, when he threw three picks in a 41–27 loss to the eventual Super Bowl champion New England Patriots. It was a learning experience for Roethlisberger, one that would only take him a season to benefit from.

In 2005 he was ranked third with a passer rating of 98.6 and was 9–3 in the regular season. The club went 11–5 and made the playoffs as the sixth seed. It was that postseason that showed just how much of a franchise quarterback Big Ben was. He played well in Cincinnati in a 31–17 win and then stunned the Colts in a January 15 win as the Steelers knocked off the No. 1 seed 21–18. Against the Colts, Roethlisberger threw two touchdowns and threw for 197 yards.

The next week in the AFC Championship Game in Denver, Roethlisberger was at his best. He raced the team out to a 24–3

Ben Roethlisberger has quaterbacked the Steelers to three Super Bowls and two championships.

halftime lead, throwing two touchdowns in the first half and making great decisions all over the place. He ran in the clinching touchdown and ended the day going 21-for-29 for 275 yards. He didn't have a great day in Super Bowl XL, throwing just 9-for-21 for 123 yards and two picks, but still hit some big plays to help the team win their fifth title in a 21–10 win.

The off-season for Roethlisberger and the team was one of disaster. On June 12, 2006, he was involved in a horrific motorcycle accident that nearly cost him his life. Roethlisberger was driving without a helmet near downtown Pittsburgh when, in an attempt to make a left turn, he slammed into a car, went over his handlebars, and shattered the windshield of the vehicle with his head.

He was rushed to Mercy Hospital, where he went into surgery for more than seven hours. He suffered broken bones in his face, a broken upper and lower jaw and nose, a nine-inch laceration to the back of his head, and lost a couple of teeth. The quarterback has stated in interviews he felt it was a wake-up call, and he used it as motivation to get back on the playing field in time for opening day 2006.

That didn't happen, either. Just a few days before the opener against Miami, he had an emergency appendectomy, keeping him out of the first game. He came back but simply wasn't 100 percent, and the team limped to a 1–3 and then 2–6 start, stopping any real hopes of a title defense. He also suffered a concussion during the season, underscoring the team's problems as a whole.

The next season was a fresh start. With new coach Mike Tomlin and offensive coordinator Bruce Arians, Roethlisberger had his best season as a pro, throwing for 3,154 yards, 32 touchdowns, and just 11 picks as the team went 10–6 to win the AFC North. It was redemption for Roethlisberger.

The 2008 season continued Roethlisberger's rise as one of the league's best quarterbacks. While his numbers were not as impressive (17 touchdowns to 15 interceptions), he was the established leader of the team, and his play in the playoffs again showed his maturity. He led the team to their sixth title with a gutsy, last-minute drive against Arizona that ended with a remarkable throw to Santonio Holmes for an amazing 27–23 win.

Roethlisberger started the '09 season with a new contract that paid him $102 million over eight seasons. While the team started hot that year, it fell on hard times with a five-game losing streak that stopped hope of repeating as champions. Still, Roethlisberger is the unquestioned leader of the new generation of Steelers, and his never-say-die play has paid off with helping the team to a pair of Super Bowls. The ceiling for this quarterback continues to rise as one of the best in the game today.

If there is a downside to the story of Roethlisberger, it's his off-the-field behavior in the 2009 and 2010 off-seasons. In the '09 off-season, Roethlisberger was hit with a civil lawsuit in Lake Tahoe, Nevada, by 31-year-old Andrea McNaulty, who was working a hotel Roethlisberger was staying at while there for a golf tournament.

McNaulty claims that when she showed up to Roethlisberger's room to fix what he said was a broken TV, the quarterback assaulted her and forced himself on her. McNaulty, though, had some questionable tactics in the case, telling people she and the quarterback had consensual sex, and even going to Pittsburgh for a game in hopes of running into him. Roethlisberger denied from the start anything happened between him and McNaulty.

Then in the spring of 2010, another woman, this time a 20-year-old college student, came forth stating that Roethlisberger assaulted her in a bathroom inside a nightclub in Georgia. The case drew national attention if, for nothing else, it was the second straight off-season Roethlisberger was in the news for the wrong reasons. The case was eventually dismissed on April 12 since the state did not have enough evidence to push forward with charges.

The league did have something to say, however, as commissioner Roger Goodell stepped in and levied a suspension upon Roethlisberger, where he was forced by the league to sit the first four games at the start of the 2010 season. The city and its fans seemed to turn on their quarterback after the latest allegations, and many felt if the team was willing to trade wideout Santonio Holmes as they did, they should also cut ties with the quarterback who helped them win two recent Super Bowls.

Instead, after sitting out the first four games of the 2010 season, Roethlisberger became the leader the Steelers and fans had waited for, both on and off the field. He returned in Week 6 and led the team into the postseason with a record of 12–4.

He and the Steelers overcame a 14-point halftime deficit to beat the Ravens in the divisional playoff game, and then in the AFC Championship Game against the New York Jets, he played flawlessly for 30 minutes, building up a 24–3 halftime lead as the team eventually won 24–19 to earn a berth in Super Bowl XLV.

On the game's biggest stage, he and the offense suffered early but worked their way back from an 18-point deficit to eventually pull the game to 21–17. Roethlisberger threw for 263 yards and two scores, but he also threw two interceptions, and in the end the Steelers lost 31–25.

The 2011 season saw Roethlisberger fail to get the team back to the Super Bowl. Again Pittsburgh went 12–4, but this time was upset in the wild card round by the Broncos and Tim Tebow. In the course of the season, Roethlisberger threw for 21 touchdowns and 14 interceptions, but a late ankle injury hurt his and the team's chances at a repeat Super Bowl appearance.

The following season, 2012, was equally frustrating, as again Roethlisberger went down in a Monday night win over the Chiefs. The QB suffered a shoulder sprain and rib injury, and the team suffered without him. The Steelers had a shot at season's end to make the postseason, but late losses to San Diego, Dallas, and Cincinnati left them on the outside looking in at the NFL postseason.

Roethlisberger holds many of the Steelers' passing records, but still wants more rings on his fingers to continue to build on his legacy as one of the greatest QBs ever to wear a Steelers uniform.

25 Super Bowl XIV: The End of the Dynasty

Super Bowl XIV was bittersweet for the Steelers. Though it was the day the team clinched their fourth title—the only team in the league to do so—it was also the last great day the team that dominated the 1970s had together. That team had its share of issues in 1979, as some of its best players were showing signs of wear and tear, while others had already seen the light at the end of their careers nearing. The club still went 12–4 and led the league in total offense. It had the second-ranked defense, but there was a belief that the Steelers' run of titles was nearing its end.

Still, this was the team of the decade, and there was no doubt this club was the best team in the NFL. They entered Super Bowl Sunday as a decided favorite (11½ points) over the upstart Los Angeles Rams, a team that was booed out of their own stadium at midseason. The Rams were also entering the big game for the first time and were playing with a backup at quarterback—starter Pat Haden was out with an injury, leaving Vince Ferragamo to step in as signal-caller.

Los Angeles had nothing to lose, and they played like it. Early on in the game they trailed 3–0 after Steelers kicker Matt Bahr nailed a 41-yard field goal, but then after a short kickoff, the Rams put together their first drive of the game. Running back Wendell Tyler went for a 39-yard run, the longest run the Steelers allowed all season. Fullback Cullen Bryant went in from the 1 shortly after that, and Los Angeles led 7–3.

The Steelers' offense was on display the following possession—Larry Anderson went 45 yards with the kickoff to Pittsburgh's 47. Then Franco Harris went 12 yards, and Rocky Bleier went for a yard. Terry Bradshaw hit tight end Bennie Cunningham for eight, and after another Bleier run, Bradshaw hit Lynn Swann for 18 yards. Cunningham then caught a pass for 13 yards to the Rams' 5, and two Harris runs later the Steelers were back up 10–7.

The Rams came back again, attacking the Steelers' defense and getting a big pass-interference penalty to set up a game-tying field goal to make it 10–10. Bradshaw and the offense couldn't do much the remainder of the half against Los Angeles, and after an interception, the Rams converted a field goal from 45 yards out to give the heavy underdogs a 13–10 halftime lead.

The big-play offense of the Steelers finally came alive in the third quarter, when Bradshaw and Swann combined for a 47-yard touchdown to give the Black and Gold a 17–13 lead, though it wouldn't last long. Los Angeles receiver Bill Waddy pulled in a 50-yard pass from Ferragamo, and the next play Los Angeles pulled some trickery.

Running back Lawrence McCutcheon took a handoff, started to the right, and then threw a 24-yard touchdown pass to Ron Smith, giving Los Angeles a 19–17 lead after a missed extra point. The Steelers' defense had been beaten to the punch all day, and the team seemed stunned. The next two Steelers offensive possessions ended with Rams picks, and with 15 minutes left between them and a fourth title, the Rams led by two.

The fourth quarter, however, showed what champions are made of. Even with Swann out due to injury, the offense struck again. From their own 27, Bradshaw wound up and fired a perfect deep pass to John Stallworth in the middle of the field. Rams defender Rod Perry just missed batting the ball away, and the pass fell into the arms of Stallworth, who went the final yards for the famous 73-yard score. It was 24–19 Steelers with 12:04 to play.

After a couple of punts, the Rams had one more drive left in them to try and take the lead. This time, the Steel Curtain bent but didn't break. Los Angeles marched up the field, combining Ferragamo passes and Tyler runs to get to the Steelers' 32-yard line. On first down, the QB made a mistake, not seeing linebacker Jack Lambert waiting for his pass down the middle. The Hall of Famer picked off the pass, saving the Steelers' lead with less than six minutes to play.

Then it was Bradshaw and Stallworth again, this time on a third-and-7 hook-up for a 45-yard gain to the Rams' 22, effectively clinching the game for the Steelers. An interference penalty in the end zone set up the ball at the 1, and on third down Harris went over, putting the game away at 31–19.

It was a coming-out party for Stallworth, who had three catches for 121 yards and a score, and Bradshaw was the MVP, going 14-for-21 for 309 yards with two touchdowns. Some felt that the Steelers' run would continue, as the "One for the Thumb" phrase popped up almost right after the win.

It was not to be, and it took the organization 26 years to win another Super Bowl, long after the players of the '70s had left the game and coach Chuck Noll had retired. In that respect, Super Bowl XIV was the end of a dynasty.

26 Harrison's Immaculate Interception

Plays can define a game or, in some cases, a career. While the career of Steelers linebacker James Harrison is yet to be completed, the play that he will forever be remembered for put him in the record books and pushed the Steelers to their sixth Super Bowl title.

The 2008 season was magical for the former Kent State Golden Flash, who had spent a good portion of his career simply trying to make it onto a roster. Hard work finally paid off for Harrison in 2007, when he became a starter for the Steelers. He made an impact right away, but he saved his best for Super Bowl Sunday in Tampa Bay.

The Steelers had controlled the first quarter and a half of Super Bowl XLIII, building a 10–0 lead, but Arizona was on their way back into it with a short touchdown. After a Ben Roethlisberger interception, they were in position to take the lead before halftime. The momentum of the game was changing.

Enter Harrison. The Cardinals had a first-and-goal at the Steelers' 1 with 18 seconds left in the first half. Everyone knew that they had to throw the football. Kurt Warner tried to squeeze the ball into Anquan Boldin at the goal line, but what he didn't see was Harrison drop back into coverage.

The NFL Defensive Player of the Year snatched the pass and started a historic trip up the sideline. It was a run for the ages,

Linebacker James Harrison returns an interception 100 yards for a touchdown during Super Bowl XLIII. The play changed the momentum of the game just before halftime. The Steelers won the game 27–23.

with no less than five Steelers protecting him as he made his way down the field. First it was Warner trying to make the tackle, but he failed. Harrison almost lost his footing, but he just kept his legs churning—even Steelers' play-by-play man Bill Hillgrove seemed surprised that Harrison stayed on his feet.

He tried to cut inside at one point, making a mini leap that again didn't exactly look graceful, but, as coach Mike Tomlin always said, "Style points don't matter." LaMarr Woodley made a block, then defensive lineman Brett Keisel helped out in getting a piece of a Cardinal along the way.

Things on the play got really sticky after Harrison went over a fallen Cardinal around the Arizona 30, as two of the fastest Cardinals, wideouts Larry Fitzgerald and Steve Breaston, closed in to try one last time to bring down the linebacker. They grabbed him around the 5-yard line, and Harrison started to fall forward. Lucky for him, as he was falling forward, he was also falling on Fitzgerald, who was grabbing him from behind on the side. Breaston was coming in to hit Harrison on his left, making him fall to his right. He landed on Fitzgerald.

As Harrison fell, he did a summersault into the end zone, holding onto the ball and not having his knees hit short of the goal line, which would have killed what was the greatest play in Super Bowl history. The official signaled a touchdown, and Harrison stayed down, laying spread-eagle in the end zone, completely exhausted.

The officials looked it over, and the correct call stood, making it 17–7 Steelers. If Arizona had scored to take a 14–10 halftime lead, who knows what the outcome of the game would have been. Harrison's play negated that scenario, and the Steelers went on to win the game 27–23.

The history-making play had so many twists and turns, and it remains a play for the ages, the greatest defensive play in Super Bowl history. Even though Harrison left the team after the 2012 season, it is still remembered as perhaps the greatest touchdown in Steelers Super Bowl history.

27 Tomlin Steps In, and the Winning Ways Continue

Much like Bill Cowher before him, Mike Tomlin's job entering the 2007 season with the Steelers was not going to be an easy one. All Tomlin had to do was maintain the winning and championship runs that Cowher had done for most of his 15 seasons on the sideline. Cowher had inherited a winning tradition from Hall of Fame coach Chuck Noll, and now it was up to Tomlin to keep the streak

Coach Mike Tomlin had big shoes to fill when he took over in 2006. Since then, he led the team to its sixth Super Bowl title, becoming the youngest coach in history to win the Lombardi Trophy.

going. It was not going to be easy, and for Tomlin, he wanted to do it his way.

Tomlin, a native of Newport News, Virginia, was a longshot at best to be the Steelers' head coach when Cowher announced he was walking away after the 2006 season. All along everyone felt that the next coach would come from within the organization—both offensive coordinator Ken Whisenhunt and offensive line/assistant coach Russ Grimm seemed ready and primed for a chance to take the helm.

Once Dan Rooney and those inside the Steelers' camp spoke to Tomlin, it was obvious it was not going to be long before he was the head coach of some franchise. He took the team by storm with his presence and impressed the club so much that he and Grimm were the final two candidates. While the Steelers didn't want to lose Grimm, in the end they went with Tomlin, making a statement that hiring from within isn't always the best decision. A few years into Tomlin's head coaching career, it's obvious they made the right choice.

Coming in as a 34-year-old head coach for a club that was two years removed from hoisting a Super Bowl trophy is never easy. Tomlin did something that most first-time coaches never do—he kept many of the assistant coaches from the Cowher era. The biggest move was keeping defensive coordinator Dick LeBeau, which surprised some, considering Tomlin practiced the 4-3 defense while an assistant in Tampa Bay and Minnesota. It took a lot for him to stay with the Steelers' 3-4 defense, but by 2008 the move paid off, and the club rode their 3-4 defense to a sixth Super Bowl title.

There were plenty of early growing pains in Tomlin's first season. He ran a physically and mentally draining training camp that first year. And some of the personnel moves he made were met with shaking heads, not the least of which was the release of longtime popular linebacker Joey Porter.

It didn't take long for Tomlin's first team to make an impact. The Steelers in 2007 started out 3–0 and were 9–3 before some injuries began to catch up with them. The club was drained by December, and they lost three of their last four games, making them the No. 4 seed in the AFC. They hosted a first-round playoff game against the Jacksonville Jaguars, where they fell behind 28–10, launched a spirited comeback, but lost 31–29 to end their season.

Tomlin did some things differently in 2008, tweaking his training-camp schedule and making sure the players were a lot fresher. They had the toughest schedule in recent NFL history, and they tore through it with a punishing defense and quarterback Ben Roethlisberger, who was getting better and better. The coach pushed all the right buttons, motivating his team and making sure they stayed humble and focused the whole season.

Tomlin Not So Bad on the Field, Either

Steelers coach Mike Tomlin was a three-year starter at William and Mary, where he finished his career with 101 catches for 2,046 yards and a school record 20 touchdowns. Tomlin was a first-team All-Yankee Conference selection in 1994 and established a school record with 20.2 yards per catch. Despite being a receiver, it was only at the start of his career with William and Mary and then Arkansas State where he coached receivers before he moved on to coach on the other side of the ball, starting with defensive backs in 1998 also at Arkansas State. He won a Super Bowl ring with the Tampa Bay Buccaneers as their defensive backs coach in 2003.

The team went 12–4 and ended the regular season as the No. 2 seed in the AFC, earning a first-round bye. They topped the Chargers after a slow start in the divisional playoff game, 35–24, and then beat the Ravens 23–14 for the AFC Championship. It was the third time Tomlin's team topped its archrival. Then, in a memorable Super Bowl against the Cardinals, the club rallied after the defense allowed a late touchdown by Larry Fitzgerald, and Roethlisberger drove his team down the field for a score to pull out a 27–23 win.

Tomlin became the youngest head coach to win a Super Bowl, was the 2008 Motorola NFL Coach of the Year, and set a Steelers record by winning 22 games in his first two seasons. The 2009 season was again full of challenges. The team started 6–2, but a hard-to-swallow five-game losing streak ended most of its playoff dreams. The Steelers ended the year 9–7 and out of the playoffs.

The following season the coach and team had to play the first four games without starting QB Ben Roethlisberger, who was suspended for his off-the-field conduct. Tomlin may have pulled off his best coaching job that season, keeping the team together under trying circumstances. Once Roethlisberger returned, they stormed to the postseason, going 12–4 and winning another AFC North title. They got to Super Bowl XLV, but fell to the Green Bay Packers 31–25.

The team was once again one of the league's best in 2011, going 12–4, but two losses to the Ravens made them to a wild card team in the AFC. Beat up and on the road, Denver pulled a stunning OT upset to knock Tomlin and the Steelers out of the postseason after just over 60 minutes of football.

Things seemed to catch up with the Steelers in 2012, as again injuries put a damper on the season, as they had to play three games without Roethlisberger, and they eventually turned a 6–3 start into an 8–8 season, and were for the second time in four seasons watching the postseason from home.

Tomlin remains one of the game's best coaches, and while some are amazed at how the Steelers always seem to be in the hunt year after year, the coach seems to flash that smile, and always seems to find a way to get the best out of his players.

28 Heinz Field

The new generation of the Steelers felt the home that had housed them for four Super Bowls, Three Rivers Stadium, had become outdated, and they needed a new home to move forward as a franchise. After much planning and $281 million dollars later, Heinz Field opened in the late summer of 2001, housing not only the NFL club but also the University of Pittsburgh Panthers. The stadium insures that the Steelers will remain in Pittsburgh for decades to come, as well as gives them extra revenue to sign free agents who they couldn't previously afford.

The team also added revenue when the locally owned H.J. Heinz Company purchased the stadium's naming rights. As part of that deal, Heinz will pay the Steelers a whopping $57 million

The Opening of Heinz Field

August 18, 2001, was the official opening of Heinz Field, but it didn't open up with 65,000-plus screaming fans rooting for the Black and Gold. Instead, the stadium was filled with mostly teenage girls rooting on their favorite band—N'Sync. The Steelers didn't get to play in their new home until the following Saturday, opening the stadium with a preseason game against the Detroit Lions, which they won 20–7.

through 2021, adding more dollars in the team's pocket for current and future players while providing a facility that is chock full of the present and past.

Groundbreaking of the new stadium took place on June 18, 1999, and construction started a month later. The design links the building to the area and includes details that acknowledge the team's rich history. The stadium is built of the material synonymous with Pittsburgh—steel—about 12,000 tons of it. Memorabilia from the Steelers and Pitt's past is also housed at the stadium, making the Coca-Cola Great Hall a fan's delight to walk though before or after games. With a 65,050 seating capacity, Heinz Field houses 129 luxury suites and approximately 7,300 club seats, all of which are

Heinz Field has been sold out for every Steelers game since the stadium opened in 2001.

Record Crowd Celebrates the Demise of Ravens

While the Steelers have celebrated a number of big home wins over the years, the largest live crowd to see a Steelers game took place in January 2009 as the team topped the Ravens 23–14 to win the AFC Championship Game. The announced crowd was 65,350. The previous record crowd at Heinz Field was 65,242, when the team lost the 2004 AFC Championship to the New England Patriots. The largest regular-season crowd in Heinz Field history was on October 26, 2008, when the Steelers lost a hard-fought game to the New York Giants. A total of 64,991 were on hand for that matchup.

sold out well in advance. In fact, every game at the stadium since its opening has sold out.

The outside of the stadium is breathtaking. Fans can walk along the river among thousands of Steelers faithful as they enter the front of the stadium. There is a bronze statue of Steelers original owner Art Rooney there, moved about 100 feet from its old position outside of Three Rivers Stadium.

One thing that still is considered a drawback to the new stadium is the field itself. In 2006 the field was voted as the worst in the league in a survey done by NFL players. A Monday night game in 2007 really brought the field's shortcomings to light. After hosting high school championship games and a college game in the preceding days, the field was a mud pit. A new layer of sod was laid down, but one and a half inches of rain made it almost impossible for either the Steelers or Miami Dolphins to gain any footing. Pittsburgh needed 59:43 to finally score the first points of the game, and in the end, they overcame Miami 3–0. To this day, likely due to the fact the city holds so many events at the stadium, the grounds crew at Heinz continues to do what they can to make sure the field is as good as it possibly can be for NFL Sundays.

Make no mistake about it, Heinz Field is a jewel among new NFL stadiums. Sure it's not easy to kick field goals there (just ask the Jets' Doug Brien, who missed two in a playoff game against the

Steelers in January 2005), but for the Steelers and their fans, they have enjoyed an advantage there just like they did at Three Rivers. The players have embraced the stadium, as the fans have, as well, making it yet another connection that brings fans and the team closer together.

29 John Henry Johnson

Before the days of famous Steelers running backs like Franco Harris and Jerome Bettis, the Steelers' real first workhorse was a 210-pound fullback named John Henry Johnson. He was the club's No. 2 draft pick in 1953, but didn't actually play for the Steelers until 1960. He opted to start his career in Canada, where he was the MVP his rookie year. The following year he played for the 49ers and then was traded to the Lions and, finally, Pittsburgh.

He was known for his great blocking and soft hands, which also made him a dangerous receiver out of the backfield. In the 1962 season he caught 32 passes for 226 yards and a touchdown. In all, he had 106 catches for 814 yards with the Steelers. He was truly a fullback in a halfback's body, able to use both speed and power to become one of the best and most underrated backs in NFL history.

Johnson's best years in his 12-year pro career were spent in a Steelers uniform. From 1960 to 1965 Johnson was the club's best back, rushing for more than 1,000 yards in 1962 and 1964, when it wasn't commonplace in the NFL to put up 1,000-yard seasons. His best year with Pittsburgh came in 1962, when he went for 1,141 yards and seven touchdowns, putting up 4.5 yards per carry. He made a significant impact during his other years with the Steelers, as well, rushing for 621 yards in 1960, 787 yards in 1961, and 773

Only One 00

The Steelers franchise has only seen one player ever wear the jersey No. 00. That player was halfback/starting quarterback Johnny Clement, who played with the team from 1946 to 1948. Clement came to the Steelers after playing one year (1941) for the Chicago Cardinals. After his three seasons with the Steelers, he finished his career with the AAFC's Chicago Hornets in 1949.

yards in 1963. His second-highest rushing season came in 1964, when he rushed for 1,048 yards and scored seven touchdowns. He ran for 26 touchdowns in his five full seasons with the team (he played in just one game for the Steelers in 1965).

Johnson seemed to be all about firsts. On October 10, 1964, against the rival Browns, he rushed for 200 yards on 30 carries, making him the first Steeler to rush for 200 yards in a game. With his efforts, the Steelers pulled off a major upset, beating the powerful Browns 23–7. He was just the ninth player in the NFL to rush for at least 200 yards in a single game.

He ended his career in 1966, playing 14 games for the Houston Oilers and rushing for a total 226 yards. In his six seasons with the Steelers, he had rushed for 4,381 yards on 1,006 carries, an average of 4.4 yards per carry. He's still highly regarded as one of the best Steelers backs of all-time, fourth all-time for most rushing yards behind just Franco Harris, Jerome Bettis, and Willie Parker. When he retired, Johnson was fourth all-time among rushers in pro football history. He was behind just Jim Brown, Jim Taylor, and Joe Perry in the all-time leading ground gainers in NFL history. He ran for 6,803 yards on 1,571 carries, putting up 4.3 yards per carry.

Twenty years after his retirement, he finally got his due in 1987, when he was elected to the Pro Football Hall of Fame. Johnson will always be remembered as one of the great Steelers of all-time. He was chosen as one of the best Steelers in history from 1933 to 1970, along with Bobby Layne, Ernie Stautner, and Bill

Dudley. He also was named one of the 50 most significant Bay Area Sports Figures of the Century in the Alameda newspaper for his playing time with the 49ers.

30 "Bullet" Bill Dudley

A throwback and one of the first Steelers to ever be recognized for just how good he was, "Bullet" Bill Dudley was a star. Dudley found his way on a couple of Steelers teams that were not all that good, and his play made them competitive. William McGarvey Dudley was 5'10", 182 pounds when he played, but some say that he was even smaller, possibly about 176 pounds, and even then some said he may be too small to take the pounding doled out to halfbacks.

Dudley was a force with the team on the field. He was even known for his mouth, yelling at teammates when he felt they were not giving their all—something that was unheard of at the time. The Steelers were never much of a powerhouse and usually found themselves at the bottom of the standings. Dudley wanted to change all that.

He could do a little bit of everything, and he did it all well. The University of Virginia gave Dudley a scholarship when he was only 16 years old, and by his third season, he was a starter and led the Southern Conference in total offensive yards. By his senior season, he was named the best college player of the year by the Washington D.C. Touchdown Club. He led the nation in four categories: touchdowns scored (18), points scored (134), rushing average (6.2 yards per rush), and total touchdowns (29). In 1941, playing in the East-West Shrine Game, he picked off four passes and threw for his team's only touchdown in a 6–6 tie.

Dudley Wins MVP Award at Three Levels

"Bullet" Bill Dudley was a dynamic player who was one of the very best of his time. He shined as a member of the Steelers for the three seasons he played there and set a number of records that will be hard to top. Dudley remains as the only player ever with a rushing touchdown, touchdown reception, punt return for touchdown, kickoff return for touchdown, interception return for touchdown, fumble return for a touchdown, and a touchdown pass. Not only that, he also has a touchdown via lateral and has kicked PATs and field goals. Dudley is the only person to win MVP awards at the college, service, and professional levels, winning the MVP award while at Virginia and the NFL MVP award in 1946 with the Steelers.

So it wasn't a shock when the Steelers took him first in the 1942 draft. They gave him the ball right away, and coach Walt Kiesling made him a feature in the team's offense. It paid off. He ran for a 44-yard touchdown and also threw a 24-yard touchdown in his first game, a 24–14 loss to the Eagles. The following week he raced for an 84-yard touchdown on a kick return as the team lost to Washington 28–14.

Dudley's play his first year helped the team improve from a 1–9–1 record in 1941 to a 7–4 mark. He also led the NFL in rushing, with 696 yards on 162 carries, and was named to the All-Pro team. Throwing the ball, he went 35-for-94 for 438 yards and two touchdowns, and even punted, kicking 18 times for a 32-yards-per-punt average. He was also solid returning kicks on both kickoffs and punts.

His NFL career was put on hold in 1943, when he went into the U.S. Army Air Corps. He shined on the football field for the Army football team, helping the team to go 12–0 in 1944 and was named the team MVP. He flew two supply missions at the end of World War II and was ready to continue his NFL career near the end of the 1945 season.

He returned to Pittsburgh and played in the last four games of that '45 season, scoring two touchdowns against the Chicago

Cardinals and even kicking two extra points. He ended the year as the Steelers' leading scorer and ran for 204 yards and returned three kickoffs for 65 yards despite playing in just four games. The team ended the season with a 2–8 record.

The next season was Dudley's best as a Steeler, and he was the NFL's MVP. He scored 48 points that season, helping the team go 5–5–1. That season he led the NFL in rushing, punt returns, and interceptions. It was a season for the record books, and one that stood out when he made the Pro Football Hall of Fame in 1966.

Dudley was traded to the Detroit Lions in 1947, earning a three-year deal worth $20,000 a season. He played there for three seasons, and in 1949 was traded to the Washington Redskins, where he played another three seasons before leaving the game in 1953 due to knee injuries.

After retiring from the NFL, Dudley became a scout for the Steelers and Lions, and eventually went into the insurance business with his brother in Virginia. He was placed in the College Football Hall of Fame in 1956, the Pro Football Hall of Fame in 1966, and the Virginia Sports Hall of Fame in 1972. He even served four terms in the Virginia House of Delegates. He passed away at the age of 88 in February 2010 after suffering a stroke in late January of that year.

31 L.C. Greenwood

L.C. Greenwood was maybe the quietest member of the Steelers' famed Steel Curtain, but in a way he was also the loudest. He and John "Frenchy" Fuqua would show off their style on Fridays in the locker room during the Steelers' glory years of the 1970s. Greenwood, who was known for wearing bell-bottoms, funky hats, and even capes, always won. But his flamboyant style off the field said little about how good Greenwood was as a player on it.

L.C. Henderson Greenwood was picked by the Steelers in the 10th round of the 1971 draft, just as the team was starting to climb out of the depths of the NFL. He quickly cemented himself on the team, becoming the starting left defensive end on the Steel Curtain. He stayed on that line until he walked away from the game in 1981. Known for his quickness, Greenwood put up some impressive career highlights, including six Pro Bowl selections, two All-Pro selections, four Super Bowl victories, 73.5 career sacks, and five sacks in four Super Bowls.

What made Greenwood stand out other than his play on the field were the shoes he wore. His gold shoes were his signature, a staple that followed him his whole career. Those gold shoes could be seen every Sunday making tackles and sacking quarterbacks. Before the shoes, the P.A. announcer often would incorrectly credit another Pittsburgh defender with a tackle Greenwood made. It made Greenwood feel slighted, so he took to coloring his shoes gold so he would always be noticed—and he made quite a few noticeable plays over his great career.

He led the Steelers six times in sacks, putting up as many as 11 in one season. He also led the NFL with five fumble recoveries in the 1971 season, 14 in his career. He always seemed to be a force in the pass rush of the Steel Curtain. His size, 6'6", 245 pounds, made him tough to block, and he also had the speed to get around most offensive linemen. His great play in the Steelers' four Super Bowls earned him a spot on the Super Bowl Silver Anniversary Team in 1991.

People still talk about Greenwood for his shoes. What many don't know about L.C. was that he believed his spiffy looks on the field were related to his play. "If you look good, you play good," Greenwood said in NFL Films' story about the 1979 Steelers, *America's Game.* "You gotta have everything in the perfect order. Your shirt gotta be tucked in. I felt if I was clean, I'd play that way."

And just about every Sunday Greenwood played clean. He likely won't ever find his way to the Pro Football Hall of Fame—despite being a finalist in 2006—but his fashion sense and gold shoes will forever go down in Steelers history.

32 Andy Russell

Linebacker Andy Russell doesn't get the credit he deserves for his intelligent play on the field. The former Steelers linebacker served as defensive captain for nine seasons and played on the first two championship teams, winning Super Bowls IX and X. Russell was selected for the Pro Bowl seven times and was the Steelers' MVP in 1970. He was a member of the NFL All-Decade Team from 1965 to 1975 and also one of the NFL's 300 Greatest Players.

Russell was born in 1941 in Detroit, Michigan, and began playing football as a freshmen in high school when his family moved to the St. Louis, Missouri, area. He played end in 10th grade, and then played fullback and linebacker the following two years, earning all-state honors his senior season. He turned down plenty of chances to play out of state, instead choosing to play for his hometown college, Missouri. He lettered for Tigers teams from 1960 to 1962, playing both ways. He shined in the three bowl games he played in, picking off two passes in MU's Orange Bowl win over Navy in 1961. He also led Missouri in rushing in 1961, and even took a pass back 47 yards on an interception in a 10–0 win over Oklahoma that season.

The Steelers liked his potential and were in need of playmakers, so they took a chance on Russell in the 16th round of the 1963 draft, picking him 220th overall. He took the field as a linebacker in 1963

First Big-Money Player Starred in Pittsburgh

Back when players would play football for a few months and then hold down other jobs, it was Art Rooney who shelled out cash for the first "rich" player in football. That player was Colorado All-American Byron "Whizzer" White, who was signed in 1938 to a contract that paid him $15,800. White went on to lead the league in rushing that year, and then rushed his way to a seat on the U.S. Supreme Court, where he served for 31 years before retiring in 1993.

and had three interceptions and one fumble recovered in his rookie season. Russell left the Steelers following that season to serve in the U.S. Army as a lieutenant in Germany.

He returned to the Steelers in 1966 at the age of 25 and quickly became the leader of a defensive squad that quite frankly wasn't very good. They never made much of an impact in the NFL against the big boys, and it wasn't until Russell was introduced to a new coach in 1969 that the Steelers finally got on track.

Chuck Noll took over and made Russell a better player. While he was already a Pro Bowl player, Noll made him more disciplined, and Russell started to click more with a defense that was filling up with future Hall of Famers. Russell, though, was the leader of that unit in the locker room, helping mold what would go on to make history as one of the greatest defenses in NFL history.

The Steelers just kept getting better, and by the time the unit was ready for its first Super Bowl in 1974, Russell was a veteran leader, guiding the young players to the next level. He was 33 years old but was still playing at a high level when the team topped the Vikings 16–6 in January 1975. The following year he received the NFL Players Association's Byron "Whizzer" White Award for the player who had done the most for his team, his community, and his country.

After the club won its second title in the '75 season, Russell began to look ahead to his post-NFL career. He played the 1976 season, then walked away with two rings and many more accolades as a key member of those two Steelers Super Bowl clubs.

After the game, he enjoyed success as an author, publishing three books: *Andy Russell: A Steeler Odyssey, An Odd Steelers Journey,* and *Beyond the Goalpost.* Russell also is heavily involved in charity work—he was the 1989 Big Brothers and Sisters Man of the Year and has raised more than $5 million dollars for the Russell Family Foundation.

33 Hines Ward

Hines Ward played with a smile on his face, and it drove the opposition crazy. Every Sunday Ward, who was with the Steelers his entire career, played with the heart, determination, and pure joy that you simply don't see from many NFL players these days. Make no mistake about it, Ward played with a fire that made him one of the best wide receivers in the NFL, but he went about it with a huge heart that made him one of the most popular Steelers in franchise history.

It didn't start out so great for Ward, though. When he was drafted by Pittsburgh in the third round of the 1998 draft, the team didn't exactly know what to do with him. Ward had played quarterback for Forest Park High School in Georgia, and then at the University of Georgia he was the ultimate "slash" player, catching 149 career passes for 1,965 yards, playing tailback for 3,870 all-purpose yards, and also holding records at the school for pass attempts, completions, and yards in a bowl game.

When the Steelers took him, he was initially used as a special-teams player and sparingly as a wide receiver. That first season in

Ward Loved to Pick on the Browns

In his career, Hines Ward had a whopping 29 games in which he had at least 100 yards receiving. Of those 34 games, five came against the rival Cleveland Browns. Ward had two 100-plus-yard games against Cleveland in the 2005 season, and of his five 100-plus-yard games in the playoffs, one was against Cleveland in the 2003 AFC wild-card game. His biggest receiving day came in the 2006 shootout against the Falcons, when he caught eight balls for 171 yards and three touchdowns.

Pittsburgh he caught 15 passes for 246 yards, and the following season as the Steelers struggled to a 6—10 record, he got into the lineup more often, catching 61 passes for 638 yards and seven touchdowns. He also started to get a reputation as a hard-nosed blocker on the field—he wasn't scared to put his defender hat on and make a play for a fellow wideout or running back.

The team moved to Heinz Field in 2001, and with it, Ward started to become a household name among NFL wideouts. While fellow receiver Plaxico Burress was the tall playmaker who captured attention, Ward kept making plays week in and week out. The club went 13–3, and Ward had his best season to date, catching 94 balls for 1,003 yards and four scores.

Still, Ward's blocking got plenty of attention, though not necessarily in a good way. That season he started getting labeled as a "dirty" player by players from other teams across the NFL. In a November 15–12 overtime win over the Browns in Cleveland, Ward laid out Browns safety Earl Little, and even stood over him admiring his handy work. In his defense, Ward said Little had made a derogatory comment about him, and he simply had heard enough.

While that 2001 season was a good one for Ward, it was simply a stepping stone for even better seasons to come. The 2002 season saw him catch a career high 112 passes for 1,329 yards and 12 touchdowns. The pass-happy club made the playoffs, but again fell short of a Super Bowl. The '03 season saw Ward go for 1,163 yards and 10 touchdowns.

The thing Ward may be remembered most for, though, was the 2005 season and Super Bowl XL. The Steelers' offense was just a step behind the Seahawks that day, but it was Ward who made a couple of fingertip catches and even ran a reverse for a first down to get things going. He made a key 37-yard catch on a third-and-28 that eventually led to the team's first score, giving them a 7–3 lead. Then, with the Steelers leading 14–10 with just less than nine minutes left, Ward was in on the key play of the game. He caught a 43-yard pass on a reverse from wideout Antwaan Randle El, where he leaped into the end zone to put the game out of reach in the 21–10 win. Ward would go on to be named the MVP of the game, catching five passes for 123 yards and a score.

It was also that '05 season against Cleveland when Ward made his 538th reception to become the Steelers' all-time leader in receptions.

Hines Ward's trademark smile, determination, and standing as the Steelers' all-time leader in receptions has made him one of the most popular players in franchise history.

Steelers Team MVPs

While the NFL is a quarterback-driven league, when it comes to the Steelers, their quarterbacks usually don't get the nod from their teammates as the team MVP. It's an award that a lot of players say means more to them than any award they can get.

Ben Roethlisberger got the honor in 2009, but he's just the third quarterback since 1995 to get it (Neil O'Donnell in 1995 and Kordell Stewart in 2001 were the other two). Since the award began in 1969, it has gone to a defensive player 23 times, and three times there were co-MVPs (1988, 2002, and 2005). Quarterback Terry Bradshaw, wide receiver John Stallworth, and linebackers Greg Lloyd, James Harrison, and Levon Kirkland have all won the award twice. Wide receiver Hines Ward, cornerback Rod Woodson, and running back Jerome Bettis are the only three who have won the award three times. The first team MVP in 1969 was wide receiver Roy "Sweet Pea" Jefferson.

And the records kept coming. On December 2, 2007, against the Bengals, he caught his 64th touchdown, setting a Steelers all-time record and further cementing himself as a future Hall of Famer.

Ward earned his second Super Bowl ring in the 2008 season as he again was a main cog of the Steelers' offense, catching 81 passes for 1,043 yards and seven scores. He was injured in the AFC Championship Game against the Ravens and fought hard the two weeks leading up to the Super Bowl just to get the chance to play in the game, and he did.

On draft day 2009 Ward inked a new deal with the Steelers for four years at $22 million, and he earned it, pulling in 95 catches that season for 1,167 yards and six touchdowns.

He was a leader in the locker room late in his career, and again in 2010 showed he still had it on the field, helping the team reach the Super Bowl, where he caught a touchdown. That year he had 59 catches for 755 yards and five TDs.

Then oddly enough the wideout seemed to be phased out of the offense in 2011. Playing in mostly third-down packages and then not at all in a number of games, Ward saw the writing on the wall, and while he celebrated his 1,000th catch in the regular season finale against the Browns, he knew that the season might be his last for the Steelers.

He was right. Following the loss to Denver, rumors started to swirl about the team releasing him, which it did at the beginning of March. Ward struggled with the thought of playing elsewhere, and instead of trying to, he announced he would retire—as a Steeler—on March 20, 2012.

"Without the support over the past 14 years this game wouldn't be the same to me," he said. "It wouldn't be as fun for me. You guys meant the world to me. The city and this organization means the world to me. So today, as sadly as it feels for me right now, I hope it will be a good day for everyone here."

Ward ends his career as a lock for the Pro Football Hall of Fame, and while his career was winding down, he even went out and won the TV dance competition *Dancing with the Stars*, always flashing that smile that Steelers fans will always love.

34 "Iron" Mike Webster

His name personified toughness on the Steelers' offensive line for 15 seasons. He played a total of 220 games at center, 150 of them in a row. His nickname told the story behind the player known simply as "Iron" Mike—Mike Webster. He was taken in the fifth round of that famous 1974 draft that was chock full of Hall of Famers, Webster among them.

He was the anchor of the offensive line. A nine-time Pro Bowl selection, you never had to worry about Webster not being there on Sunday...or even making a mistake. He was that good. "Nobody could outwork Mike," former Steelers tight end Larry Brown said. "He was a good student, a tough guy who wanted to play."

Webster was one of the fastest centers in the league's history when it came to getting off the ball and being able to throw a block. He could open holes for Franco Harris or Rocky Bleier, or he'd protect his quarterback and close friend, Terry Bradshaw.

Standing 6'1", 255 pounds, Webster dominated the Big Ten as the best center in the conference while playing at the University of Wisconsin. He came into the Steelers' system and was the backup for another great center, Ray Mansfield, who showed Webster what it took to excel in the NFL. After two seasons as backup, Webster took over the starting job in 1976. He would stay there for 150 straight memorable games, until 1986.

He ran the line during the Steelers' four Super Bowls and was a great influence to the young guys in the locker room. "He gave you everything he had," Dan Rooney said. Webster played hurt quite a bit throughout his career, something that really didn't come to light until after his playing days ended in 1990. Those who played with him or against him knew how good he was. He was named to the NFL's 75th Anniversary All-Time Team in 1994. He also was a member of the NFL 1970s All-Decade Team, and then made it again in the 1980s.

"Webster was flat out the best," fellow Steelers offensive lineman Tunch Ilkin said. "I don't know that I've ever met anyone who was more focused and dedicated than Mike Webster," former Steelers quarterback Mark Malone wrote upon Webster's passing in 2002. "Mike would do whatever he possibly could to achieve greatness. He always had a good attitude. His energy, enthusiasm, and dedication always amazed me."

Webster ended up being the last of the 22 Steelers who played on all four Super Bowl championship teams to leave the club. He signed with the Kansas City Chiefs as a free agent after the 1988

Steelers Dominate the 1970s Pro Bowls

While it comes as no shock, Steelers players were a staple in the Pro Bowls in the 1970s. In its first Super Bowl year, 1974, the team sent eight players to the game. Two seasons later it had a team record 11 players in the Pro Bowl. The 1977 season saw nine players selected, and then in '79 10 players represented the AFC. Even in 1980 10 players were part of the AFC squad.

season. He was at first hired in Kansas City as an offensive line coach, but then talked the team into letting him start at center for two more seasons until he finally walked away in 1990.

While his life after football was one of sadness and pain—he suffered from amnesia, dementia, depression, and acute bone and muscle pain—Webster never seemed happier than when he was inducted into the Pro Football Hall of Fame in August 1997. The sadness of the end of Webster's life was documented in an ESPN. com piece by Greg Garber. He died of heart failure in Pittsburgh on September 24, 2002, at the very young age of 50. Those who knew him said he had spent months living in his black pickup truck and at an Amtrak station in downtown Pittsburgh. It was a sad end for a man who gave so much on the field but could not live life the way he wanted to off of it.

Some in the NFL today say that the things Webster faced and the injuries that eventually cost him his life are a lesson to remember for NFL stars of today and the future. The league is much more aware now of the head trauma that players face, and there are more precautions a player has to go though before he can make it back on the field after an injury. These things can be directly linked back to the life and story of Mike Webster.

35 Title No. 5 Comes 26 Years Later

Redemption. February 5, 2006, in Detroit was a day of redemption for Bill Cowher and the Black and Gold, as they finally won their long-awaited fifth Super Bowl trophy. The Steelers had run through the AFC's top three teams—the Bengals (No. 3), Colts (No. 1), and Broncos (No. 2)—and had earned the right to take on the NFC's No. 1 Seattle Seahawks.

The focus of the game was on Steelers veteran running back Jerome Bettis—a local product of the Detroit area. He was given the key to the city during the two weeks of pregame hype, and much was made about Bettis playing what would be his final game of his Hall of Fame career.

Seattle ran a West Coast offense, and while the Steelers' defense was expected to be able to shut them down, this was by no means a gimme. The Steelers entered the game as three-point favorites, and though the momentum and crowd seemed to be well on their side, the Seahawks had other ideas.

Seattle dominated the first quarter. They came out throwing, as quarterback Matt Hasselbeck picked his spots against the Steelers' defense. And on the other side, the Steelers' offense was in disarray. Ben Roethlisberger was a victim of an O-line that started the game with a couple penalties, and the team couldn't do anything against Seattle—they didn't even record a first down until the second quarter.

Seattle was able to convert on a drive, and kicker Josh Brown booted a 47-yard field goal, giving the Hawks a 3–0 lead with 22 seconds left in the first quarter. There was a sense of relief that the score wasn't worse—it seemed the Steelers avoided what easily could have been a seven- or 10-point deficit based on how lackluster their first 15 minutes were.

They finally showed some signs of life in the second quarter, despite Roethlisberger's first mistake of the game, a pick by Seattle's Michael Boulware. The quarterback combined with Hines Ward to help the team with an 11-play drive that got them in position to score the game's first touchdown. It looked like the drive was going to stall after Roethlisberger took a sack to set up a third-and-28 from the Seattle 32, but this time, the offense came through. Roethlisberger scrambled on the play to buy time, then just before getting hit, he fired a ball downfield that Ward came back for, making a great catch at the Seattle 3 and setting up first-and-goal.

Bettis gained two yards on the first two plays, then on third down Cowher called for Roethlisberger to take it on a sneak. In a controversial play that Seattle fans still say was a wrong call, Roethlisberger dove for the goal line, and official Bill Leavy hesitated but eventually ruled it a touchdown. A replay confirmed the call, and the Steelers led 7–3 at the half. Even Cowher admitted that, walking up the steps to the locker room, he wasn't sure how they were ahead—but they were, and they were 30 minutes away from a title.

The big plays for the Steelers continued on the second play of the third quarter. A handoff was called to running back Willie Parker, and the back who wasn't even drafted sprung loose. Thanks to a crushing block by All-Pro guard Alan Faneca, Parker was able to spring through a hole, and his burners did the rest. The back raced a Super Bowl record 75 yards into the end zone to give the Steelers a 14–3 advantage.

The Steelers continued to play tough on defense, and midway through the third quarter they had a chance to put the game away after a missed Seahawks field goal. Pittsburgh went on a drive led by two pass plays from Roethlisberger to Ward, and they found themselves with a first down at the Seattle 11. Two runs by Bettis put them in a third-and-6 from the Hawks' 7.

After a timeout, Roethlisberger made a game-changing error when he tried to float a pass over the head of Kelly Herndon, but

Seahawks Cry Foul Over Super Bowl XL Officiating

The Steelers were the nation's favorites to win Super Bowl XL. There was the Jerome Bettis storyline, plus it was the return to glory for the team that had dominated the 1970s. The Seahawks, however, were not seeing it that way, and they said as much after some calls didn't go their way in the 21–10 Steelers victory.

Seattle coach Mike Holmgren was vocal about the calls that didn't go to the Seahawks, saying the following to a crowd of Seattle fans at a rally after the game: "I didn't know we were going to have to play the guys in the striped shirts as well." Bill Levy, the head official, heard it from Seattle fans mostly about two calls. The first was over the Steelers' first touchdown and whether quarterback Ben Roethlisberger broke the plane with his dive, and the second was a holding call that stopped Seattle from having a first-and-goal at the Steelers' 1 when they trailed 14–10. The possession for Seattle ended with an Ike Taylor interception that killed the Seahawks' last chance to take the lead. The Steelers scored on Hines Ward's touchdown catch the following drive.

"The game was properly officiated, including, as in most NFL games, some tight plays that produced disagreement about the calls made by the officials," NFL spokesman Greg Aiello said in a statement.

the ball floated right into his hands, and the Seattle defensive back returned the ball 76 yards to the Steelers' 20. The celebration was going to have to wait, and fans and the team were going to have to sweat this thing out after all.

It took just three plays until Hasselbeck threw a 16-yard touchdown pass to tight end Jerramy Stevens to make it a 14–10 game. Game on, to say the least. Things got even more tense when the Hawks went on a drive that saw them get to the Steelers' 19-yard line with a shot to take the lead. After a questionable holding call on a pass play that would have put the ball on the Steelers' 1, Casey Hampton came up with a big sack to set up a second-and-25.

A pass play got the Hawks seven yards, Hasselbeck took a shot downfield, and Ike Taylor came up with a huge pick, taking the ball to the 29. Then the Steelers got another somewhat strange call when Hasselbeck got called for a low block, adding 15 yards to put the ball on the 44.

It was time not to play it safe, and offensive coordinator Ken Whisenhunt agreed. The Steelers got a first down after Roethlisberger went for five yards on a third-and-2 to the Hawks' 43. Then came the play that became the staple of Super Bowl XL, and one that cemented the team's fifth title.

The first-down play started with Roethlisberger handing off to Parker, who then gave it to wideout Antwaan Randle El on a wide receiver reverse. But, after a great block by Roethlisberger, Randle El, who was a quarterback in college, fired a perfect pass downfield to a wide-open Ward, who made the catch and leapt into the end zone with the final nail in the Seattle coffin to make it 21–10 with 9:04 to play.

The Steelers' defense needed to make sure they didn't give Seattle another chance. Seattle got to the Pittsburgh 47, but then a corner blitz by Deshea Townsend saved the day—he took down Hasselbeck with a five-yard sack, forcing a punt. The offense, led by Bettis on what proved to be the final carries of his career, chewed up 4:15 of the clock, and by the time the Steelers punted with two minutes left, the celebration in Steeler Nation had already started.

Seattle made one last gasp, and a final desperate drive fell short. The real celebration could start after Roethlisberger kneeled down to secure the team's fifth title. Cowher's postgame grin, hugging of his wife and daughters, and hoisting of the Lombardi Trophy told the real story. The coach, always known as one who couldn't win the big game, had finally done it. Ward, who had five catches for 123 yards with a score, was the MVP, and Parker ended the day with 93 yards on 10 carries.

Twenty-six years after winning Super Bowl XIV, the Steelers finally had new hardware to display in their front office. At last.

36 Rocky Bleier

Robert Patrick Bleier, better known to Steelers fans and most everyone else as Rocky Bleier, is one of the great stories not only in Steelers history, but in NFL history in general. He came back from what he was told was a football-ending injury in Vietnam to become a main cog in the Steelers' lineup during the Super Bowl runs in the 1970s. The nickname "Rocky" came to Bleier as a baby, according to the Steelers' running back.

"As the first-born of the family, my dad was proud, as all parents are," he said. "And the guys would come into the bar and say, 'Bob, how's that new kid of yours?' And my dad would go, 'Aw, you should see him, guys, looks like a little rock sitting in that crib. He's got all these muscles.' I'm a little fat baby. So they'd come back in the bar and they'd say, 'Hey, Bob, how's that little rock of yours?' So after that, that's how I got it. It stuck."

He quickly got rid of the baby fat, and by the time he graduated from Xavier High School in Appleton, Wisconsin, he was a star in both football and basketball. He was a three-time all-state pick as a running back, a spot he would continue to develop at the University of Notre Dame, where he enrolled in 1964.

While at the school, he played on the memorable national championship team in 1966 and earned a degree in business management. Bleier showed his leadership qualities as the team captain for the Fighting Irish in 1967. The following year, despite his somewhat smaller size for a running back (5'9", 210 pounds), the Steelers took him in the 16th round of the NFL draft, 417th overall.

Bleier was determined to make an impact in the league, though he didn't get many chances in his rookie year. He rushed the ball just six times for 39 yards, and caught just three passes for 68 yards. After that, Bleier was drafted by the Army and sent to serve his country in Vietnam. It was on August 20, 1969, that his life changed. He and his platoon were ambushed in a rice paddy near Chu Lai. He was wounded in his left thigh, and when a grenade hit nearby and exploded, it sent pieces of shrapnel into his right leg and foot.

At a hospital in Tokyo, doctors told him that he would never play the sport he loved again. But it was also there he got a postcard from Steelers owner Art Rooney, who said the following: "Rock— the team's not doing well. We need you. Art Rooney." It was there and then that Bleier decided he would do whatever it took to make it back to the Black and Gold.

Bleier returned to the team, and it took him two full years to get back into the lineup. He was waived by coach Chuck Noll twice and couldn't walk without a limp. He went from 180 pounds to 212, and in the summer of 1974 he finally made it all the way back. That season he finally had the chance to make his mark in Week 4.

He started as a backup at halfback despite leading the team in rushing in the preseason. He got the chance to play alongside Franco Harris in a Week 7 Monday night game against the Atlanta Falcons. With the pair the team needed finally in place, Bleier opened the door for Harris, and they combined for 219 rushing yards. Harris and Bleier would not be broken up again, and, as they say, the rest is history.

The Steelers won the Super Bowl that season and the year after that. From there, Bleier never lost his starting spot, and he became one of the best lead blockers in the NFL. He also was a great back himself, going more than 1,000 yards with Harris in the 1976 season. He even made a leaping touchdown catch from Terry Bradshaw in Super Bowl XIII, putting the team ahead for good.

He left the Steelers with four rings and, at the time, was the team's fourth all-time leading rusher, and 3,865 yards. He also pulled in 136 catches for 1,294 yards and 25 combined touchdowns. Bleier went on to write *Fighting Back: The Rocky Bleier*

Story, which became a movie in 1980 starring Robert Urich as Bleier. Today he runs Rocky Bleier Inc. and speaks to companies and groups.

37 The Bus Arrives in the Steel City

The Steelers knew after the 1995 season that the run game was in flux. The team had already said good-bye to Barry Foster the season before, and while they had some decent backs in Byron "Bam" Morris and Erric Pegram, there was that desire on the part of Bill Cowher and the front office to go out and get a back who would pound away and be able to wear down defenses.

The club's leading rusher in '95 was Pegram, who came to the team in the off-season from the Falcons. He was a shifty back and showed heart and ran hard, putting up 813 yards and five touchdowns, with an average of 3.8 yards per carry. Morris was the bruiser, a guy who would come in for those tough one-yard runs with the game on the line—like in that season's AFC Championship Game when the team needed that final yard to go up for good against the Colts 20–16.

Morris ran for 559 yards on 148 carries, nine touchdowns, and an average of 3.8 yards per carry. Overall, though, Morris was a disappointment. He was expected to be the team's lead back that season, but with the 3–4 start, he was replaced by the smaller Pegram. Morris did come back and play better near the end of the year, but the team didn't feel comfortable with him as the franchise back. Things became even worse when in March 1996 he was arrested for marijuana possession. The Steelers knew it was time to act.

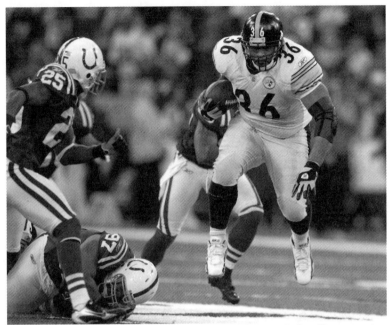

Running back Jerome Bettis, seen here in a 2006 divisional playoff game against the Colts, ran for more than 1,000 yards in each of his first six seasons with the Steelers. He retired in 2005 as the NFL's fifth all-time leading rusher.

The club seemed to have interest in a running back in Los Angeles by the name of Jerome Bettis. He had fallen out of favor with head coach Rich Brooks, and after going for 1,429 yards his rookie season, had dropped to 637 yards and three touchdowns in 1995. Brooks had also said some not-so-flattering things about Bettis, calling him lazy. Bettis was in a system not meant for him. The Rams wanted to throw more, and Bettis simply wasn't in their plans. Plus, they wanted to draft troubled running back Lawrence Phillips, which would mean they really wouldn't need Bettis any longer.

So the two teams began talking about a trade that would send Bettis and the Rams' third-round pick to the Steelers. The asking price—the Steelers' second-round pick that season along with their fourth-round pick in 1997. As the two teams kept speaking, it became evident they both felt that it was a deal that could be made. The Rams took Phillips, and that opened the door even more for Bettis to be moved. Los Angeles ended up taking tight end Ernie Conwell with the Steelers' second-round pick, and the fourth-round pick ended up being moved to the Dolphins, who used it on guard Jerome Daniels, who was cut in training camp.

Bettis fit the Steelers' offensive game plan like a glove. The team released Morris, who eventually pled guilty to drug possession, leaving Bettis and Pegram as the two main running backs on the roster. Pegram started the season as the No. 1 back, but by the Steelers' third game of the season, Bettis quickly took over. He ran for 133 yards and two scores in a Monday night win over the Bills, setting the pace for the big back to have a big season and a bigger career.

The Bus, as he is so well known, ran right into the hearts of Steeler Nation. He ran for more than 1,000 yards in each of his first six seasons with the Steelers, from 1996 to 2001. He also went to the Pro Bowl four times as a Steeler, was the 1996 NFL Comeback Player of the Year, and was the 2001 Walter Payton Man of the Year.

By the time Bettis walked away following the team's Super Bowl win in 2005, he was the NFL's fifth all-time leading rusher with 13,662 yards and 91 touchdowns. He also caught 200 passes for 1,449 yards and three touchdowns—not bad for a trade that some felt the Steelers were getting robbed on. As for the Rams, they went 15–33 over the next three seasons with Lawrence Phillips as their running back, and it wasn't until the team traded for Marshall Faulk and Kurt Warner became quarterback that they had any success.

The Bettis trade gave the Steelers one of their most all-time beloved players, and a player who helped march the team into history with its fifth Super Bowl title in 2005.

38 Forbes Field

As Pittsburgh football's first home, Forbes Field will not be remembered for many great memories, but it's still a piece of Steelers history worth mentioning. Ground was broken for the stadium in the Oakland neighborhood of Pittsburgh on March 1, 1909. Known primarily for baseball, it officially opened for the hometown Pittsburgh Pirates the following June 30 for a game against the Chicago Cubs.

The football team purchased by Art Rooney in July 1933 was also known as the Pirates. Their first game at Forbes was against the New York Giants on September 20, 1933. The game was played in front of a crowd of about 25,000, and the Giants won 23–2. But the football Pirates came back the following week to beat the Chicago Cardinals. It wasn't until 1940 that the Steelers took their name, and they spent the next 23 seasons at Forbes Field, playing mostly poor football that most Pittsburgh natives would choose to forget.

The clubs were bad, managing to play just one playoff game during their tenure at Forbes Field, losing a 1947 Eastern Divisional playoff game to the Eagles 21–0. They did manage to play in the not-so-famous Bert Bell Benefit Bowl in 1962 against the Lions, a game that was played as a postseason exhibition for third place. They couldn't even win that, falling 17–10.

One shining moment came on November 30, 1952, when the Steelers gave their fans a reason to celebrate in a 63–7 win over the New York Giants. They set a number of records, including scoring nine touchdowns. A number of the 15,140 fans who attended the snowy game stormed the field, tearing the goal posts out of the ground.

This isn't to say that Forbes Field didn't see any good football along the way, as the Pitt Panthers, who shared the stadium, excited

A Decade of Playoff Silence at Three Rivers

While the Steelers were the team of the decade in the 1970s, the team went through a period of not playing any playoff games at home throughout the following decade. They hosted the San Diego Chargers in a first-round playoff game on January 9, 1983, after a strike-shortened season. It would be exactly 10 years to the day when the team would host another playoff game, taking on the Buffalo Bills on January 9, 1993. The team lost both playoff games, 31–28 to the Chargers and 24–3 to the Bills.

the city's fans with national championships in 1910, 1915, 1916, and 1917. For the most part, they were the standard bearer for football in the city, even boasting five undefeated seasons at the ballpark.

Most of the time, when it came to the NFL, when the Steelers took the field, they simply couldn't match up with the other teams. The team regularly sat between third and fifth in the standings. The team managed just five finishes better than third in their history at Forbes Field, and those were all second-place finishes—they never won their division at Forbes.

While the baseball Pirates had their share of success at Forbes Field, the University of Pitt acquired Forbes Field in 1958, giving the Steelers some options as to where they could play their future games. The Steelers started to play some of their games at the much bigger Pitt Stadium in '58, and they played their last game at Forbes Field on December 13, 1958, scoring a 38–21 win over the very team they had beaten for their first win at the stadium, the Chicago Cardinals.

Forbes Field officially closed on June 28, 1970, as the MLB's Pirates played a pair of games against the Chicago Cubs. The city's new jewel, Three Rivers Stadium, opened on July 16, 1970, for both the Pirates and Steelers. The Steelers' first game at Three Rivers was played on September 20, 1970—a 19–7 loss to the Houston Oilers.

39 Dermontti Dawson

The Steelers under Bill Cowher ran the ball better than any other team in the NFL, and one reason for that was due to an offensive line that was built not only for power and being able to get off the ball, but also with big men who could move. No other lineman had those traits under Cowher more than center Dermontti Dawson. Without Dawson, who knows what type of shape the Steelers' O-line would have been in for the 13 years that he played in the Steel City?

Dawson was a quiet leader on the line, never one to be loud or have an attitude. But when it came to being a steady leader, Dawson was there every Sunday to call the blocking assignments on the line and make sure whoever was under center would get the ball and be protected at the same time.

Dawson was taken in the second round by the Steelers in the 1988 draft, and within a year took over the center spot for another Hall of Famer, the late, great Mike Webster. Many Steelers fans were stunned when Webster left Pittsburgh for Kansas City, but the Steelers knew what they were doing, and they knew that Webster was quickly heading toward the end of his career. It was time to give the starting center spot to Dawson, who played elsewhere on the line his rookie year despite knowing that the center spot would soon be his.

He fit in right away as the anchor of Chuck Noll's O-line, and despite never getting the attention he deserved, Dawson was consistently opening holes for backs like Merrill Hoge, Tim Worley, and Barry Foster, as well as protecting quarterbacks Bubby Brister, Todd Blackledge, and Neil O'Donnell. The Steelers' teams in Dawson's first three seasons under Noll went a combined 23–25, but they did reach the second round of the playoffs in 198. Their lack of success was not due to the play of Dawson, who was solid at the center spot.

Things changed quickly under new head coach Bill Cowher in 1992, and Dawson quickly started to get the pub that he deserved as one of the top linemen and centers in the NFL. With new offensive coordinator Ron Earhardt, the Steelers became a running team with a conservative approach to throwing the football. The backfield would consist of Hoge playing the fullback/blocking back role, and the halfback would be the bruising Foster, who in Cowher's first season shattered records in carries and yards. It was the Steelers' O-line, led by Dawson, that opened the holes for "Bananas" Barry, and it was that 1992 season that Dawson was named to his first Pro Bowl.

The Pro Bowl became an annual stop for Dawson—from 1992 to 1998 he was named to seven straight, and he played in 171 consecutive games, becoming the rock of the line that saw the team either lead the league or be near the top in rushing year after year. You could count on No. 63 to be out there ready to play every Sunday, and his quiet, effective demeanor is what Steelers fans loved about him. His teammates nicknamed him "Ned Flanders," after the character from *The Simpsons* due to his personality, that of being a pleasant guy who didn't seem the type to push 300-plus-pound nose tackles aside to open holes for running backs.

The run of Pro Bowls and games played, however, stopped almost as quickly as his career took off. In 1999 he was forced to miss nine games due to a hamstring injury. The severe hamstring also forced him to miss seven more games in 2000, and following that season the team made a tough decision, opting to release Dawson. Instead of trying to overcome the injury quickly and sign with another team, the quiet leader of the Steelers' O-Line for 13 seasons decided he'd had enough and retired. The Steelers do not retire numbers, but out of respect for Dawson they have never given out No. 63.

Dawson's career was finally showcased for all to see in 2012, as the center was picked to be in the Pro Football Hall of Fame, an honor that he truly deserved as one of the best players ever to wear a Steelers uniform.

Now living in Lexington, Kentucky, he is a real estate developer and also runs the Dermontti Dawson PRO Foundation, which was established to benefit at-risk children.

40 Mike Wagner

While the front four was responsible for their destruction of offenses back during the Steelers' dynasty run in the 1970s, there was also a pretty formidable secondary led by safety Mike Wagner. The Steelers' 11th-round draft pick in 1971 was a steady force in the team's backfield, playing in four Super Bowls and ending his career in 1980.

Wagner was born in Waukegan, Illinois, on June 22, 1949. He grew up rooting for the Bears and the Cubs, playing sports and excelling in football. He played college ball at Western Illinois University, and in 1969 earned NAIA All-America status. The Western Illinois Leathernecks were not exactly a well-known college team, which is why the Steelers were able to snag Wagner in the 11th round, 268th overall.

The club was in the process of developing their defense, which would become one of the best ever with players like Joe Greene, Jack Lambert, L.C. Greenwood, and others paving the way for the famed Steel Curtain. Wagner was installed right away in the secondary, playing in 12 games of the 6–8 1971 season and picking off two passes.

The next season he was even a bigger impact player on defense, intercepting six passes as the Steelers began to assert themselves. They improved to 11–3 and won their first-ever playoff game in the famous Immaculate Reception game at Three Rivers Stadium, beating Oakland 13–7. The following week they lost to Miami in the AFC Championship Game, but Wagner and the defense were well on their way to building a dynasty. Wagner tied for the lead in the NFL with eight interceptions in 1973, and the team continued to mature into an AFC contender.

In the championship season of 1974, Wagner only picked off two passes but sealed the team's first Super Bowl with an interception of Fran Tarkenton. The team defeated the Minnesota Vikings 16–6 for its first Lombardi Trophy.

The defense got even better the next year, when the curtain fell on opposing defenses all season long. In an interview with NFL Films, Wagner recalled a 1975 game where he never had to make a tackle. He said it was almost frustrating not having to be on the ground after a number of plays, as the front four and linebackers were so good, he could simply sit back and watch.

He did more than that in Super Bowl X, where in a critical stretch of the fourth quarter, Wagner baited Cowboys quarterback Roger Staubach into throwing a pass over the middle that he picked off. The play was key—it led directly to a field goal to give the Steelers a 15–10 lead in a game they would win 21–17 to secure their second world title.

Wagner continued as the starter in the team's Super Bowl wins in Super Bowls XIII and XIV. He retired in 1980 after a successful 10-year career that included two games with three interceptions: one in 1973 against Cincinnati, and a second one in his final year against the team he grew up rooting for, the Chicago Bears.

His career concluded with 36 interceptions, the third most in Steelers history at that time. He also recovered 12 fumbles and forced five, and was a two-time Pro Bowl selection in 1975 and

1976. Always known for his smarts on and off the field, Wagner works as an investment banker in the Pittsburgh area with HT Capital Markets.

41 Super Bowl XLIII: Call Them Six-Burgh

The Steelers arrived in Tampa brimming with confidence for Super Bowl XLIII. They had run the course of one of the toughest schedules any team had seen in years, and it seemed that nothing, much less the Arizona Cardinals, were going to stop them from earning their NFL-record sixth Super Bowl title.

The evening before the game, Ybor City, a hot party spot in Tampa full of bars and restaurants, was chock full of Steelers fans. Finding a Cardinals jersey was hard to do, and much like the Super Bowl three years earlier in Detroit, the following day at Raymond James Stadium would be a home away from home for the Black and Gold.

Most odds had the Steelers favored by between six and seven points, and most thought their first-ranked defense would be able to handle Cardinals quarterback Kurt Warner and the high-powered Arizona offense. The Cardinals were an unlikely opponent for the Steelers, having entered the playoffs at 9–7, beating the Falcons then the Panthers on the road, then the Eagles at home just to make it to the big game. To say it was a shock they were even in the Super Bowl is an understatement.

At first it looked like the Steelers were going to turn Super Bowl XLIII into a cakewalk. They were denied a first-possession touchdown after a reversal on a third-down play that was first ruled a touchdown after Ben Roethlisberger bulled his way into the end zone. The officials ruled his knee was down, and the Steelers settled for a short field goal to make it 3–0.

The Steelers' defense dominated early. Warner and the Cardinals' offense seemed tight, and it played right into the Steelers' hands. The Black and Gold offense took their second possession the distance, going 69 yards in 11 plays in 7:12 as Gary Russell went in from one yard out to make it a 10–0 game. All seemed to be going the Steelers' way, but not for long.

The Cardinals rallied as Warner led his team quickly down the field, hitting Anquan Boldin for a big 45-yard gain to the Steelers' 1. On the next play, Warner threw a touchdown to tight end Ben Patrick to make it a three-point game again at 10–7. Two possessions later the Steelers' offense committed a turnover when Roethlisberger's pass was batted in the air and intercepted, giving Arizona the ball at the Steelers' 34 with two minutes to play in the half.

The Cardinals drove to the Steelers' 1-yard line, and with 18 seconds left to play in the half, one of the most memorable plays in Super Bowl history took place. Warner went back to pass and tried to hit Boldin quickly, but the NFL Defensive Player of the Year, James Harrison, jumped the route and picked the pass off.

Helped out by a convoy of Steelers, Harrison started up the sideline, leaping over players and avoiding being knocked out of bounds. It appeared twice that Harrison was about to get tackled, and starting at about the Cardinals' 25, it was easy to see a race to the end zone was on. Harrison, gassed beyond belief, got to the 3 when Cardinals wide receivers Larry Fitzgerald and Steve Breaston tried to bring him down. He was tackled, but fell into the end zone, and the officials correctly ruled a touchdown, giving the Steelers a 17–7 halftime lead.

Even with that, there was an uneasy feeling as the Steelers scored the only points of the third quarter. They drove from their 18 to the Cardinals' 2, but had to settle for a short Jeff Reed field goal to make it 20–7. The Arizona offense caught a break, and as the fourth quarter started, the game was still not over by a longshot. Arizona went to their no-huddle at the 11:30 mark, and it worked. They went 87 yards in just eight plays and less than four minutes, scoring on a one-yard Fitzgerald catch to make it 20–14. The Steelers' offense, stuck in the mud for most of the second half, needed to do something to avoid a collapse. Instead, they made a critical mistake. The teams traded punts, and the Steelers got the ball at their own 1. After an incomplete pass, then a run by Willie Parker that went nowhere, Roethlisberger took a shotgun snap in his own end zone. He completed what would have been a huge 19-yard pass to Santonio Holmes, but there was laundry in the end zone. Center Justin Hartwig was called for holding, and since it happened in the end zone, it was a safety. The two points made it 20–16 Steelers with 2:58 left.

The defense then had a chance to make a stop and save the game. They failed. Arizona had the ball at their own 36, and on the second play of the drive, Warner threw a slant pass to Fitzgerald. He quickly broke into the open field, and within a matter of seconds Fitzgerald was in the end zone, celebrating a 64-yard touchdown and a Cards 23–20 lead with 2:37 left. Gulp.

It would be on Roethlisberger and the Steelers' offense to rally. On the sideline, Mike Tomlin told his team with a sense of confidence that if the Cardinals were going to score, that's how you wanted them to do it—fast. This gave the Steelers more than enough time to mount a rally and cement their place in NFL history.

It's safe to say that the Steelers' final drive to a title didn't start out so well. On the first play, guard Chris Kemoeatu was flagged for holding, moving the Steelers back to their own 12-yard line. Roethlisberger had to scramble for his life on the next play, but found Santonio Holmes with a big 14-yard pass to set up a second-and-6. After an incomplete pass, it was Ben to Santonio again, this time for 13 yards to put the ball at the Steelers' 39 with a first down.

A pass for 11 yards to Nate Washington, then a four-yard run by Roethlisberger put the ball at the Arizona 46 with 62 seconds left. After a Steelers timeout, the real key play of the drive took place. Going back to the pass, Roethlisberger pumped once, then threw to a wide-open Holmes, who caught the ball and quickly turned upfield, weaving through the Cardinals tacklers until he was taken down at the Cardinals' 6-yard line.

At that point, you got a sense that something special was about to happen. The Steelers took their last timeout after the play and set up their plan for the final six yards. In the huddle, Holmes, who had already made three big catches in the drive, told Roethlisberger he wanted the ball. The QB looked for him on the first play from the 6 and threw to him in the back of the end zone. The pass was on target, but Holmes' hands were not, and the ball went through them, falling incomplete.

On second down, again a pass-play was called. The primary look for Roethlisberger was running back Mewelde Moore in the flat, but he wasn't open. Then he looked to Hines Ward, who was also covered. Tight end Heath Miller wasn't an option, either. Next he looked for Holmes, who was going toward the right corner of the end zone. Roethlisberger threw a pinpoint pass over the outstretched arms of three Cardinals defensive backs and perfectly into the hands of Holmes, who took a shot as he caught it, but held on.

The officials signaled touchdown an after a few tense moments of review, confirmed the call, giving the Steelers the 27–23 lead with 35 seconds left. Tomlin huddled his defense one last time, telling them that if they could make one last stand, they would go down as legendary. The Cardinals started at their 23, Warner quickly hit Fitzgerald for 20 yards, and they called a timeout with 22 seconds left.

After the timeout, Warner found running back J.J. Arrington for 13 yards but had to use his last timeout with 15 seconds left and Arizona standing at the Steelers' 44. The next play would be

Arizona's last, as Warner scrambled in the pocket for what seemed to be at least seven or eight seconds. He finally ran out of luck, LaMarr Woodley crunched him, and the ball squirted loose. Brett Keisel fell on the ball, and history was in the Steelers' back pocket.

One Roethlisberger knee later, the Steelers were able to take their rightful place as the premiere NFL franchise with six NFL titles. Holmes took home the MVP for his heroics, and Roethlisberger had redeemed himself for a poor outing three years earlier in Detroit in Super Bowl XL. More importantly, it was another title and celebration for the Steel City.

42 San Diego Stunner in '94

January 15, 1995, was a day Steelers fans had waited a long time for. It had been exactly 10 years and nine days since the Steelers had appeared in an AFC Championship Game, and 15 years since Pittsburgh had hosted one. The city was alive for another Super Bowl—all the Steelers had to do was beat the San Diego Chargers.

The Steelers were eight-and-one-half point favorites entering the game, and for good reason. They had the league's top rushing attack with Barry Foster and Byron "Bam" Morris, and their defense was even better. Dubbed "Blitzburg," the Steelers' defense had put up a franchise high 55 sacks and also was dangerous with players like Hall of Famer Rod Woodson, Kevin Greene, Greg Lloyd, and Levon Kirkland.

Just eight days before the game the Steelers had whipped a team that many thought was their biggest challenge on the road to Super Bowl XXIX, the Cleveland Browns. The Steelers had beaten Cleveland twice in the regular season, and in the playoffs the game was a severe beating. Pittsburgh won 29–9, rushing their way to a 24–3 lead at halftime and never looking back. Players doused coach Bill Cowher with a Gatorade shower after the game, and it appeared they were unstoppable. They were wrong.

The week leading up to the AFC Championship Game against San Diego, the Chargers got wind of a Super Bowl rap video that mouthy tight end Eric Green bragged about making. Then there was defensive lineman Ray Seals, who said that the Chargers would be lucky to score against the Steelers at all. Mind you, San Diego had beaten the Steelers 37–34 on Christmas Eve that season, but it was a meaningless game, and most of the Steelers starters sat out since they had already clinched the AFC's best record.

One thing that didn't seem to be in the Steelers' favor on game day was the weather. Mother Nature must have not gotten the memo for snow and cold, and instead doled out rain and temperatures in the upper 50s. Still, the game was at home, and from top to bottom the Steelers were the better team. Right?

Things looked great for the Black and Gold when they scored on their first possession—Neil O'Donnell hit running back John L. Williams with a 16-yard touchdown to give the Steelers a 7–0 lead at the 7:28 mark of the first quarter. The defense was doing its part, holding the Chargers in check for most of the first half.

San Diego got back in the game in the second quarter after a pass-interference call put the ball at the Steelers' 1. The defense stopped San Diego running back Natrone Means on three straight plays, though, and a short field goal made it 7–3 Steelers. Pittsburgh answered and went up 10–3 at the half with a Gary Anderson field goal after they got to the Chargers' 12, but a holding call forced them to settle for three.

The third quarter saw the Steelers go up 10 as Woodson picked off Chargers quarterback Stan Humphries. The offense got to the 6, but again had to settle for three and a 13–3 lead. Things seemed to be well in order, but not for long. A play fake by Humphries

Some Not-So-Good Records

While the Steelers' record number of Super Bowl wins might be the most important in the NFL, the team also holds some less-than-prideworthy records. Among those:

- Fewest touchdown passes in a season: 0 (1945)
- Most turnovers in a game: 12 (vs. Philadelphia on 12/12/65—nine of those were interceptions, also an NFL record)
- Most rushing yards allowed in a game: 426 (vs. Detroit on 11/4/34)
- Most punts blocked in a season: 6 (Harry Newsome, 1988)
- Most times sacked in a game: 12 (vs. Dallas on 11/20/66)
- Most touchdowns allowed on kickoff returns in a season: 3 (1986)
- Most touchdowns allowed on punt returns in the postseason: 2 (2001)

left Steelers corner Deon Figures looking into the backfield, and tight end Alfred Pupunu ran right down the middle of the field. A perfect pass and 43 yards later, it was 13–10 with 8:23 left in the third quarter.

The offense could not run on the slick turf. Foster got most of the carries and was held in check. That left O'Donnell to try to win with his arm, which his AFC title record 54 pass attempts clearly shows. The offense couldn't do much, though, and it was going to be on the defense's shoulders to win the game.

They did their best, but all it took was one more long stunning play to knock out the Steelers and quiet a nation of rabid Steelers faithful. It took place with 5:13 left in the fourth quarter, when Steelers corner Tim McKyer was caught deep on a pass play by Humphries and Chargers wide receiver Tony Martin. The veteran wideout leaped in the air and caught a 43-yard bomb that landed him in the end zone, putting San Diego up 17–13.

It was a true punch to the stomach, and the Steelers would have to find a way to respond if they wanted their season to continue. They got the ball at their own 17, and O'Donnell led the team on a frantic but effective drive that eventually put the team at the San Diego 9 with two minutes left on the clock. A first down run went nowhere, then a pass to Green was nearly picked off. Third down saw a pass to Williams net six yards, setting up a now famous fourth-and-3 for the Steelers with a minute left.

After a timeout in which Cowher was clearly laughing with O'Donnell, a pass play was called to try and get the final three yards. They sent four receivers out, and it was thought that Green was the go-to guy, but he was double-teamed. As O'Donnell dropped to the 10-yard-line, he saw Foster flash open at the 1 and quickly tried to sneak a pass to him—a pass that would have carried him into the end zone had he caught it. He didn't. It was not to be.

O'Donnell threw low, and Foster slid down to make the catch, but Chargers linebacker Dennis Gibson came over the top and knocked the pass down. Within seconds of the incomplete signal the Charger's sideline went into a zealous mode of celebration. Three kneel-downs later, the Chargers were off to Miami to play a superior San Francisco 49ers team that punished the Chargers 49–26.

Records were set by O'Donnell, completing 32-of-54 passes for 349 yards. The Steelers outgained San Diego 415 to 226. It didn't matter. Little did Steelers fans know that it would be the first of four losses in AFC Championship Games at home under Cowher's direction. This one, though, seems to have hurt the most—they simply let it slip away over three yards.

43 Iron City Beer

When it comes to beverages and the Steelers, there's really only one drink that stands out—Iron City Beer. It's a Pittsburgh original, and one that Steelers fans have been enjoying for many generations.

Iron City Brewing Company was founded by Edward Frauenheim, a young German immigrant, back in 1861. The company started when the city of Pittsburgh was starting to become a thriving American city, one that had steel mills that were producing a lot of the nation's steel, and jobs were aplenty in the area. It wasn't uncommon for workers to work long hours at the mills, then enjoy the city's beer.

Iron City not only has enjoyed a relationship with the Black and Gold, but it also helped establish some of the groundbreaking things that drinkers enjoy to this day, such as:

- the "snap top" can (1962)
- the twist-off resealable bottle top (1963);
- draft beer packaged in cans
- the aluminum bottle (2004)
- the original light beer, Mark V (1976)

Iron City was also the first brewery to have its own presidential candidate: Dan Crawley of Churchill, Pennsylvania.

Iron City cans have filled tailgate lots around Three Rivers Stadium and Heinz Field through highlight years—the dynastic 1970s and the most recent Super Bowl seasons—and the low times, as the steel mills closed and the team slumped in the '80s. The brewery survived prohibition, so it can certainly weather the storms of a few off seasons. Throughout the years, Iron City has undergone some tweaks, including the addition of Iron City Light, which was introduced in 1977 to help the brewery survive some of the tough economic years.

The company also took advantage of its connection to the Steelers by releasing specialty cans that paid homage to the teams as they were winning titles. Steelers fans from the 1970s still relish those old cans that sit as collectors' items showing off the four Super Bowl teams from that decade. Many of those very cans have been passed down from generation to generation. And as recently as March 2009 the company released a special "six-pack champs" edition to honor to the Steelers' six Super Bowl titles. Of course, the company omitted the team's logo on the cans to stay out of trouble with the NFL, which does not permit unauthorized use of team logos.

The company continues to enjoy what has been a fruitful relationship with the Steelers, and it's been a relationship with the fans that can been seen in tailgate lots all over Steeler Nation to this day.

44 Donnie Shell

While everyone loves to remember the glory days of the Steel Curtain, people tend to forget just how good some of the other players behind that front four really were. One of those classic players that could be counted on week in and week out as a rock of the secondary was strong safety Donnie Shell. The five-time Pro Bowler was a big hitter who had a nose for the ball, and when he retired in 1987, his 51 career picks made him the NFL career leader in interceptions for a strong safety.

The Steelers knew how important Shell was to them, as he was rewarded for his stellar NFL career with a number of honors once it ended. He was selected to the Steelers' All-Time Team, as well as to the NFL Silver Anniversary Super Bowl Team, and the Steelers' 75th Anniversary Team. Shell has been up for induction into the Pro Football Hall for Fame a number of times, making it as a finalist in 2001, but has not been able to crack into the Hall. With so many 1970s Steelers already there, some critics may feel adding Shell would be overkill.

Shell's life revolved around sports since he was young. Growing up in Whitmire, South Carolina, he played on state championship teams in baseball (as a left-handed pitcher) and basketball, ran track, and

Pick-Pocketing

While there have been a couple Steelers with two- and three-interception games in their careers, a four-pick effort has only been done once, and that was by defensive back Jack Butler on December 13, 1953. In front of 22,057 fans at Washington, Butler picked off four Redskins passes, including one for a touchdown in the fourth quarter to give the Steelers a 14–13 come-from-behind victory. The team wrapped up the season at 6–6, fourth in the NFL Eastern Division. Butler was a four-time Pro Bowler for the Steelers, and in October 2008 was named as one of the greatest 33 Steelers of all-time. He was enshrined in the Pro Football Hall of Fame in 2012. No opponent has ever picked off four passes in a game against the Steelers.

made a postseason football all-star game. He was offered a full scholarship to South Carolina State, half for football and half for baseball. He played linebacker and guard in high school and, once he got to South Carolina State, was convinced to give the safety position a shot. He did to great success, earning All-America and all-conference honors. To think that Shell entered the NFL as an undrafted free agent in 1974 is mind-boggling. It's also a testament to the Steelers' scouts at the time, who took a chance on him. The gamble clearly paid off.

Shell was 5'11", 190 pounds, and he rarely made mistakes when quarterbacks would try and hit receivers in coverage. He was a master of making up ground fast on receivers, and he was also known for his bone-jarring hits, one of which was on Oilers running back Earl Campbell near the goal line in 1978. Campbell, who had his share of good days versus the Steelers, dashed through the line for a couple yards, and then Shell came out of nowhere to lay a hit on Campbell that lifted him off the ground. The hit even made the montage of highlights at the start of the *NFL Live* pregame show on NBC for a few years in the early '80s. "Donnie Shell delivered some of the toughest hits ever on Campbell," ESPN columnist John Clayton wrote in 2007. Yes, Shell was not afraid to use his body as a battering ram to lay out opponents.

While he made life tough for opponents, Shell earned it by being in great shape and always being in position to make a play. He was a staple wearing No. 31 in the Steelers' backfield for 14 seasons. From the 1979 season to 1984, he had at least five picks per season, and even had a three-interception game against the rival Browns in 1981. Even if Shell never gets the honor of being placed in Canton, his legacy will remain forever as one of the greats in Steelers history.

45 Super Bowl XXX: Setback in Loss to Dallas

Super Bowl XXX in Tempe, Arizona, was a long time coming for the Steelers and their fans. They had waited 16 seasons for the team to return to the big game, their last appearance coming in Super Bowl XIV in 1980 against the Rams. The team had made an amazing run from 3–4 at one point in the 1995 season. They ran off eight in a row to clinch the AFC Central, then beat the Bills and Colts to get to the Super Bowl.

Reaching the big game was about putting the demons of the 1994 season behind them, as well. They had lost the AFC Championship Game at home against the Chargers and were anxious to show the NFL they were for real. In reaching the Super Bowl, they would be matched up against the team of the '90s and an old foe—the Dallas Cowboys.

It would be the third time the two teams would meet in the Super Bowl, the Steelers having bested Dallas in Super Bowls X and XIII. Now, though, Dallas was the class of the NFL. They came into the game as heavy favorites (13 points in most books), and had won two of the last three Super Bowls. They had an offense led by a massive offensive line, Hall of Fame quarterback Troy Aikman, and Hall of Fame running back Emmitt Smith. Not to mention a Hall of Fame wideout named Michael Irvin, and, oh yeah, another sure future Hall of Fame cornerback/wideout Deion Sanders.

If the Steelers were going to pull the upset, they would have to slow down Smith, pressure Aikman, and hit some big plays against Sanders. To say it was going to be tough was an understatement. The team started the game looking like it was out of its league. The defense played scared to start the game, allowing Dallas to march down the field on their first two drives to quickly take a 10–0 lead.

The Pittsburgh offense underwent a change in the '95 season. From a one-time power running attack to a wide-open passing affair, the club used four- and five-wideout sets during the season, and quarterback Neil O'Donnell was bombs away through points of the season. He had solid players to throw to—Yancy Thigpen, Ernie Mills, Andre Hastings, wunderkind Kordell Stewart, and even tight end Mark Bruener.

To start Super Bowl XXX, though, O'Donnell and the offense were out of sync. They went three-and-out on their first drive, then after they did get a drive to the Dallas 36 later in the first half, they were stopped after a bad snap by center Dermontti Dawson when O'Donnell was in the shotgun. It looked like Super Bowl XXX was going to be a runaway.

Dallas even added to the lead with another Chris Boniol field goal, this time from 35 yards to make it 13–0 in the second quarter. If the Steelers were going to recover, they would need to settle down and put together a drive, and also find a way to stop Aikman and the Cowboys' offense.

Pittsburgh's offense finally got things going late in the second quarter. Starting at their own 46, they got a few big pass plays to Hastings, and then converted a fourth-and-1 when Stewart went for three yards. They drove to the Dallas 6 and went on a slant pattern to Thigpen, who made the touchdown catch in front of

Fallout from Super Bowl XXX

In the aftermath of Super Bowl XXX, the Steelers lost three key parts in the off-season after their title run. Maybe the most important was the departure of quarterback Neil O'Donnell. He took the brunt of the beating by Steelers fans and the media for the loss, but many don't remember how important he was to simply getting the team to the title game. O'Donnell bolted for the Jets, and his career quickly went downhill.

Also gone were linebacker Kevin Greene, who combined with Greg Lloyd to form a great 1-2 punch at the outside linebacker spot. Greene took more money to land with the Carolina Panthers. Also leaving was offensive coordinator Ron Erhardt, who didn't see eye to eye with Bill Cowher on the play-calling. He ended up back in New York, but this time with O'Donnell and the Jets. After a 1–15 season, he walked away from the game in January 1998.

Sanders with just 13 seconds left in the half. Suddenly the score was 13–7 Dallas, and Super Bowl XXX was a game again.

Just as the Steelers seemed to have momentum, things turned to disaster in the third quarter. O'Donnell went back to pass, and the ball slipped out on him. It sailed right to Dallas corner Larry Brown, who took it 44 yards to the Pittsburgh 18. It took Dallas just two plays to reach the end zone on a Smith one-yard run to make it 20–7.

The third quarter continued as the Steelers' defense finally started to assert itself. Aikman was pressured, and Smith had nowhere to run, giving the Steelers' offense a shot at getting back into the game. First they got a drive going with Byron "Bam" Morris carrying the load and O'Donnell hitting passes. That set up a Norm Johnson 46-yard field goal with 11:20 left in the game to make it 20–10.

Then, in his first Super Bowl as coach, Bill Cowher made one of the gutsiest calls in Super Bowl history. An onside kick. It was perfect and came at a perfect time, and Deon Figures recovered it, giving the Steelers the ball right back at their own 48. The offense went back to work, and after they got down to the 1, Morris waltzed into the end zone, cutting the Dallas lead to three with 6:36 left.

It was time for the defense to step up and stop the Cowboys, and once again, they did their job. Levon Kirkland made an amazing sack of Aikman, leaping over a blocker to force a punt, giving the Steelers the ball back at their own 32 with plenty of time—4:15 remaining.

What happened next would go down as a dark moment in Steelers history. On second down, O'Donnell saw a blitz coming and threw the ball where he felt Hastings would be on a hot route read. Instead, Hastings ran his route as was called, to the inside, and as O'Donnell threw the pass, the only player in its path was, again, Cowboys corner Larry Brown. He took the ball back to the Pittsburgh 6, giving Dallas a rather easy chance to put the game away. They did.

Two plays after the pick, all doubt was lifted as Smith dove in from four yards out to give Dallas the 27–17 victory. For being in the right place at the right time, Brown walked away with the Super Bowl MVP award. It was tough to watch ego-filled owner Jerry Jones and his handpicked coach, Barry Switzer, celebrate with the Lombardi Trophy on a stage that easily could have been filled with black and gold.

46 Greg Lloyd

The Steelers' attitude on defense in the mid-1990s was led by an angry man. Greg Lloyd from small Fort Valley State used being drafted in the sixth round in 1987, as well as never getting the respect he felt he deserved, to go out and punish players on a week-in, week-out basis. Wearing No. 95, Lloyd made making big plays and inspiring teammates on defense a weekly occurrence. He was the mouthpiece of the early years of Bill Cowher's coaching reign, and in his 11-year NFL career was named to five Pro Bowls and three NFL All-Pro teams.

He played every game angry and came out each week with a passion to physically pummel the opposing offense. From his karate-like chop to knock the ball out of quarterbacks' hands, to stopping running backs coming at him at full speed, Lloyd was truly a throwback linebacker. He could have played with the Steelers of the 1970s, and while players like Jack Lambert and Jack Ham would have still gotten a lot of the press, Lloyd might have been as good as those guys during his tenure in Pittsburgh.

His Steelers career began when coach Chuck Noll drafted him in 1987. He spent two seasons fighting back from a knee injury just to make it on the field, and once he was able to get there, he wanted to give his coaches a reason to keep him there. He did. From a knockout of Jets wide receiver Al Toon in December 1989 to a goal-line stop of Patriots running back Leonard Russell a few weeks later, Lloyd always seemed to come up with a *SportsCenter* highlight clip.

When Cowher was hired in 1992 as coach, one of the first things he wanted to do was move Lloyd from the outside linebacker spot. It was a move that Lloyd balked at, and in the end, the player won out—and it was a good thing he did. He was always a hit with the fans, who loved his jarring hits and his "just plain nasty" attitude that made the Steelers' defense what it was.

The 1994 season may have been Lloyd's best. Playing opposite Kevin Greene on the other side of the defense, Lloyd simply dominated games. He was voted as team MVP for the second time in his career and was named Defensive Player of the Year by UPI. He put up 91 tackles (73 solo), with a career-high 10 sacks and seven forced fumbles. He led the defense again in 1995, the season the team made the Super Bowl but suffered a tough 27–17 loss to the Cowboys.

Then, just like that, it was over for Lloyd. He tore the patella tendon in his left knee during the first game of the 1996 season in Jacksonville. Then in 1997 he suffered an ankle injury in the final half of the season, which developed into a staph infection, ending his year and his Steelers career. He was released the following off-season, ending what was a memorable career for Lloyd, who was voted onto the Steelers' 75th Anniversary Team.

After one season with the Carolina Panthers, Lloyd retired, moving on to his second career, where he could continue to bring it from a physical standpoint—instructing tae kwon do. The fourth-degree black belt has been teaching in Fayetteville since 1998 and probably still uses the same intensity in the martial arts studio that made him a big fan favorite on the football field, and one of the best linebackers in Steelers history.

47 Troy Polamalu

The Steelers have always felt that the best way to build a championship team is through the NFL Draft, and the drafting of Steelers safety Troy Polamalu in 2003 once again proved that theory correct. The club had not made a Super Bowl since the 1995 season, and they knew they needed a playmaker on the defensive side of the ball. Polamalu was the player they targeted when draft day arrived in 2003.

Several off-season events led up to Polamalu coming to Pittsburgh. First, the team was shunned by free agent safety Dexter Jackson, who left Tampa Bay and, after agreeing to a deal with the Steelers, backed out to ink with Arizona. Then, on draft day, though the Chargers were eyeing Polamalu to replace Rodney Harrison with their 15th pick, they traded down. With Polamalu still available, the Steelers moved up, making a deal with the Chiefs to move from 27 to 16 to grab the USC safety.

The pick was historic for Pittsburgh—Polamalu was the first safety the team had ever taken in the first round. Since then, he has become the unqualified face of the franchise, playing with reckless abandon every play, saying a prayer after every play, and seemingly coming up with a play that makes the highlight films every week. That abandon was his worst enemy though in the 2009 season, as playing on special teams in Week 1 versus Tennessee he injured his knee and was limited to just three games the entire season.

It didn't start so hot for Polamalu. He struggled his rookie year, playing in all of the team's 16 games in their 6–10 season but not picking off a pass, and defending just four passes. By his second year, though, No. 43 started to show why he was a first-round pick. As the club went 15–1 and reached the AFC Championship Game, he became a star in the making, picking off five passes, collecting a sack, and defending 14 passes. He set up a score in the team's divisional playoff win over the Jets with a pick, and teams started game-planning for the physical safety.

Since that second season, Polamalu has been a playmaker. In the Steelers' miracle playoff run of 2005, he played at an incredible level, making big plays in all three wins on the way to Super Bowl XL, including showing the ability to take over a game like he did in Denver, when the team won the AFC title by topping the Broncos.

Polamalu a TV Star

While he may be quiet for the most part off the field, Troy Polamalu introduced Steelers fans to another side of the safety when he starred in a remake of the famous Joe Greene Coca-Cola commercial during Super Bowl XLII. The commercial was so popular that Polamalu scored another commercial, this time doing an ad for Head and Shoulders shampoo. The comedic ad showed that Polamalu has another career once his NFL days are over.

Troy Polamalu runs for a 40-yard touchdown after intercepting a pass from Baltimore quarterback Kyle Boller during the fourth quarter of the AFC Championship Game in Pittsburgh in January 2009.

Every season Polamalu comes up with his own highlight reel. From crazy hits that opposing players don't even see coming to one-handed interceptions, the safety never fails to amaze even his own teammates. His interception for a score against the Baltimore Ravens in the AFC Championship Game in the 2008 season was the backbreaker that led to the team's 23–14 win on the way to Super Bowl XLIII.

Also evident every week is Polamalu's humility. Deeply spiritual, he does not allow himself to get caught up in the superstar lifestyle that causes so many NFL players to find themselves on the front pages for all the wrong reasons. He doesn't hang out in nightclubs or drive 100 miles an hour on the freeway, instead he spends time with his family. His hobbies include growing flowers, making furniture, and playing the piano.

While it's not exactly typical of the way you would expect one of the hardest hitters in the NFL to act, Polamalu is cut from a different cloth, and it's made him one of the most popular Steelers in years. There's no telling what the long-haired Samoan safety will do next. From starring in commercials to making amazing plays, the Steelers' decision to move up and pick Polamalu in the 2003 draft was one that has paid off in countless ways.

48 Fats Holmes a Force on the Steel Curtain

Taking a backseat to no one when he played and being part of the greatest defensive line in NFL history, Ernie "Fats" Holmes knew how to punish an opponent every time he took the field. Combined with Joe Greene, L.C. Greenwood, and Dwight White, Holmes was a steal in the eighth round of the 1971 draft. He was the forgotten member of the Steel Curtain, but some say he was the most fierce of the four players.

Holmes did have his issues both on and off the field. Some said he was wild and not very disciplined when he played, which was a reason why he was traded by the Steelers in 1978 to Tampa Bay. He did win two titles as a member of the Curtain and unofficially collected 40 sacks while a Steeler.

During a stretch in 1974, Holmes had a streak of having a sack in six straight games, which ties him with Joe Greene and Greg Lloyd for the longest stretch in team history. That season, as the Steelers' defense rounded into form and won its first NFL championship in Super Bowl IX, Holmes put up 11.5 sacks.

This is not to say Holmes was all about sacks, streaks, or numbers, he was more about winning—and hurting the opposition along with his Curtain teammates. "I don't mind knocking somebody out," Holmes told *Time* magazine in 1975. "If I hear a moan and a groan coming from a player I've hit, the adrenaline flows within me. I get more energy and play harder."

And that happened just about every time he and his teammates took the playing field. They terrorized opponents—Holmes even sported an arrow on his head, making him appear even more of a menace when he got into the opposition's backfield.

The problems that haunted Holmes during his career may have overshadowed just how good he was. In March 1973, distraught over the breakup of his marriage and the ensuing custody dispute, he suffered an emotional breakdown and began firing a pistol at trucks while driving on the Ohio Turnpike. He even shot at a police helicopter and wounded an officer who was chasing him through the woods. He ended up pleading guilty to assault with a deadly weapon and spent two months in a psychiatric hospital. His life, with help from the Steelers, got back on track, and he was a big part of the line that helped the team win their first two Super Bowl titles.

He was a two-time All-Pro in 1974 and 1975, and while he continued to play at a high level, the Steelers eventually grew tired of his weight issues, trading him to the Buccaneers in 1978. The team must have known something—Holmes failed to make the team out of preseason. He did go on to play three games for the New England Patriots in 1978 before finally retiring.

His post-NFL career included some appearances in pro wrestling, including an outing in the WWE's *WrestleMania II* as part of a "football-wrestler" battle royal in Rosemont, Illinois. He then became an ordained minister in Wiergate, Texas. In interviews after his career, Holmes said that he remained a Steelers fan and even followed the team as much as he could in Texas. He served as captain for a Steelers-Browns game at Heinz Field, as well.

Holmes' life was cut short when on January 17, 2008, he was killed in a one-car accident near Beaumont, Texas, about 80 miles outside of Houston. He was not wearing a seat belt at the time of the accident, was ejected from his automobile, and was pronounced dead at the scene. He was just 59 years old.

49 A Catch for the Ages

In NFL lore, Dwight Clark's game-winning touchdown in the NFC Championship Game in January 1982 is widely known as "The Catch." In Pittsburgh, Steelers fans have a "catch" of their own that they will talk about for years to come, and that is the grab of wide receiver Santonio Holmes that won them Super Bowl XLIII over the Arizona Cardinals 27–23. Holmes went from rising star to superstar in the matter of one drive that won the Steelers their sixth ring, an NFL record. On the drive, Holmes had four receptions for 71 yards as the Steelers rallied back after giving up the lead with 2:37 left on a 64-yard touchdown to the Cardinals' Larry Fitzgerald.

The third-year wideout could be seen on the sideline telling his teammates, "It's time to be great," and great he was. As the Steelers made the frantic march down the field, Holmes became the primary target on a number of passes from quarterback Ben Roethlisberger, including a huge one that converted a third down, and another that saw him make a catch on an 11-yard curl at the Cardinals' 35, then turn and race toward the end zone as Aaron Francisco slipped. Holmes was taken down at the Cards' 6, setting up one of the great finishes in NFL history.

The first-down play saw Roethlisberger again look for Holmes in the left corner of the end zone. Holmes had beaten Dominique

Santonio Holmes (10) brings down the game-winning touchdown in the corner of the end zone late in the fourth quarter of Super Bowl XLIII against the Arizona Cardinals. Pittsburgh won 27–23.

Rodgers-Cromartie and Antrel Rolle, but as the high pass came in, the wideout went up and twisted to make the grab...and the ball went through his hands. "I thought I lost the Super Bowl," Holmes said after the game about the play that almost was.

All that play did, though, was delay the inevitable. Holmes was actually the third option on the second-down play for Roethlisberger. Running back Mewelde Moore was the first, and receiver Hines Ward was the second. Both were covered, leaving Roethlisberger to look for Holmes, who went to the right corner of the end zone and had three Cardinals racing to get back to him— Rodgers-Cromartie, Francisco, and Ralph Brown, who was at first covering Moore in the flat.

Roethlisberger looked around and decided to try to squeeze it in to Holmes. "It's one of those throws where you just don't think," Roethlisberger said. "You're just trying to put it where the receiver can catch it, but if you don't, he's the only one who can catch it. When I let it go, I thought it was his ball or no one's. But a second later, I see the corner [Brown] and I think, 'He's gonna pick it off.'"

The slow motion of the play tells the story: as the ball went over the outstretched hands of Brown, Francisco was ready to lay out Holmes if he made the grab. Rodgers-Cromartie could do nothing as Holmes, keeping his feet down, extended his arms as high as he could, making a finger-tip grab as Francisco hit him in the back with his right forearm, hoping that he could jar the ball loose. It didn't happen. Holmes fell straight down, but kept the ball tucked away while keeping both feet down. Replay after replay showed that the officials made the correct call—a touchdown, and one that remains as vivid as ever to the players involved and Steelers fans all over the world.

50 Attend Steelers Training Camp in Latrobe

The city of Latrobe, Pennsylvania, is abuzz each and every July and August, as Steelers fans far and wide come to the city to welcome back their team to training camp. For the past 43 seasons, the Steelers have held their training camp at St. Vincent College, a suggestion made over 40 years ago by Art Rooney Jr., a St. Vincent alum.

It is a rite of summer for Steelers fans to see the position battles and watch their favorite Steelers get ready for the season. It's been a tradition since 1966, and the college has seen some of the greatest Steelers players of all-time take the field there to hone their craft.

Players take up temporary residence for four weeks at Rooney Hall, which is named after legendary Steelers owner Art Rooney. They spend their summers getting ready for the season in meetings, long afternoon and sometimes night practices, and bonding with the fans—young and old—by signing autographs and taking pictures.

There's many things that make camp at St. Vincent College in Latrobe a special place to visit. The overall atmosphere is amazing. Steelers fans, who we already know are like no other, come out like fans of no other team in the league, most days with space at St. Vincent College limited with the amount of fans on hand, just to watch their favorite players simply run through the drills that make them a top-notch NFL team.

It's really quite a sight to behold the fans all clad in black and gold sitting on blankets on the rolling hills at the college with their rosters watching the team in the heat of the summer. There never seems to be a summer that goes by where there's not a few days of 100-plus temperatures there, and that makes for some intense practices at the site.

Latrobe is also the best place to get up close and personal with the players. Most players are more than willing to interact with the fans, taking the time to sign autographs as they go down that long hill from Rooney Hall to the practice field—some will even take personal photos with the fans lined up on the steps and the hill as they go in from a long day's work.

As a young fan in 1993, I recall being able to catch up with some of the biggest names on the roster—Barry Foster, Greg Lloyd, Rod Woodson, Carnell Lake—in training camp that year. I still even have a cherished photo with the starting quarterback of that team, Neil O'Donnell. While Mom was never one to want to sit through those two-and-a-half-hour practices, there was always a shady spot to relax and read a book while Dad and I went through the roster, watching drills and pointing out what players we felt would step up with big seasons.

Another great aspect of the Steelers training camp is the fact that it's all free. There's plenty of parking at the college for fans and families, and there's no charge to watch the team take the field and practice each day of the summer. This is a departure from a growing trend in the NFL to charge just to see training camp.

If you need another opinion on how grand the stage is in Latrobe at St. Vincent to watch the Steelers, consider the words of Peter King, an excellent *Sports Illustrated* writer, who wrote, "It's the best training camp in the NFL, the best venue for watching real football in the NFL, and my favorite place to soak in what sports should be."

51 Cowher Arrives in the Steel City

When the Chuck Noll coaching era in Pittsburgh came to the end after the 1991 season, the organization had to do something they had not done in an amazing 23 seasons—find a new head coach. It was not going to be easy. The Steelers needed a voice, a strong one that could come in and take a group of players who had talent—but didn't show it on the field at times—and lead them to the next level. Under Noll, the Steelers had only made the playoffs once in his last seven seasons.

The coaching search following Noll's retirement was vast, and ended up with a final group of four candidates. Those four men were former Steelers great Joe Greene, Houston Oilers offensive coordinator Kevin Gilbride, Dallas Cowboys defensive coordinator Dave Wannstedt, and Kansas City Chiefs defensive coordinator Bill Cowher.

Anytime you hire a coach, it's a dramatic and franchise-changing decision. Pick the right guy, and you could be set for 10 to 15 seasons. Choose the wrong guy, and it could put your club in a tailspin that could take years to turn back around in the right direction.

Tom Donahoe, who took over football operations when Noll left the team, was responsible for the final decision. Dan Rooney told Donahoe one simple thing—don't screw this up for us. Sure, no pressure, all he was asked to do was replace a Hall of Fame coach who lead the team from being a laughingstock in the decades before his arrival to being a powerhouse franchise that took home four Super Bowls in his 23 seasons. No pressure at all.

Entering the 1991 off-season, there were nine NFL teams looking for a head coach. In true Steelers fashion, they did their homework and filled their post last, not panicking and going after big names who brought more bark than bite. Once the team decided on their final four, they did their research, and the four all brought interesting traits and qualities to the table.

There was no doubt that Greene was the fans' choice. He was probably the only name most fans really knew on the list. He was a Pittsburgh guy through and through, and Rooney knew all about him for the 13 seasons he spent as a terror on the field and the five he had already spent with the team as an assistant head coach under Noll. It would be hard to pass up a guy who had meant so much to the franchise.

Gilbride was by far the oddest choice as a finalist. He was a run-and-shoot coach with the Oilers, a hooky offense that was more like arena football than the NFL, where on just about every play the quarterback was zipping the ball all over the field. It was not uncommon to see Oilers quarterback Warren Moon putting up 350- to 400-yard passing games, and throwing the ball 40 to 50 times. Bottom line, he would have never fit in, in Pittsburgh.

Both Greene and Gilbride were eventually pushed aside, Greene mostly because the team wanted a clean break from Noll and his staff. The final choice for the job came down to two—Wannstedt and Cowher. Both were young—Wannstedt was 39, Cowher was 34—and both were natives of the Pittsburgh area. Both were defensive guys first, and both were emotional guys who

Bill Cowher came from Kansas City to beat out Dave Wannstedt for the Steelers' head coaching job. Fifteen years later, Cowher left the Steelers with a Super Bowl win and a 161–99–1 record.

were not afraid to speak their minds. The decision would be interesting, to say the least.

The two men did their best to sell themselves to Donahoe, as well as to Rooney. In the end, one thing that Rooney could not get past was just how young Cowher was. But as Rooney talked time after time with him, he got more and more past the fact that Cowher was graduating high school the year the Steelers won their first Super Bowl.

Rooney called Cowher on January 17, 1992, to invite him and his wife, Kaye, up to Pittsburgh for the weekend. After a dinner and talk with key members of the organization on January 19, Dan and Art Rooney and Donahoe offered Cowher the job. Two days later Cowher took the podium at Three Rivers Stadium and told Steeler Nation that the team he was about to take over would play with a fire, and there was a wealth of talent to work with.

The rest, as we all know, is history. In 15 seasons Cowher was a Super Bowl champion, led the team to two AFC titles, was the

Sporting News NFL Coach of the Year twice, and ended with a record of 161–99–1. It's safe to say that the coaching search of the post-Noll era worked out just fine for the Black and Gold.

52 Two Passes Define O'Donnell's Legacy

The career of former Steelers quarterback Neil O'Donnell is summed up in two completions. The problem is, those two completions were to the other team. It was January 28, 1996, and the Steelers were in the Super Bowl for the first time since January 20, 1980. O'Donnell was a leader, and he led the team to the dance with his best season as a pro, throwing for 17 touchdowns and just seven interceptions as the team overcame a 3–4 start to end the season 11–5.

In the playoffs, he was very good against the Bills, and then in the AFC Championship Game against the Indianapolis Colts, he rallied the team with a late fourth-down completion and then a long pass to Ernie Mills that led to a 20–16 victory. It was on to the Super Bowl and the Steelers' third title game against the Dallas Cowboys.

Early on, the game belonged to Dallas, as the Cowboys built a 13–0 lead midway through the second quarter. Then the Steelers' offense got going. O'Donnell led the team on a drive right before the half, and a short touchdown pass to Yancey Thigpen made it 13–7 at halftime.

The third quarter saw O'Donnell make his first critical mistake. He helped the team get to the 48-yard line, but then on third down a ball sailed on him and landed right in the hands of Cowboys cornerback Larry Brown. He took it back to the Steelers' 18, and then two plays later Dallas scored to make it 20–7.

O'Donnell Almost Delays Big Ben

The Steelers almost derailed starting quarterback Ben Roethlisberger in 2004 as the man they really wanted under center after starter Tommy Maddox was hurt in Week 2 against the Ravens. Coach Bill Cowher put a call in to his former quarterback, Neil O'Donnell, asking if he would consider coming back to the Steelers for the '04 campaign. O'Donnell thanked his former coach but rejected the offer and decided to stay retired. Of course, Roethlisberger got the call after that and went on to win his first 15 starts at QB before losing a game. If O'Donnell would have come back, who knows what would have happened?

The team had to rally again. They got a field goal and an onside kick, after which they drove down the field, and Bam Morris scored to make it 20–17. The defense was red hot, they stopped the Cowboys and gave the Steelers the ball back at their own 32 with 4:15 to go. That's when disaster struck the usually careful quarterback.

On a Cowboys blitz, O'Donnell threw to where wideout Andre Hastings should have been, but the receiver went inside instead of staying outside, and the only person standing where the ball arrived was Larry Brown. He made the easy pick, took it down near the goal line, and two plays later the game was iced when Emmitt Smith scored to make it 27–17.

O'Donnell's final desperate pass was also picked off, but no one remembers or cares about that one. All anyone talks about is the first two. The sad thing about the final pick was it was his last pass as a member of the Steelers. The following off-season, O'Donnell was a free agent, and he and his wife made a decision that killed what could have been a long run as the club's quarterback for years. He picked the New York Jets and more money over being with a winning team in Pittsburgh.

The deal to move to New York was unheard of at the time—five years for $25 million with an $8 million signing bonus. At first he decided he wanted to stay in Pittsburgh, but then just before midnight on February 28, 1996, he took the Jets' offer. His career went nowhere fast playing for the Jets. He lasted there just two seasons, going 8–12 as a starter and throwing 21 touchdowns and 14 picks in those two seasons.

He went on to play one season for the Cincinnati Bengals in 1998, winning just two games, but one was a memorable one against his former Steelers team, as he threw a late 23-yard touchdown to Carl Pickens to beat his former team 25–20. Then he played five seasons as Steve McNair's backup in Tennessee, and started only eight games in five seasons. His final game came on December 28, 2003, against the Tampa Bay Buccaneers, and as a starter he was 18-for-27 for 232 yards with two touchdowns in a 33–13 win.

O'Donnell's career numbers with the Steelers saw him have some very productive seasons. When he was given the green light to throw the ball, he put up impressive numbers—not huge numbers, but numbers that put the Steelers in the best position to win. O'Donnell's career saw him hold the NFL record for lowest career interception percentage with 2.11 picks every 100 pass attempts. It was almost cruel that two interceptions defined his career in the Steel City.

With the Steelers, he won 39 of 61 starts and threw for 12,867 yards with 68 touchdowns and 39 interceptions. He never got the credit he deserved as a quarterback who could manage the game as well as make some tough throws when needed. One can only wonder what would have happened if those two throws in Super Bowl XXX would have been completed—to Steelers receivers instead of to Larry Brown.

53 Super Bowl XLV: Packers Rain on a Steelers Parade

As the Steelers entered Super Bowl XLV in Dallas, many pundits felt that their defense was good enough to hold down Green Bay quarterback Aaron Rodgers and a Packers team that needed three wins to make it to the big game.

But Green Bay was red-hot, beating the Eagles, the top-seeded Falcons, and the rival Bears to earn the right to play the Steelers in the 45th anniversary of the biggest game on earth. The Steelers, on the other hand, needed just two wins and had the luxury of playing both of them at home.

Pittsburgh rallied from a 21–7 halftime deficit to beat the rival Ravens in the AFC divisional playoff game. The Steelers next faced the New York Jets, who had upset the Patriots on the road. The Steelers built a 24–0 lead and then had to hang on for dear life, but they did enough to beat Rex Ryan and the Jets 24–19 to punch their ticket to the big dance.

The Steelers were slight 2½-point underdogs, but with a defense that looked like it was ready to hoist another trophy, they spoke all week long leading up to the game about having to hold Rodgers in check. Little did they know that the replacement for the legendary Brett Favre was on tap to have maybe the greatest game in his NFL career.

Rodgers picked apart the Steelers all day, taking home MVP honors and throwing for 304 yards and three touchdowns in the Packers' 31–25 win. The score would have been worse were it not for a couple of key drops in the game that seemed to keep the Steelers in it.

The favorite target for Rodgers was Jordy Nelson, who seemed to pick on Steelers corner Willie Gay all afternoon. Nelson caught nine passes for 140 yards, and while he had three drops of his own, he seemed to always have a big catch in him to keep a drive going. He started the scoring by getting behind Gay for a 29-yard score with 3:44 left in the opening quarter.

While seven points isn't impossible to overcome, little did the Steelers know that just 24 seconds later the deficit would be 14. Quarterback Ben Roethlisberger was hit on the arm on a long pass down the sideline, and Packers safety Nick Collins made the easy pick and went 37 yards the other way for a score to make it a two-touchdown game.

Things would get worse before the Steelers finally started to mount a comeback that nearly earned them their seventh title. A Shaun Suisham 33-yard field goal made it 14–3 about four minutes into the second quarter, but with 2:24 to play in the half, the Packers would go up by 18 at 21–3.

Roethlisberger threw his second pick, this time to Packers CB Jarrett Bush, who jumped in front of Mike Wallace for the Steelers' second turnover. The Packers didn't wait long to cash in, as four plays later from the Steelers' 21 Rodgers hit Greg Jennings for a score to give the Pack a lead that looked like it would make for a blowout Super Bowl.

But as he has been known to do, Roethlisberger rallied his troops, and got things going just before the half. He led the team on a frantic 77-yard drive that ended with Hines Ward's last Super Bowl TD with 39 seconds to play in the half to make it 21–10. It seemed like the momentum in the game was shifting to the Steelers, who continued their comeback in the third quarter.

After the Packers' first drive stalled at the 25, the Steelers offense went to work, and it was the run game led by Rashard Mendenhall that did most of the damage. A 17-yard run by Mendenhall was followed a few plays later by a 16-yard run by Issac Redmen. Mendenhall capped the drive with an eight-yard TD run that closed the gap to 21–17, and suddenly it was a ballgame again.

After a quick three-and-out for the Packers, it looked like the game was about to be totally taken over by the Steelers offense, who again started to mount a drive. From their 40 the Steelers converted a third-and-1, and found themselves at the Packers' 29 after a Ward 15-yard catch.

The Green Bay defense finally stepped up, and three plays later Roethlisberger was sacked for a two-yard loss, setting up Mike Tomlin's decision to throw out Suisham to try a 52-yard field goal. The kick was a disaster, going wide left, and even worse, it gave the Packers back the advantage of field position with the ball at the Green Bay 43.

Once again the Steelers D did enough to stop the Packers offense, with Rodgers guiding Green Bay to the Steelers' 38 before stalling. The Steelers had nothing going on offense either, and gave the ball back to the Pack, who again were stuffed.

It set up the Steelers with great field position at the Packers' 40. Mendenhall carried for eight yards on the final play of the third quarter. The next play, however, would set off a chain of events that sealed the Steelers' fate.

Clay Matthews saved the Packers with a hit on Mendenhall on his next carry that popped the ball out, and the Packers recovered at their own 45. It was as deflating a turnover as a team could have, and it started a fourth quarter that cemented the Packers' championship.

Rodgers went to work picking on a tired Steelers defense, and hit a huge 38-yard pass to Nelson on a third-and-10 from the Steelers' 40 that set up a two-yard touchdown throw to Jennings that made it 28–17. The drive seemed to take the wind out of the Steelers' sails, and with 11:57 left, they had to score—and score quick.

Roethlisberger did his part, hitting passes downfield four times to Mike Wallace, the last a nifty 25-yard score that closed the gap to 28–23. The Steelers went for two and Antwaan Randle El ran in the conversion to make it 28–25. If the Steelers could just force a Packers mistake, the game could have still been theirs.

Didn't happen. Green Bay again went on a back-breaking drive, with Rodgers taking the Pack from their 25 to the Steelers' 5, the huge play a 31-yard pass to Jennings to set up a short Mason Crosby field goal to make it 31–25.

The Steelers had one more shot, but unlike three years earlier against the Cardinals, the football gods were not on their side this time around.

An awful penalty by special teams captain Keyaron Fox put the Steelers at the 13 to start the final drive, but Roethlisberger hit Heath Miller for 15 yards to get them up to the 28. Ward then caught a five-yard pass, setting up a second-and-5 from the 33.

From there, the Packers defense rose up. A deep incomplete pass was followed by two bad attempts to hit Wallace, and the confetti that could have been black and gold instead was green and gold for a Packers team that celebrated its fourth Super Bowl and 13th NFL championship.

"I feel like I let the city of Pittsburgh down, the fans, my coaches, and my teammates, and it's not a good feeling," said Roethlisberger, who later put his head in a towel and wept. The Steelers fought hard, but three turnovers and a lack of pass defense when they needed it most cost them what would have been a memorable seventh Super Bowl trophy.

54 Big Ben's History-Making Rookie Year

Tommy Maddox had stepped in and manned the front for the Steelers in the 2002 and 2003 seasons, and to his credit, had done some amazing things. He helped the team reach the playoffs in the '02 season and even won a shootout over the Browns in a 36–33

AFC wild-card victory. In '03, however, the bottom dropped out on Maddox and the club. The team took on a pass-happy look on offense, and things quickly went south as the team went 6–10. Bill Cowher knew that a change had to be made, and the club moved swiftly in the off-season to do just that.

The 2004 NFL Draft saw a number of high-profile quarterbacks enter the draft. Eli Manning, Philip Rivers, and Ben Roethlisberger were the biggest names. It would have been a shock to see one of them drop down to the Steelers at 11, but that's exactly what happened.

The club had the chance to take the 6'5", 241-pound, Lima, Ohio, native in Roethlisberger, and they jumped at the chance. They hadn't drafted a quarterback in the first round since Mark Malone in 1980, and in the team's history they had only drafted a quarterback in the first round five times before Roethlisberger's arrival.

The early thought process was that Roethlisberger would learn from veteran quarterbacks in Maddox and his backup, the arriving Charlie Batch. How quickly things would change. Batch was injured in the preseason, pushing Roethlisberger up to the backup role. After an opening day win over Oakland, Maddox and the club went into Baltimore in Week 2.

The Ravens beat up Maddox, and in the third quarter he was hit from behind, hurting his elbow and forcing Roethlisberger into the game. The rookie threw two touchdowns, but it was too little too late as the Steelers fell 30–13. It was the only time the team would lose in the regular season that year.

Roethlisberger took over the team and took the NFL by storm. He started his first game the following week in Miami in the last winds and flooding rains of Hurricane Jeanne, helping the team to a 13–3 victory. The next week against the Bengals he threw for 174 yards and a score as the team moved to 3–1 with a 28–17 win.

The league really started to take notice the next week when he faced the Browns at home. Missing on just five passes, the rookie threw for 231 yards and a score as the Steelers rolled to 4–1 with a 34–23 win. The roll continued with a comeback win against Dallas the next week on the road, as Roethlisberger put up a QB rating of 125.5 with two touchdowns. He cemented his early rise to fame two weeks later, stopping the Patriots' NFL record 21-game win streak with a 34–20 victory, throwing for 196 yards and two scores. The wins kept coming, the next week it was the unbeaten Eagles that the Steelers beat up 27–3, then it was Cleveland again to move to 8–1 with a 24–10 road win. Many seemed to think that Roethlisberger was simply managing the team to wins, but at the same time, no rookie quarterback had ever been able to put together such a win streak.

By the time the end of December rolled around, Roethlisberger and the team were 14–1 entering the final game of the year. He sat against Buffalo, but the backups led the club to a 29–24 win to finish the year at 15–1, only the fourth team in NFL history since the league adopted a 16-game schedule in 1978 to finish with such a record.

The only downfall to Roethlisberger's rookie season was when the divisional playoffs started two weeks later, he was mentally and physically drained. He didn't play well at home versus the Jets, throwing two picks and relying on some late heroics to win in overtime 20–17.

A rematch with the Patriots took place the following week. Again, Roethlisberger struggled, as did the rest of the club as New England walked out of Heinz Field with a 41–27 win. It was a tough lesson for Roethlisberger and the team, but one they would learn from the following year when the then-23-year-old became the youngest quarterback ever to win a Super Bowl.

Despite the setback in the AFC Championship Game in 2004, Roethlisberger's rookie season was a preview of a franchise quarterback who would put two more Lombardi Trophies in the Steelers' front office over the next four seasons.

55 Joey Porter

Joey Porter was a solid Steelers linebacker from 1999 to 2006 who usually let his bark be backed up by his bite. He followed a long line of solid outside linebackers, such as Greg Lloyd, Kevin Greene, and Jason Gildon. When he came in, the team wasn't the powerhouse it had been under Bill Cowher, but he was around for some of Cowher's final good seasons, including the Super Bowl XL win in February 2006.

Porter was a Steelers third-round draft pick, the 73rd overall pick of the 1999 draft. He started his Steelers career wearing Lloyd's old No. 95, but changed to No. 55 before the start of the regular season. Even with the number switch, through a large part of his career, many felt that Porter was a Lloyd clone, playing with the same intensity as well as with the same vocal barrage on opponents.

During his first year, Porter shined on special teams, and since the team was going nowhere fast in '99, his playing time on defense increased. In that first season he put up six tackles and two sacks, and also returned a fumble of former Steelers quarterback Neil O'Donnell 46 yards for a score in the team's season finale against the Tennessee Titans.

By the following season, Porter was lined up opposite Gildon, and he shined, putting up 10½ sacks as the team went 9–7, missing the playoffs by one game. He also put up 74 tackles and had a pick, two forced fumbles, and one recovery. For his efforts, he was named the AFC Defensive Player of the Month for October. One game that month in particular stood out—against the Bengals on October 15 he had eight tackles (seven solo), three sacks (including one for a safety), four quarterback hurries, and a forced fumble.

It was that season when his mouth also stared to get the better of him. In a game against Cleveland he got into it with Browns punter Chris Gardocki. The punter was seen flipping off Cowher after Porter verbally laid into him, earning the Steelers a roughing-the-punter penalty. It was all in a day's work for Porter, who was becoming the vocal go-to guy on the Steelers' defense.

In 2001 Porter had another solid year, and the team shined, going 13–3 in its new home in Heinz Field. Porter finished the season with 59 tackles and nine sacks, but the team fell in the AFC Championship Game to the New England Patriots at home, leaving Porter and the club unfulfilled entering 2002.

Two years later Porter suffered a gunshot wound to his backside outside a Denver bar on August 31. He missed the first few games of the year, but returned and gave the team an emotional lift. Despite that, he had his lowest sack total of any season other than his rookie year, and the team suffered as well, going 6–10.

He was back to Pro Bowl form in 2004, though, putting up three sacks against the Pats on Halloween in a win, and another two sacks versus the Redskins on November 28. The team went 15–1 in the regular season, and Porter led on defense. He again let his emotions get the better of him before a game in Cleveland on November 14, when he and Browns running back William Green threw punches before the game, both getting ejected.

In a strange twist of fate, while Porter was in the locker room, some unknown Steeler named James Harrison came in, took over, and played lights out, doing a great imitation of Porter as the team won the game and continued a winning streak. The season continued to go the Steelers' and Porter's way until the AFC Championship Game, where again the Patriots topped them, this time running over the Steelers' defense in a 41–27 win.

Finally in 2005 all the hard work that Porter put into his Steelers career paid off. He was again a Pro Bowl player, and he had 10½ sacks to go along with 56 tackles, two picks, and four forced

Linebacker Joey Porter was known for his vocal style of hard-hitting football.

fumbles. He was stellar in the playoffs, getting huge plays against Peyton Manning and the Colts in the Steelers' divisional playoff win in Indy, then the following week stripping Jake Plummer early in the game to set up a touchdown as the Steelers beat Denver to advance to Super Bowl XL.

Of course once they got to the big dance, Porter started talking. He and Seattle Seahawks tight end Jerramy Stevens got into a verbal battle when Stevens said that he and the Seahawks were going make Steelers running back Jerome Bettis lose his final NFL game. Needless to say, that didn't sit well with Porter, who spent the week firing back at the tight end. Porter won the war with Stevens, who dropped a couple passes in the 21–10 Steelers victory. Porter finally was able to celebrate, as he and the Steelers had reached their goal of a Super Bowl title.

The following year was his last as a member of the Steelers. He had seven sacks and overall put up 55 tackles when the team stared the year 2–6 but rallied to 8–8. They missed the playoffs, Bill Cowher stepped down as coach, and the team felt it had seen the best of Porter, releasing him March 1 instead of paying him a $1 million signing bonus.

Porter was unhappy to leave the only football city he knew but nevertheless moved on. Just a week after he was released, he inked a five-year deal worth $32 million with the Miami Dolphins. He took his vocal style of hard-hitting football with him, and in 2008 shined as he led the AFC with 17½ sacks. He retired from the game wearing Steelers colors again, waving a Terrible Towel at Steelers training camp in August of 2012.

"This is home. Even when I left—it was okay to go and play for Miami and Arizona—but there's nothing like home," Porter said. "Pittsburgh, once you come through here, it's a special piece in your heart here, in Pittsburgh. That void wouldn't have been filled if I didn't come back and retire as a Steeler."

56 Merril Hoge

If there was ever a member of the Steelers in the mid- to late 1980s who seemed to wear his heart on his sleeve and get more than he ever could have thought out of his talent, it was running back Merril Hoge. Known for his hard-nosed play and shoulder blocks into defenders, Hoge was a Steeler at heart and played more like a '70s-version member of the team than one from the sometimes struggling '80s version.

Chuck Noll took a chance on Hoge in the 10th round, the 261st pick overall. He right away showed his fight on the field. In his rookie season he was fifth on the team in special-teams tackles. In

From Player to Broadcaster

There are a number of former Steelers players who are known for their faces and voices on TV and radio more than on the field. Terry Bradshaw may be the most famous off-the-field Steelers player, going on to star in films and is a full-time studio host for *Fox NFL Sunday*. Mark Malone went on to report for ESPN, as did running back Merril Hoge. Bill Cowher is a cohost for *NFL Today* on CBS, and Tunch Ilkin is the Steelers' current color-commentator. Jack Ham did some radio work after his career, and Rod Woodson appeared on the NFL Network. Even "Slash" is on TV, as Kordell Stewart is an ESPN commentator.

1988 he finally got to make his mark on the field as a running back, where he didn't disappoint. He bowled over defensive players for a team-high 705 yards to go along with three touchdowns, and even shared the team lead with catches (50) for another 487 yards and three scores. He brought his lunch pail to work every Sunday and quickly became a fan favorite in Steeler Nation despite the team having some down years, going just 5–11 in 1988.

It was the 1989 season when people outside of Pittsburgh started to notice Hoge. He had another productive year with 621 yards and a team-high eight rushing touchdowns, but it was on the national stage where eyes were opened. On New Year's Eve in a wild-card game against the Houston Oilers, Hoge pounded his way for 100 yards on 17 carries and a score as the Steelers upset Houston 26–23 to move to the AFC divisional playoffs in Denver.

The following week, Hoge was on display. He put up 7.5 yards per carry as he rushed his way to 120 yards on 16 carries and a score. He added eight catches for 60 yards as the Steelers nearly pulled off another big upset before eventually bowing out to the eventual AFC-champion Broncos 24–23.

He followed up his productive '89 season by leading the team in rushing in 1990, going for 772 yards and seven scores as the team went 9–7 but missed the playoffs. In 1991, Noll's final season as coach, Hoge ran for 610 yards and two scores with 49 catches for 379 yards.

When Bill Cowher came in to start the 1992 season, Hoge's role changed. No more would he be getting the ball 10 to 20 times a game. Instead, he would now play the role of fullback, opening holes for upcoming AFC leading rusher Barry Foster. While Foster set team records, Hoge stayed in the background, carrying the ball just 41 times for 150 yards. He also had only 28 catches.

After a 1993 season in which he had 51 carries for 249 yards, Hoge took advantage of free agency and moved to the Chicago Bears. He managed to play in just five games before retiring at the end of the 1994 season due to post-concussion syndrome. At that time he had the longest consecutive playing streak in the NFL.

Hoge didn't go quietly into retirement. In 1995 he joined ESPN, becoming a valuable member of the network's NFL crew. In February 2003 Hoge was diagnosed with non-Hodgkin's lymphoma. But even cancer wouldn't stop him: by the following July, Hoge was cancer-free. While he is successful on the air, he is most remembered by fans as an old-school player in a new era of Steelers football.

57 Heath Miller

If there's an offensive skill position that has always seemed to get pushed to the back burner for the Steelers, it's the tight end spot.

In the history of the franchise, the tight end position has been mostly filled by players who were known more for their blocking than their pass catching. A couple names do jump out, such as Randy Grossman and Bennie Cunningham from the Super Bowl years, as well as more recent names like Eric Green and Mark Bruener.

Bruener was a popular player, brought to the team with a first-round pick back in 1995. He had nine productive seasons for

Pittsburgh, but left following the 2003 season, leaving a void the team knew it would have to fill.

And fill it they did.

On draft day 2005, the team selected the 2004 John Mackey Award winner (best collegiate tight end in the country), Heath Miller. All Miller has done throughout the course of his career is redefine the tight end position for the Steelers, far and away becoming the best tight end the Steel City has ever seen.

Miller has been part of two Super Bowl winners and was on the team when they fell to the Packers in the 2010 season in Super Bowl XLV. He's a two-time Pro Bowl selection, and was selected by his peers in 2012 as the team MVP, the first time in team history that the honor went to a tight end.

"I have been saying for years that he is my favorite player, but we just never coached it up to where he got the opportunity to come out and show what he has been able to do," Steelers safety Ryan Clark said after the passing out of the award. "If you look, game in and game out this year, when he got opportunities to deliver, he delivered."

In 2012, Miller led the team with 71 catches and 816 yards, good for second on the team, and he tied Mike Wallace for the team lead with eight touchdowns. The season didn't end well for Miller, as in the second-to-last game he tore his ACL and MCL, an injury that could sideline him into the 2013 season.

Miller will take on the injury with the same quiet, unassuming passion that has made him one of the best tight ends in the game today. He's the ultimate team player, always putting his teammates first and never drawing attention to himself.

Born October 22, 1982, to proud parents Earl and Denise Miller, Heath grew up in Richlands, Virginia. He played football in high school at Honaker High School, and actually was the guy throwing the passes, not catching them, as the team's quarterback.

While playing QB, Miller earned the Associated Press Player of the Year honor as a senior and was a two-time AP All-State selection.

He also earned the All-Southwest Virginia first-team honors at quarterback and was a second-team all-state selection at defensive back, adding Region D Offensive Player of the Year honors.

Miller set several school records in passing and led the team to its first state championship game his senior year, in which they lost to King William High School 25–15. Football wasn't the only sport Miller excelled at; he also was a very good baseball player, playing first base and earning the Black Diamond District first-team honors, and was an All-Region and All-State selection.

He also took to the hardwood, playing basketball as a forward, earning the All-District and All-Region honors. Following high school, Miller decided to take his talents to the University of Virginia.

While he started as a QB, Miller made the transition to the tight end spot, and just like in high school, he took to it right away. He was a three-year starter for Virginia, making big plays and big catches. Miller certainly earned his nickname: "Big Money."

Miller wrapped up his college career putting up big numbers, leading the ACC for most career receptions (144), yards (1,703), and touchdowns (20) by a tight end. In Virginia history, these totals place Heath second in receptions, seventh in yards, and tied for fourth in touchdown receptions, regardless of position.

He won the John Mackey Award as the nation's best tight end, and with the Steelers needing a tight end, he was the perfect fit for the club. As a blue-collar player who always works hard on the field and during the week to get ready for games, Miller was a perfect fit for Bill Cowher's Steelers.

Pittsburgh drafted him with the 30th pick overall in the 2005 NFL Draft, and it didn't take him long into his rookie season to start producing. As the Steelers made a run to Super Bowl XL, Miller pulled in 39 receptions for 459 yards and six touchdowns. He was the starting tight end in the Super Bowl, and earned his first ring with the Steelers as they topped Seattle 21–10 in Detroit.

Davis Goes 100-plus against the Panthers

Little-remembered Steelers safety Travis Davis had one of the few highlights of the Steelers' 6–10 1999 season. It came the day after Christmas on December 26 as the Steelers broke a six-game losing streak at home against the Carolina Panthers with a 30–20 win. The Steelers led the game 3–0, when the Panthers were driving for the go-ahead score in the first quarter. Panthers running back Fred Lane got a handoff, and the ball squirted out of his hands. Davis, who played with the Steelers for just that season, scooped up the ball two yards into the end zone and took off, covering a record 102 yards into the opposite end zone at Three Rivers Stadium for a touchdown to give the Steelers a 10–0 lead. The return remains the longest in Steelers history.

With his career off and running, Miller worked hard and his numbers seemed to get better and better with each passing season. His biggest season came in 2009, when he grabbed 76 catches for 789 yards and six touchdowns. In July of 2009 the Steelers rewarded Miller with a six-year deal for $35.3 million, including a $12.5 million signing bonus.

The numbers continued to pile up for Miller, but the husband and father of two sons remains grounded, always putting the team first and doing his best. "This game is about more than individual players," Miller said during the 2012 season. "It's never about one person. It's the epitome of a team sport. I understand that and respect that."

Miller has also been one of the most durable players in recent memory, missing just five games in his Steelers career, including the season finale of 2012 after tearing his ACL and MCL. With the numbers he put up in 2012, Miller became the third Steeler in club history with 400 career catches, and he broke Elbie Nickel's record of 37 touchdowns by a tight end.

As he enters 2013 trying to come back from his injuries, he will do it ranking third in team history in receptions (408), seventh in yards (4,680), and tied for fifth in receiving touchdowns (39).

Even more important than catching touchdowns and setting team records are the things that Miller does off the field.

Heath has been a big part of local charities, contributing to the Salvation Army and WTAE TV's Annual Mini Golf Classic as a host to raise money for the Salvation Army. Miller can also be seen doing high school fundraising at local basketball games.

If Miller can overcome the injuries that derailed him late in the 2012 season, there's no doubt that he will continue to add to his legacy as the best tight end in Steelers franchise history.

58 Steelers Survive Wild Showdown with Cleveland

The 2002 season was quite amazing for Steelers quarterback Tommy Maddox. He reinvented himself that season as a quarterback, coming from just about nowhere to lead the Steelers to an AFC North title and into the playoffs with a 10–5–1 record. He took over for an ineffective Kordell Stewart in the fourth quarter of the third game of the season and never lost the starting job the rest of the season. His numbers on some weeks were rather gaudy, as the Steelers got away from a power offense to a pass-happy party led by "Touchdown" Tommy.

Maddox threw for 2,836 yards with 20 touchdowns and 16 picks during the regular season, and two of the wins that season were over Cleveland, each of them by three points. They entered the playoffs having to play the first weekend and drew a Browns team that needed a win and some help on the last week of the regular season to set up the third meeting.

Cleveland entered the game having to go with backup quarterback Kelly Holcomb, playing for Tim Couch, who had suffered a fractured leg in the regular-season finale against the Falcons. Many felt that Holcomb would melt under the pressure of a playoff game versus a good Steelers defense, but the Steelers and their fans were in for a surprise that cold, somewhat snow-filled day at Heinz Field. During the pregame it looked like that weather would mean that both teams may have to lean on their running games. Light snow fell, it was cold, and there was some wind. Instead of a usual slug-it-out affair between two rivals, the game seemed more like a classic AFL matchup between two pass-happy clubs looking to score and score often.

Three plays into the game, Cleveland's Holcomb hit wideout Kevin Johnson for 83 yards to the Steelers' 1, setting up the high-scoring battle. Cleveland scored on the next play to make it 7–0, then, after a muffed Steelers punt, Holcomb threw to Dennis Northcutt for a 32-yard score early in the second quarter to make it 14–0. The Steelers faithful were shell-shocked.

Antwaan Randle El, who had fumbled a punt earlier that set up the Browns' second score, got the Steelers on the board with a 66-yard punt return to close the gap to 14–7. The half closed 17–7 Cleveland, and there was an unsteady feeling in the crowd with the Browns controlling the momentum.

Those uneasy feelings continued in the third quarter, when early in the quarter the Browns' air show continued. Holcomb hit Northcutt for his second touchdown less than three minutes into the quarter to make it 24–7, and things seemed to be getting worse. Finally Maddox got the team on track, and a 10-play, 61-yard drive late in the quarter made it 24–14 when Plaxico Burress caught a six-yard score.

As the third quarter ended with the Steelers down 10, it was clear Maddox was going to have to have a special fourth quarter to pull this thing off. He didn't disappoint. The Browns did their best to steal the show with an offense that simply could not be stopped. Holcomb again gashed the Steelers' defense after a Maddox drive

Don't Call it a Comeback

The Steelers have had a couple of big comebacks in their history, their two biggest when they were behind 21 points. The first 21-point comeback was December 15, 1985, when the team rallied from a 21–0 deficit in the second quarter against the Buffalo Bills to win 30–24. The second came in October 1997, when the team trailed Baltimore on the road 21–0 in the second quarter. Led by quarterback Kordell Stewart, they came back and beat the Ravens 42–34 in a season that saw them reach the AFC Championship Game.

and touchdown pass to tight end Jerame Tuman to bring the Steelers within six at 27–21. Holcomb needed all of 1:58 to get that score back. An 18-yard pass to Northcutt, followed by a 23-yard run by William Green got the ball to the Steelers' 20. Three plays later, with Holcomb rolling out, he found wide receiver Andre' Davis open in the end zone for what seemed to be a back-breaking score. Now it was 33–21 Browns. Even after Cleveland missed the two-point conversion, the mood in the stadium was a combination of shock and sadness. It seemed the 2002 season was all but over.

But Maddox and the offense would not be denied. Getting the ball back at the 5:30 mark, the quarterback went to work right away, hitting four passes and combining with a couple of big Browns penalties to get the ball to the Cleveland 5. Two plays later Maddox hit Hines Ward with a pass that probably shouldn't have been thrown, given there were three Browns standing right there, for a touchdown to make it 33–28 with just over three minutes left.

It was time for the Steelers' defense to finally stop Holcomb, and they did. A three-yard run was followed by an incomplete pass. Then, with the game on the line after a delay-of-game penalty, Holcomb's pass attempt to Northcutt went right threw his hands, saving the Steelers and allowing them to get the ball back with 2:35 to play. It was time for Maddox to shine.

A pass to Burress gained 24 yards to the Cleveland 37, then two plays later a pass to Ward gained 10 to the Browns' 27. A sliding

Playoff Game Draws a Thumbs-Up Review

Sports Illustrated writer Michael Silver put the wild playoff win over the Browns into perspective on the magazine's website shortly after the game concluded:

I've seen some amazing games—Music City Miracle included—but this one certainly ranks right up there. There was such an outpouring of emotions after Chris Fuamatu-Ma'afala's touchdown.... And I can't remember when the last time I heard Renegade by Styx blaring through a stadium. It was a resounding moment. Then I was thinking: 50 seconds to go, Kelly Holcomb is hot, the Browns have taken most of their games down to the last second.... It was a greatly entertaining game—two very flawed teams, but very gutsy and with explosive offenses. But the cynic in me wants to take the Browns to task for going into the Prevent defense, and you could make an argument against both coaches for some of the play-calling. Of course, Bill Cowher is beyond reproach now that the Steelers won.

catch by Burress near the sideline gained 17 to the Cleveland 10. Maddox quickly hit Ward for seven yards to the Cleveland 3, and the Black and Gold called a timeout with 58 seconds left.

Finally Maddox's arm got a rest, and he handed off the next play to fan favorite fullback Chris Fuamatu-Ma'afala, who stunned the Browns, going for the final three yards into the end zone to make it 34–33 Steelers with 54 seconds left. Pittsburgh got the two-point conversion to make it 36–33, and the energy in the stadium made the day of fear melt away. Now all the defense had to do was hold down Holcomb for less than a minute.

They almost didn't do it, allowing the Browns to get to the Steelers' 45 with seven seconds left. Holcomb, with some faint shot left, hit wide receiver Andre King at the 29. With no timeouts, King frantically tried to get out of bounds but was a second too late, allowing the Steelers to escape with a most memorable 36–33 win.

Maddox's record-setting day didn't start great, but he rebounded to set the team record for most passing yards in a playoff game with 367 yards and two interceptions with three touchdown passes. The three scoring passes all came in the final 19 minutes. Holcomb, who would go on to win the starting job for the Browns the following year, threw for 429 yards and three touchdowns.

The Steelers would go on to lose in overtime to the Titans the following week in another memorable game, ending their season. But many won't forget the day that "Touchdown" Tommy led their team back against their archrivals.

59 Jefferson Street Joe

"Jefferson Street Joe" Gilliam broke new ground as a member of the Pittsburgh Steelers, and while his story has a sad ending with his passing on December 25, 2000, Gilliam overcame a lot in his life and is remembered for his ability and play in his few seasons with the Steelers. Gilliam played quarterback for Pittsburgh right at the start of their 1970s dynasty, and for a while, it appeared that he could have been the quarterback who would be winning Super Bowls, not Terry Bradshaw.

Gilliam was chosen by the Steelers in the 11th round of the 1972 draft after wrapping up a career as quarterback at Tennessee State. While there, Gilliam was a two-time All-American with a big-time arm that impressed the Steelers and head coach Chuck Noll.

What made Gilliam so different was the position he played. While most African American college quarterbacks entered the NFL at another position, such as wide receiver or defensive back, Gilliam stayed at quarterback, and it paid off in the few seasons he spent with the Steelers.

Gilliam paved the way for future black quarterbacks, players like Doug Williams, who went on to win a Super Bowl with the

Washington Redskins in 1988. "Joe made it all possible for every one of us black quarterbacks," Williams said at Gilliam's funeral in 2000. "The struggles he went through eased the struggles we had to endure. That's why I had to be here today. I wouldn't have been comfortable with myself had I not come here to pay respect to Joe for all he did to help the rest of us."

He was not the first black starting quarterback in the pros—that distinction belongs to Marlin Briscoe of the Denver Broncos in 1968—but Gilliam broke ground with early success in the 1974 season. By starting that season, he beat out the first overall pick in the 1970 draft and a player who would eventually take the starting role and ride it to the Pro Football Hall of Fame—Terry Bradshaw. The strong-armed Gilliam made heads turn early in the season, and the team started 4–1–1 with him under center. In a Week 1 win over the Baltimore Colts, he threw for 257 yards, and then the following week in a 35–35 tie with the Denver Broncos, Gilliam threw for 348 yards.

Things for Gilliam would start to go downhill from there. He threw for just 106 yards against the Oakland Raiders in a Week 3 17–0 loss. And even though the team topped the Houston Oilers 13–7 and then the Kansas City Chiefs 34–24, Gilliam wasn't as effective, and rumblings about putting Bradshaw into the lineup began. Finally, after throwing for just 78 yards against Cleveland in Week 6, Noll had seen enough, putting Bradshaw in and sitting Gilliam. The Steelers would go on to win their first Super Bowl that season, but it was with Gilliam on the sideline. He ended the year throwing for 1,274 yards with four touchdowns and eight interceptions. The following season he played little, and then was released. Gilliam moved on to play for New Orleans in 1976, but was released for breaking team rules.

Despite his early success with the Steelers, Gilliam at times was homeless, and also was in and out of rehab centers trying to get clean from addictions to cocaine and heroin. He ended up selling

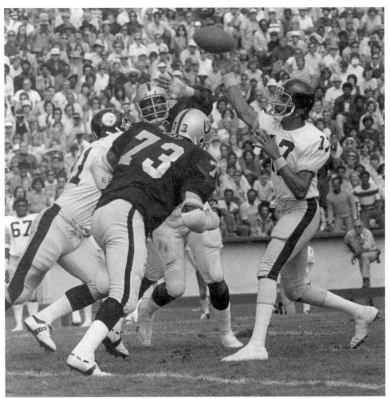

"Jefferson Street" Joe Gilliam paved the way for future black quarterbacks by starting the 1974 season with the Steelers.

his two Super Bowl rings, and it wasn't until the late 1990s that Gilliam finally appeared to have turned his life back around.

Gilliam opened a football camp for teens at Tennessee State and also started to counsel drug addicts. He was on hand for the Steelers' final game at Three Rivers Stadium when the Steelers topped the Washington Redskins on December 16, 2000. Nine days later, he was gone, passing away from a heart attack after watching a Cowboys-Titans game.

How different Steelers history might have been if Gilliam's fast start to the 1974 season would have continued, and how his life might have also been radically changed, as well.

60 The Bus Rides Home a Winner in Super Bowl XL

January 24, 2005, was a day of depression for Steeler Nation. It was one day after the team's stunning 41–27 setback to Tom Brady and the New England Patriots in the AFC Championship Game at Heinz Field. Not only had the Steelers taken a 15–1 regular-season record and wasted it with another AFC title loss at home, it also appeared to have marked the end of the stellar career of the Steelers' bruising back Jerome Bettis.

"I was on the sideline thinking, 'I can't believe this is happening. This was supposed to be a celebration,'" Bettis wrote in his book *Driving Home.* "I was looking at the seconds ticking away, asking myself what happened."

The day after the game, tears flowed freely in the Steelers' locker room as Bettis told his team he was not sure about next year, but that it was a pleasure to play with this group of men. Hines Ward spoke to the media, crying like he had just lost his best friend, saying that Bettis deserved to go out a champion. He was right.

What happened next was a story not even Hollywood could invent. Bettis made the decision to come back for the 2005 season, and it was a decision that paid off with one memorable ride. "The Bus," as Bettis is so affectionately known, came back and helped the Steelers go 11–5 in the regular season, through a most memorable three-game ride in the playoffs, and to a trip to Super Bowl XL.

And wouldn't you know that the game was to be played in Ford Field in Detroit, Bettis' hometown. Here was a future Hall of Fame back ready to play what ended up being his final game of his great NFL career, in front of family, friends, and a crowd that clearly was on the Steelers' side.

Bettis wasn't even the starting running back in the game for the Steelers—Willie Parker had cemented that role by the time Super Bowl XL against the Seattle Seahawks rolled around, but that didn't matter in the least. The Steelers' intros for the contest started with their emotional leader doing his famous trot onto the field—alone.

"When I went out, it was surreal," Bettis said. "It was a longer run than normal because of the MVP banners, so I had to run a pretty good distance. I was screaming and going crazy and had never been so jacked up in my life. I turned around thinking the guys were right behind me, but they were some ways back, and I thought, 'Great, what do I do now?'"

Soon Bettis was joined by his teammates, and the Steelers' ride to a title was underway. The team played tight early on and didn't get a first down until the second quarter—and Bettis didn't get his first carry until three minutes into the second quarter. The Steelers trailed 3–0, but with their leader determined to go out a winner, Bettis played a role in helping the team get the lead.

After a circus throw and catch from Ben Roethlisberger to Hines Ward that got the team out of a third-and-28 jam to the Seahawks' 3, it was time for Bettis to give the team the lead. While the Hollywood script would have had Bettis scoring and winning the MVP, it just didn't play out that way.

Bettis got two carries, taking it to the Seattle 1. On third down, Roethlisberger took a quarterback sneak, going right behind Bettis. Roethlisberger leapt, and while it was a call that some say was wrong, the referee ruled touchdown, and thanks to a solid block by Bettis and the flight of Big Ben, the Steelers were up 7–3 at the half.

The second half started with Bettis' protégé, Parker, breaking off a 75-yard run for a score to make it 14–3. The game went back and forth for some time, and Bettis helped the Black and Gold get into the fourth quarter up 14–10. The Steelers went for the knockout blow with 9:04 left on a play that Bettis says he didn't even want to see the team run. A pitch out to Parker, followed by a handoff to wideout Antwaan Randle El, who then fired a bomb to Ward for a clinching 43-yard touchdown.

The celebration for Bettis and the Steelers began, even with some work left to do. The club got the ball back with 6:15 left. Bill Cowher told his "closer" to do one thing—hang on to the ball. And he did. Bettis got seven carries to help the Steelers run the clock to the two-minute mark before having to punt. The runs cemented the championship, with Bettis playing a solid supporting role.

His linescore wasn't great—14 carries for 43 yards—but his mission to earn a ring was complete. He announced his retirement right there on the Super Bowl podium at the 50-yard line, hoisting the Lombardi Trophy. Bettis went out a winner—one year after it appeared his career would end with a major letdown.

61 Louis Lipps

While the Steelers were a dominant franchise in the 1970s, full of names that eventually would end up in the Pro Football Hall of Fame in Canton, Ohio, in the '80s it was almost the opposite. The Steelers took a major step backward, struggling to the point where they made the playoffs only twice, 1984 and 1989. The players got older, and the young ones were mostly misses. Except one.

That one player, known for his big play-making ability as well as memorable name, was wide receiver Louis Lipps. The Steelers' first-round pick in 1984 came in and made a huge impact on the franchise, both as a punt-return specialist as well as receiver. What also was memorable about Lipps was his relationship with the fans, who chanted his name every time he touched the ball…or took the field for that matter.

"As soon as the defense stopped the other team on third down, I wasn't even out on the field yet, and you could hear it coming," Lipps said. "And it was just like, 'Aw, man. I've got to make something happen now.' That's a big motivator. The fans motivate you just as much as you getting yourself together. You never want to let them down."

Lipps, from Southern Mississippi, had a big rookie season for the Steelers, taking home the honor of NFL Offensive Rookie of the Year. He also made the AFC Pro Bowl roster, taking in 45 passes for 860 yards and nine touchdowns. He broke the NFL rookie record for punt-return yardage, with 656 yards, and returned a punt for a score, as well. He was electric when he had the ball in his hands and helped the team reach the AFC Championship Game that season before they fell to Dan Marino and the Miami Dolphins.

He always enjoyed returning punts, but coach Chuck Noll was more interested in Lipps' rounding out into a complete wide receiver. "I just thoroughly enjoyed returning punts because in the blink of an eye you could change the momentum of a whole football game—on one single play," Lipps said in 2008. "When you're at Three Rivers Stadium and you have 65,000 people screaming your name, it makes you want to go out there and make something happen. And that's what I did."

He did round into an even better receiver in 1985, pulling in 59 passes for 1,134 yards and 12 scores. He also averaged an amazing 19.2 yards per catch, again establishing himself as a big-play wideout who made things happen every time he hauled in a pass. He took two punts back for scores, putting up 12.1 yards per return for the 36 returns he had that season. He again made the Pro Bowl and also was an All-Pro.

Despite his big-play ability, he began to struggle with injuries the following season. He played in 13 contests in the team's 6–10 season of 1986, but made 21 fewer catches than the year before, with 38 receptions for 590 yards and just three scores. The next year he was even worse, playing in just four games where he made 11 catches for 164 yards with no touchdowns. By then he was a non-factor in the return game since the team couldn't count on him to stay on the field.

Lipps finally was able to return to form in both the 1988 and '89 seasons, making 50 catches in each season and playing in all 16 games both years. In '88 he put up 973 yards, again going for 19.5 yards per catch, and five touchdowns. In '89 he was named as the team's MVP for the second time, leading the team with 944 yards and five touchdowns. He was a factor in the team reaching the divisional round of the playoffs before losing to the Broncos.

By 1990 Lipps' numbers started to trend down again. He had 50 catches for the third straight year, but only put up 682 yards, close to 300 less than the season before. In 1991 he had 55 grabs, but again fewer yards (671) with two scores. Entering Bill Cowher's first season as coach in 1992, Lipps and the team could not see eye to eye on his contract, and he eventually left the organization that had given him his start.

He went to play for the Saints, but he was a non-factor in 1992, playing in just two games and making one catch for one yard. Lipps came back to Pittsburgh for a short period of time in the 1993 season but never made it on the field again as a member of the Steelers.

62 Tony Dungy

While Tony Dungy will always be remembered as a Super Bowl–winning coach and a best-selling author with Christian morals and values, many don't realize that he had a very strong link to the Steelers early in his career, both as a player and a coach.

Tony Dungy was a part of the Steelers' 1978 Super Bowl team and was a coach and defensive coordinator under Noll from 1982 to 1989.

Dungy attended the University of Minnesota, where he played quarterback for the Golden Gophers from 1973 to 1976. He had a stellar college career, leading the Gophers in pass attempts (576), completions (274), touchdown passes (25), and passing yards (3,577). Not only that, he was fourth in career total offense in the Big Ten Conference and was Minnesota's Most Valuable Player twice. He entered the NFL as a free agent with the Steelers in 1977, but came in not as a quarterback but as a defensive back.

Dungy played for the Steelers in 1977 and '78, earning a Super Bowl ring as a player his second season. He also led the Steelers in interceptions, playing the safety spot in the 1978 season. But while Dungy was picking off passes, he was also picking the brain of head coach Chuck Noll. Dungy credits Noll for his coaching philosophy, which has a lot to do with the famed Tampa 2 defense that employs four defensive linemen, three linebackers, and four defensive backs.

Steelers First to Hire African American Coordinator

While the Rooney Rule has opened up jobs for many African Americans in the NFL, the Steelers were ahead of everyone when it came to hiring in that department. In 1981 the Steelers hired Tony Dungy, who of course went on to become the first African American coach to win a Super Bowl with the Indianapolis Colts in the 2006 season. Dungy broke the barrier, and now, thanks to the Steelers, many African Americans are getting the chance to shine in the NFL. The team continued to follow its own lead with the hiring of Mike Tomlin in 2007, and Tomlin became the second African American coach to win a Super Bowl with the team's win in Super Bowl XLIII.

"My philosophy is really out of the 1975 Pittsburgh Steelers playbook," Dungy said in a media interview before coaching the Colts in Super Bowl XLI. "That is why I have to laugh when I hear Tampa 2. Chuck Noll and Bud Carson—that is where it came from, I changed very little."

Dungy's Steelers career as a player ended after that '78 season in which the team secured its third Super Bowl. Then he was traded to the San Francisco 49ers, where he lasted one season before moving on to the New York Giants. His playing career ended in Giants training camp in 1980.

But Dungy moved quickly into the coaching ranks, going back to the University of Minnesota as an assistant coach and taking charge of the team's defensive backs. After just one season he was invited back to Pittsburgh, where he was an assistant under Noll. In 1982 he became the Steelers' defensive backfield coach, and by 1984 was the club's defensive coordinator.

He left Pittsburgh for good in 1989, when he left to be the defensive backs coach for the Chiefs. He was the Minnesota Vikings' defensive coordinator in 1992, leading them to the top spot in the NFL while assisting then Vikings head coach Dennis Green.

Dungy's lifelong dream of being an NFL head coach finally came true on January 22, 1996, when he was hired by Rich McKay to take over the floundering Tampa Bay Buccaneers. It was there that Dungy installed the same Tampa 2 defense that he credits learning under Noll and Carson.

It took some time, but Dungy molded the Buccaneers into a winner, and after a few playoff berths the Bucs' higher management got restless and fired him, giving the coaching job to Jon Gruden, who then came in and took Tampa Bay to their only Super Bowl win in 2002. Dungy moved to Indianapolis, where just eight days after he was fired by Tampa Bay he was a head coach once again, this time with the Colts.

The Steelers had a hand in giving Dungy possibly his most bitter defeat as a coach. In January 2006, the No. 1–seeded Colts were stunned by the Steelers 21–18 in Indianapolis in the AFC Championship Game. The loss was also tough for Dungy, coming just a few weeks after the loss of his 18-year-old son, James.

Both coach and team moved on, finally securing a championship in Super Bowl XLI when they beat the Chicago Bears 29–17. Dungy announced his retirement on January 12, 2009, and joined the NBC *Sunday Night Football* crew the following June.

Dungy will likely enter the Pro Football Hall of Fame, and it's a given that while he is giving his speech he will talk of his playing days with the Steelers and will credit Noll and the coaching crew in Pittsburgh that taught him the importance of defense and how to motivate players to be the best they can be.

63 Harrison Brings Attitude Back to the Steelers

It's hard to believe that the Steelers linebacking machine continues to crank out to this day all-world linebackers, but the club did it again starting in 2007 with a little-known linebacker form Kent State University by the name of James Harrison. No. 92's career didn't exactly take the fast road to being the dominant defensive player that he eventually became. Starting in the 2002 season with the Steelers as an undrafted free agent, Harrison spent the first two seasons on and off the practice squad.

He played a little bit on special teams that season but really made very little impact. Late in the 2003 season he signed with the rival Baltimore Ravens, but, after playing in Europe with the Rhein Fire, Harrison was once again cut, this time by the Steelers' biggest foe.

Maybe the fourth time was the charm for Harrison and the Steelers—he rejoined the team in 2004 after Clark Haggans was hurt in an off-season weightlifting accident. He shined with the club, showing potential in training camp to make plays, and he made the squad as a backup linebacker and special-teams ace.

In 2004 he finally got his shot as a starter, and again, it was due to a fellow linebacker's issues. This time it was Joey Porter, who on November 14 threw a punch at Browns running back William Green and got thrown out before the game in Cleveland even started. Harrison had six tackles and a sack in the 24–10 Steelers victory.

He got another chance to start the following season when another injury to Haggans allowed Harrison to start three games. He made a memorable play in a Monday night game that year, picking off a Drew Brees pass in San Diego and jumping over Pro Bowl running back LaDainian Tomlinson during the return. On Christmas Eve that year he body-slammed a fan who ran onto the field in Cleveland during the team's eventual 41–0 win.

Harrison got a Super Bowl ring with that Steelers club and made three tackles on special teams in Super Bowl XL, but always felt he wasn't a major factor with that team. In Bill Cowher's last year, 2006, Harrison missed five games and had just 20 tackles, but things would finally pick up for him when new coach Mike Tomlin released Porter, opening up a spot at linebacker for Harrison.

It was finally his time, and he took complete advantage of it. Playing with a fire from day one, Harrison put up 8½ sacks, forced six fumbles, and had 98 tackles as the Steelers went 10–6 before being beaten in the wild-card round by the Jaguars. He was the team MVP and had a career game that year on Monday night at home versus the Ravens, putting up nine tackles, 3½ sacks, a pick, and a fumble recovery.

Things only got better for him the following year, as Harrison was the best defensive player in the entire league. He broke the Steelers' record for sacks in a season with 16 and also forced seven fumbles, two against the Patriots in a 33–10 win on November 30. He was named the AP NFL Defensive Player of the Year on January 5, but again, with Harrison, the best was yet to come.

He and the club beat the Chargers and Ravens in the playoffs to reach Super Bowl XLIII in Tampa against the Arizona Cardinals. It was in that game that Harrison made what many consider to be the greatest play in Super Bowl history. On the final play of the first half, with the Cardinals driving to take what would have been a 14–10 lead, Kurt Warner threw a pass from the Steelers' 1-yard line. Harrison jumped the route, picked off the pass, and started heading down the sideline.

He slowed down a few times, made a few cuts, and even at one point took a leap like he did against the Chargers on Monday night a few years before. Finally Cardinals wide receivers Steve Breaston and Larry Fitzgerald made a last-ditch effort to take down Harrison at about the Cardinals' 3-yard line, but the linebacker was able to dive into the end zone for a touchdown that gave the team a 17–7 lead.

Of course the Steelers went on to win the game in dramatic fashion 27–23, but they would not have been able to do it without Harrison and his unreal 100-yard interception return. It's a play that will go down in Steelers history as one of the most exciting ever.

In 2009 Harrison's numbers were not as good as the season before, but the entire defense had its moments of struggle as well.

Harrison still played at a high level, though, going for 10 sacks and 79 tackles with five forced fumbles.

The youngest of 14 children, Harrison worked hard to become the team's fiery leader on defense, and cashed in that April, signing a six-year deal worth more than $50 million. He played at a high level in the Super Bowl year of 2010, collecting 10½ sacks with two picks and six forced fumbles as the team made it to Super Bowl XLV before losing to the Packers.

Harrison was slowed down by a broken orbital bone in 2011, and before the 2012 season he had to have surgery on his left knee. It never seemed to let him get into stride for the season.

The two years combined he had 15 sacks, and while he still had the attitude, he just didn't have the power to be the same big-play LB for the Steelers. With the club having major salary cap issues following the 2012 season, the club tried to get Harrison to take a pay cut, and once he and the team were unable to come to an agreement, the Steelers released him on March 9, 2013. He signed with the team's division rival, the Cincinnati Bengals.

64 Bubby Brister

After Terry Bradshaw took his last snap in 1983, the team went through a period where there was some pretty dark times at quarterback. See if these names ring a bell—Cliff Stoudt, David Woodley, Mark Malone, Scott Campbell, Steve Bono. And who could forget Todd Blackledge? Needless to say none of these players were able to get the Steelers back to the level where Bradshaw took them. In the third round of the 1986 draft the team decided to take a shot at another quarterback, a player who was in the style of the great Bradshaw—a big arm and a southern accent. Yes, the Bubby Brister era in Pittsburgh was about to begin.

Much like Bradshaw, Walter "Bubby" Brister didn't start his career with a ton of success. Making quite a few mistakes his first few seasons when given the chance to play, Brister was 0–2 as a starter in 1986, then two years later was 4–9 as the starting quarterback of a club that went 5–11 under Chuck Noll.

But Steelers coaches saw potential in Brister. He had a knack for keeping plays alive and was a gutsy player on the field who wasn't afraid to put his body on the line. He also had a rocket of an arm, and every now and then was able to fire off a great deep ball to players like Louis Lipps or John Stallworth, who was getting near the end of his stellar career.

Brister took over as the team's full-time starter in 1989. The season started with disastrous losses to Cleveland (52–0) and the Bengals (41–10), but he recovered to help the team go 9–7 and sneak into the playoffs. He threw for 2,365 yards with nine touchdowns and 10 picks that season. Not all that impressive from the numbers players put up today, but he went 8–6 as a starter and helped the team to a 26–23 overtime playoff win in the wild-card game versus the Oilers on December 31 in Houston. Despite going just 15-of-33 for 127 yards, he and the team walked out of the Astrodome as winners.

That game is when maybe the most unlikely thing about Brister popped up on TV screens all over America. His parents. Yes, Brister's parents followed their son's startling run into the 1989 postseason, and, for whatever reason, they were shown quite a bit those two weeks of the '89 postseason. The following week in Denver, Bubby's parents were shown what seemed like a dozen times sitting in the rafters of Mile High Stadium as the Steelers

Longest through the Air

The longest pass play in Steelers history is 95 yards, a throw from Ben Roethlisberger to Mike Wallace in a 32–20 victory over Arizona in 2011, breaking the record of 90 yards that had been done three times in franchise history—most recently in a 2001 Sunday night win over the Ravens when Kordell Stewart threw a 90-yard touchdown to Bobby Shaw. One of the three 90-yard pass plays didn't even go for a touchdown, and that was in Denver when Bubby Brister hit Dwight Stone to set up the Steelers in an October 1990 win over the Broncos. Maybe the strangest 90-yard pass play was in Seattle in 1981 when Terry Bradshaw hit future quarterback Mark Malone with a long touchdown.

battled Denver and John Elway for the right to play in the AFC Championship Game the following week.

Brister, looking to make his parents proud, did what he could. The team held a 17–7 lead, but in the end, Elway's magic was too much to overcome. Down 24–23, Brister had a chance to make history with a last-minute drive, but a low snap got away from him, and the Broncos fell on the ball to secure the win.

The following season the team also went 9–7, and Brister had his best season playing under a confusing offensive system put together by recently hired offensive coordinator Joe Walton. The team didn't score an offensive touchdown in its first four games, but once it did start to find a rhythm, its members actually played well. Brister threw for a career-high 20 touchdowns, a career high 2,725 yards, and a quarterback rating of 81.6. The team imploded in the last game of the season, though, losing out on a chance to win the AFC Central with a 34–14 loss to the Oilers.

Brister was hurt the following year and almost split time equally with rookie Neil O'Donnell. The team struggled to a 7–9 mark in Noll's last season, with Brister throwing nine touchdowns and just as many interceptions. The following summer in Bill Cowher's first training camp, Brister lost a competition with O'Donnell, and while he went 2–2 filling in for O'Donnell, Brister's time as a Steeler was clearly over.

He left the club that off-season and went on to be a journeyman over the next eight years, playing for five teams—the Eagles, Jets, Broncos, Vikings, and Chiefs. He's a footnote in Broncos history, playing as Elway's primary backup on the team's back-to-back Super Bowl teams. He had maybe the most success at any point of his career in 1998, going 4–0 in place of an injured Elway, throwing 10 touchdowns and three interceptions, and compiling a 99.0 quarterback rating.

Brister now runs a quarterback academy where he offers one-on-one training for youngsters looking to play the position, and also runs summer quarterback camps in the Denver area.

65 Barry "Bananas" Foster

The start of the Bill Cowher era for the Steelers brought upon a shift in how the team was going to win games. The primary offense was going to be to pound the football with a physical and fast offensive line that was going to use quick-hitting plays to amass chunks of yards and eat up the clock while controlling the ball on the ground. In his rookie season as coach, Cowher brought in Ron Erhardt as his offensive coordinator. Erhardt ran the Giants' offense during their Super Bowl year of 1990 and always loved to have a back who could pound defenses. He did it that season with rookie back Rodney Hampton, then turned to old vet Ottis Anderson to secure a title with an MVP outing in the Super Bowl win over the Bills that season.

Erhardt and Cowher needed a running back who could simulate that Giants' offense, and on the Steelers' roster entering 1992, the best candidate to do that was a little-known back named Barry Foster. The former fifth-round pick of the Steelers in 1990 had a few shining moments his first two seasons, the biggest of which was a 121-yard game against the AFC-champion Buffalo Bills in the second game of the 1991 season. He also had a memorable 56-yard touchdown run in that game. The issue with Foster was twofold—he seemed injury-prone, missing five games with an injured ankle in 2001, and he wasn't the friendliest guy in the locker room.

Those things didn't matter to Cowher and Erhardt, who needed someone to carry the ball and make their offense go. They didn't think likeable Merril Hoge could get the job done, and they liked what they saw in the off-season and preseason from Foster. He moved into the starting lineup as the team took the field in Week 1 in Houston. No one could have imagined the season Foster would have, as he not only broke the Steelers' single-season rushing record, he shattered it, going for 1,690 yards and 11 touchdowns and putting up an average of 105.6 yards per game.

The league quickly started to take notice of Foster in Week 2, when he went for 190 yards and two touchdowns in a win over the Jets. As the Steelers started to gain national attention, Foster and the ground game did, as well. With Hoge as fullback, Foster and the Steelers punished teams with a solid game plan that took them to 11 wins that season. He was named the 1992 UPI AFL-AFC Offensive Player of the Year. But behind the scenes, Foster, who grew up poor and left college at Arkansas early to support his family, never was the most popular player due to his sometimes cold attitude when it came to dealing with those outside his inner circle.

After his record-breaking season in '92, Foster staged a holdout. "Money talks and everything else walks," he said in that '92 season when asked what motivates him as a player. He got a new deal, and while he ran well early in the year, Foster's history

Running back Barry Foster was named the 1992 UPI AFL-AFC Offensive Player of the Year but suffered injuries the following season, was traded, and then retired in 1994.

of being hurt returned—he managed to play in just nine games that year, rushing for 711 yards and eight scores. He combined to help the 1994 team lead the league in rushing along with rookie Byron "Bam" Morris, and Steelers fans will never forget he was the intended receiver on the final fourth-and-goal play from the 3-yard line against the Chargers in the AFC Championship Game that the Steelers lost 17–13.

That off-season, the Steelers decided they had seen enough of Foster. Despite being just 26 years old, the Steelers felt they had a star in the making in Morris, and so shipped Foster to the expansion Carolina Panthers for "future considerations." They had shopped him around, and the fact the Steelers got so little for him showed what other teams truly felt of the player Foster was. It really showed when Foster was cut by Carolina before he ever played in a regular-season game. After a half-hearted attempt that lasted just a few days to come back and play for the Bengals, Foster retired and has been very much out of the public eye ever since. Most say that Foster's success in his short stint with Pittsburgh was due to the high level of play of the offensive line, as well as the game plan Erhardt and Cowher put together.

He's a footnote in Steelers history, and one that every now and then prompts a fan to say, "Yeah, I remember that guy."

66 Levon Kirkland

Lorenzo Levon Kirkland followed a long line of very good Steelers inside linebackers not only known for their run-stuffing ability but also for their size and speed. It was common on Sundays in the 1990s to see Kirkland, who at numerous times in his career topped the 300-pound mark, racing toward a ball carrier or dropping in coverage to cover a running back or tight end.

Kirkland stepped in as the Steelers' second-round draft choice in 1992 and quickly made an impact on special teams in Bill Cowher's rookie season as head coach. Kirkland also had the privilege of learning behind another very good Steelers inside linebacker, former Pro Bowler David Little. The hungry Kirkland learned well, and by just his second season was ready to assume the role as starter as Little's career was coming to an end.

It was that 1993 season when Kirkland quickly established himself. He put up 103 tackles, forced four fumbles, recovered two, and had a sack in the 13 games he started. He had that rare ability to use both power and speed, and at 6'1" and listed at 270 pounds, Kirkland was a force to be reckoned with on the inside of the Steelers' defense.

He opened up chances for outside linebackers Greg Lloyd and Kevin Greene to fight their way to the quarterback, and in 1994

Kirkland had three sacks and 100 tackles to go along with two interceptions. He became one of the vocal leaders on the defense as the Steelers pushed their way to having the top defense in the league before falling in the AFC Championship Game.

While the team continued to have success on defense over the next few seasons, Kirkland's game rose to a new level. His best season may have been 1997, when he recorded 126 total tackles and had a career-high five sacks and two picks to go along with a forced fumble. Kirkland was named to his second Pro Bowl that year, and was the cornerstone of a defense that got the Steelers into another AFC Championship Game before losing to the eventual Super Bowl–champion Denver Broncos.

Starting in 1998, the Steelers had a couple of down seasons under Cowher, though Kirkland's play continued to be high. In the team's 7–9 '98 season, Kirkland again played well and earned the honor of being named the Steelers' MVP. "He can run like a 235- or 240-pound 'backer," Bill Cowher once said of Kirkland. "But, he hits like a 260 guy."

His colorful demeanor on and off the field made him a fan favorite during his nine seasons with the Steelers, and it came as somewhat of a shock that the team would release him due to salary-cap pressure before the 2001 season. Kirkland landed on his feet in Seattle and then wrapped up his career in 2002 with the Philadelphia Eagles.

He was named to the NFL 1990s All-Decade Team and wrapped up his 11-year career with 19.5 sacks, 1,026 total tackles, 16 forced fumbles, and nine fumble recoveries. In 1996 Kirkland was named to Clemson University's All-Centennial Team and was inducted into the university's Hall of Fame in 2001. He was always good for a big hit on the field and a big smile off of it.

Today Kirkland coaches high school linebackers in South Carolina and serves as an Educational Speaker for the National Collegiate Scouting Association.

67 Steeler Nation

Being a Steelers fan hasn't always been the "in" thing. The team played in just one playoff game from 1933 to 1972, and they usually found themselves lying at the bottom of their division by season's end. They had one-win seasons in 1939, 1941, and 1969, Chuck Noll's first season as coach. And they went 0–10 in 1944. In other words, they spent many Sundays getting laughed at as power-houses in the league beat on them week in and week out.

The organization turned the corner as it entered the 1970s and has never looked back. An NFL-record six Super Bowls wins, countless playoff appearances, and a fan base that is the most rabid in the NFL—and possibly all of sports—have secured the Steelers as a force to be reckoned with.

Steeler Nation is a nation of worldwide fans who live and die with Steelers football, taking their love of the Steelers to another level. They watch their team, read about them, travel distances unheard of to see them play, and go to great lengths to be involved with anything to do with the Steelers.

It is amazing to think that a city that has undergone some of the toughest times in the country has a fan base that is second to none. They have a massive waiting list for season tickets at Heinz Field, and year after year they sell out every game, with the current streak at more than 300. In 2008 ESPN.com ranked Steeler Nation as the best fan base in the NFL. To say that the fans travel is, well, an understatement—there have been plenty of articles written about Steelers fans invading opposing stadiums, waving their Terrible Towels in support of their team.

Steeler Nation is not only about the average fans, there are plenty of famous folk who proudly wear black and gold, as well.

Pittsburgh Steelers fans are devoted to their team and dominate the stadiums of opponents, as they are seen here at this 2009 game in Denver.

Among those famous fans include musician and rocker Bret Michaels, political talk show host Rush Limbaugh, country music star Hank Williams Jr., rapper Snoop Dogg, and actors Burt Reynolds, Michael Keaton, and even President Barack Obama.

Other teams around the NFL have done what they could to keep Steeler Nation out of their stadiums, but no matter what, Steelers fans always find a way. Once, the San Diego Chargers didn't allow fans to purchase tickets to only a Steelers-Chargers game, instead requiring them to buy tickets to two other games, including a preseason game, as well. Despite the outrageous demands, yellow towels could be seen all over Qualcomm Stadium.

When Steeler Nation gets rolling, it simply can't be stopped. It's no secret that the most recent Super Bowl battles between the Steelers and the Seattle Seahawks and Arizona Cardinals have been "home" games. In Detroit for Super Bowl XL there were reports of the attending fans being 70–30 in favor of the Steelers, and in Tampa for Super Bowl XLIII it was about the same.

Other teams such as Green Bay, Dallas, and even Cleveland feel that they have large and boisterous fans, but there is no question that Pittsburgh has the best fans in the NFL. Take the words of Ross Tucker, now a member of the media who works for CNN/SI and NFL Radio, when he wrote the following after the Steelers fans showed up in force in Jacksonville for a game in 2008: "The Steelers have the most dominant fan base in the National Football League, and their ability to consistently travel, en masse, and infest other team's stadiums gives the Steelers a competitive advantage that no other franchise can claim."

Steelers fans have set the bar high for the rest of the NFL when it comes to fans, and Steeler Nation shows no signs of slowing anytime soon.

68 An Upset Opens the Door to Super Bowl XL

The Steelers' run to Super Bowl XL was filled with as many memorable moments as any playoff run in recent history. Many thought the Steelers, entering the playoffs as a No. 6 seed, would be lucky to win one game, despite that first game being at a site where they had won earlier in the season—Cincinnati.

Most Steelers fans recall that game as being the one where Steelers defensive lineman Kimo von Oelhoffen barreled into Bengals quarterback Carson Palmer, tearing up his knee and ending his season. The Steelers went on to win the game 31–17, to earn the right to move on the following Sunday to meet the No. 1 seed in the AFC, the 14–2 Indianapolis Colts.

The Colts were double-digit favorites entering the January 15, 2006, contest at the RCA Dome. They started the 2005 season 13–0, including a rather dominating 26–7 win over the Steelers in Week 12 on November 28 on a Monday night. There was really no reason to think that the Colts wouldn't be able to repeat the performance. Or was there?

Instead of playing like a heavy underdog, the Steelers came out the aggressors, putting together two long touchdown drives to start the game, quickly silencing the Dome crowd, and making Colts quarterback Peyton Manning play catch-up all day. The Steelers appeared to put the game away with another touchdown early in the third quarter to make it 21–3. But again, this was Indianapolis, and you knew that if given the chance, Manning and the Colts would make it a game—and they did.

The Colts scored quickly in the fourth quarter on a 50-yard pass from Manning to tight end Dallas Clark. After the Steelers gained some first downs and then punted, the real drama began. From the Colts' 44, Manning threw a pass that was clearly intercepted by safety Troy Polamalu. The wild man then got up, but as he did, his own knee knocked the ball out of his hands, and he decided at that point to fall on it.

Colts coach Tony Dungy had no choice but to throw a challenge flag, even though it looked hopeless in terms of a reversal. But even coach Bill Cowher sensed there might be an issue with the call, and he told his defense to keep their guard up and be ready. He must have been on to something. Head official Pete Morelli made a call that the league would later say was a mistake—he ruled the pass incomplete since Polamalu never got two knees off the ground before he knocked the ball out of his hand.

Manning quickly struck after the reversal, and after a short Edgerrin James touchdown run and a two-point conversion to wideout Reggie Wayne, Steeler Nation hearts began to pound a little faster. It was 21–18 with 4:29 left. The Steelers went three-and-out and punted, and the defense stepped up for a memorable stand. Joey Porter, who said he was so mad at the officials for reversing the Polamalu interception he couldn't even speak in the huddle, sacked Manning twice, the second time on fourth-and-16 to put what should have been the finishing touches on a huge playoff upset.

But wait.

Enter Jerome Bettis, who was called upon to seal the deal for real with a short touchdown from the Colts' 2-yard line. Bettis took the first-down snap and went into the line only to have the helmet of Gary Brackett, a Colts linebacker, smack into the ball, which popped up into the air. The ball was scooped up by Colts cornerback Nick Harper, who starting racing the other way for what would have been a Colts touchdown. Ben Roethlisberger was the only man who could get to Harper, and he made a great shoestring tackle, bringing Harper down at the Colts' 42 with 1:01 left.

"Once in a blue moon Jerome is going to make that fumble, and once in a blue moon I'm going to make that tackle," Roethlisberger said about the play. "Luckily for us they happened on the same play."

Manning was at it again, throwing his way to the Steelers' 28-yard line, giving Indy a chance to tie the game with the foot of Colts kicker Mike Vanderjagt, who had been perfect at home in the playoffs. But as luck would have it after Cowher called a timeout to ice Vanderjagt, who during the timeout pointed at Cowher, the cocky kicker shanked the 46-yard game-tying field-goal attempt wide right with 17 seconds left.

Steelers players and fans went into a frenzy. The team not only overcame a heavily favored Colts club, but it also avoided what may have gone down as the biggest playoff collapse in team history.

69 Top Five Rivals

They're the teams that Steelers fans have grown to hate over the years. When you see these teams on the schedule, your blood starts to boil just a little bit more, and you start counting the days until those games. Here are the top five all-time Steelers rivals:

1. Cleveland Browns

Okay, maybe over the past few years this matchup hasn't been quite as competitive as it used to be. After all, it takes two to make a good rivalry, and considering that the Browns have beaten the Steelers just three times since a Sunday night game in October 2003, this matchup has been pretty one-sided as of late. The Steelers had beaten the Browns 12 straight before their late 2009 loss. In those 12 games they outscored the Browns 330–142 (27.5–11.8 average per game), recorded two shutouts, and held them to six and seven points twice each. This makes Cleveland more of a whipping boy than their toughest rivals. Of course, from a Steelers standpoint, it's been a lot of fun to watch.

2. Baltimore Ravens

While some may say that the Ravens should be combined with the Browns, they really are considered two totally different franchises. The Ravens have been a thorn in the Steelers' side for the past 12 seasons, and these matchups are always the most hard-hitting of the season. The three games in 2008 took on a whole new meaning when the Steelers won by three in overtime in the first meeting, by four on a controversial ending in the second battle, and then by nine in the AFC Championship Game in January at Heinz Field. As Mike Tomlin told Ravens wide receiver Derrick Mason after the AFC title game, "I love these matchups, you guys bring out the best in us." He's right, and when these two bitter rivals meet, there are always some teeth missing from a few players afterward. The Steelers lead the series 22–15.

3. Oakland/Los Angeles Raiders

These two teams met 15 times over a 15-season span, from 1970 to 1984, but have only locked horns nine times in the 25 seasons since. But, boy, oh boy, those games in the '70s and early '80s sure were memorable. The Raiders and Steelers littered the field during those glory days with a number of Hall of Fame players on each side, and usually when they played there was a spot in the Super Bowl—or at least advancement in the playoffs—on the line. The matchups always got going well before the games themselves, with plenty of bickering in the papers. Following the 1976 season opener, Steelers head coach Chuck Noll accused the Raiders of harboring a "criminal element," which of course the Raiders make no bones about. Oakland still has issues with the Immaculate Reception of Franco Harris in the 1972 playoff game, saying the play was illegal. No matter, the Steelers actually went just 6–9 from 1970 to 1984 versus Oakland. In the past 11 meetings, they have gone 6–5, but none of those games have even come close to the legendary battles of yesteryear.

4. Houston Oilers/Tennessee Titans

The Steelers-Oilers games were always a blast to watch, and Houston always gave the Steelers a run for their money in the Steel Curtain era of the 1970s. From Bum Phillips to Earl Campbell, the Oilers were a threat to the Steelers when the two foes met in back-to-back AFC Championship Games in 1978 and 1979. The Steelers won both matchups at home 34–5 and 27–13, respectively. Then Houston underwent a change, employing the now defunct run-and-shoot offense of Warren Moon and his wideouts in the late '80s and early '90s. The Oilers then bailed to Tennessee before the 1996 season, but the teams still battled twice per year until Tennessee moved to the AFC South after 2001. Now they are two of the better teams in the AFC, but the years of Bum Phillips versus Chuck Noll is still the highlight of this feud.

5. New England Patriots

It's a rivalry that really didn't take shape until Bill Belichick showed up in New England to guide the Pats, and Bill Cowher and the Steelers started having issues with the boys dressed like soldiers. The rivalry had seen the Steelers dominate from 1972 to 1995, winning 10 of 13 regular-season games. Then in 1996 a Bill Parcells–led Pats team pounded the Steelers, who were led by a hobbled Jerome Bettis and Mike Tomczak at quarterback 28–3 in a playoff game on the road. From there, the Steelers got some revenge the following year in a lackluster 7–6 home playoff win.

Four years later things between the two clubs started taking shape when New England strolled into Pittsburgh and upset the heavily favored Steelers 24–17 in the AFC Championship Game at then-new Heinz Field. Pittsburgh got a little revenge, stopping the Pats' 18-game winning streak in 2004 with a 34–20 Halloween thrashing. The Pats again got the last laugh, beating Ben Roethlisberger and the Steelers 41–27 in that year's AFC Championship Game—again in Pittsburgh. Since then the two teams have met five times, with the Steelers winning twice. The series currently stands at 15–11 in the Steelers' favor.

70 Steelers Exorcise Demons in 1995 AFC Title Game

The focus of the Steelers in 1995 was to make up for the mistakes of the previous season, which ended with the team falling three yards short of the winning touchdown in the AFC Championship Game against the San Diego Chargers at home.

Problem was, the '95 season didn't get off to the start that many experts felt it would. The team won on opening day against the Lions, but lost quarterback Neil O'Donnell for a few weeks to a broken finger and also all-world cornerback Rod Woodson to a torn ACL when Barry Sanders made a cut on him on the turf at Three Rivers Stadium. Woodson went one way, his leg stayed planted in the turf, and the Steelers lost their biggest playmaker on defense.

While the team was able to hang in for a few weeks, losses started to mount, and suddenly after a stunning 27–9 loss to the Bengals on October 19 at home, the team was 3–4 and reeling. That's when Bill Cowher declared that it was a nine-game season, and it was time to take it one game at a time. The message worked. With a new-look offense that used a lot of five-wideout sets, and a defense that got back on track, the team went 8–1 in its final nine games, losing only the final, meaningless regular-season game in Green Bay.

They steamrolled the Bills in the divisional round of the play-offs, then got a gift when the Chiefs, the AFC's No. 1 seed, fell at home to the Colts the following day, meaning that Pittsburgh would host the AFC Championship Game the following Sunday against the upstart Colts. Just like the season before, the Black and Gold were heavy favorites to beat Indianapolis and make it to Tempe, Arizona, for Super Bowl XXX against the winner of the Packers-Cowboys NFC Championship Game in Dallas.

The Steelers seemed to approach the game knowing they needed to put the ghosts of the '94 title loss behind them, but they seemed to keep it neatly tucked away in their minds, playing tight throughout against a much looser Colts team that played like it had nothing to lose. Helped out by an early turnover, the Colts held a 6–3 lead late in the second quarter. But the Steelers finally put a drive together and were able to crack the goal line when a scrambling O'Donnell found Kordell Stewart in the back of the end zone to take a 10–6 halftime lead. Of course Stewart was out of bounds and came back in to make the catch, but the officials didn't make the call, and the Steelers had their first lead of the day.

Pittsburgh had its chances in the third and fourth quarters, but was unable to put the Colts away for good and held a slim 13–9 lead midway through the fourth. That's when the Colts, much like San Diego the season before, struck, as quarterback Jim Harbaugh hit a streaking Floyd Turner with a 47-yard touchdown to give the Colts a 16–13 lead. To say that Three Rivers Stadium was tense was an understatement, with the crowd already taking on a feeling of "here we go again," after last year's letdown.

After the teams traded possessions, the Steelers got the ball on their own 33 with 3:03 left. O'Donnell led the team into Indy territory and hit Andre Hastings on a fourth-and-3 at the Colts' 38. Then the team went for broke. O'Donnell perfectly hit Ernie Mills, who made a great catch and dragged his feet in bounds to the Colts' 1-yard line. Three Rivers erupted, and the Steelers were in business. Two plays later, Byron "Bam" Morris went in for the go-ahead score to make it 20–16 with 1:29 left.

But as Steeler Nation has come to expect, nothing comes easy. The Colts started with the ball at their own 16 after a great special-teams play by Fred McAfee to bring down returner Aaron Bailey. Indy moved the ball to their 49 when Harbaugh hit Sean Dawkins on fourth-and-2 to put the ball at the Steelers' 38. Then with outside pressure by linebacker Kevin Greene, Harbaugh took off and got to the Steelers' 29 with six seconds left when he spiked the ball, leaving time for one more play.

One more play—one more agonizing play.

It was the play that "almost was" for the Colts—Harbaugh threw up a prayer, and it was a prayer that came close to being answered. As the ball started to come down in the right corner of the end zone, it was tipped several times by Steelers defenders before it fell to Colts receiver Bailey, who, falling backward, nearly closed his hands around the ball as it came into his chest. Instead, as he turned, the ball hit the turf, and the officials, right on top of the play, made the correct call.

Steelers color man Myron Cope gulped out an "Oh, my Lord" when he thought Bailey had made the grab, but thankfully, he was wrong. Cowher pumped his fists in the air, and you could see his and O'Donnell's relief as they hugged to celebrate the well-deserved Steelers AFC Championship, one that many felt was a season later than it should have been.

The game was over, and the Steelers had won. This was possibly the most dramatic NFL game of the 1990s. It was certainly one of the great games in Steelers history.

71 Slash Has a Roller-Coaster Career in Pittsburgh

Other players in NFL history have played various positions, but no player seemed to have the type of impact that former Steelers quarterback/wide receiver/running back/punter Kordell Stewart had. The former Colorado quarterback's career was so up and down, you never really knew what to expect, good or bad.

He was drafted in the 1995 Super Bowl season by the Steelers, who selected him in the second round with their 60th pick overall.

"Slash" Sticks

Just as with pretty much every other famous Steelers nickname, Kordell "Slash" Stewart got his name from longtime Steelers radio color man Myron Cope. As Stewart started making appearances as a wideout in 1995, Cope started calling Stewart "Slash" when he would take the field. The name took hold during a Monday night game in November against the rival Cleveland Browns. Stewart caught two passes in the 20–3 win, ran the ball twice for 13 yards, and made a memorable sideline-to-sideline scramble in which he eventually threw a two-yard touchdown pass to Ernie Mills for his first NFL touchdown. "Slash" was truly born, and the NFL was never the same.

He had a solid career quarterbacking at Colorado, where he set passing records for the Buffaloes, including most completed passes, most passing yards, and most touchdown passes. In his senior season Stewart was selected as a second-team All-American, and there was no question that he would find his way onto an NFL roster as a rookie.

Many football fans who didn't follow Colorado or even college football on a regular basis knew about Stewart from his 1994 Hail Mary touchdown pass to future Washington Redskins wide receiver Michael Westbrook that sailed 76 yards to win a game against the University of Michigan.

When the Steelers took Stewart, the team was coming off a devastating 17–13 AFC Championship Game loss at home to the San Diego Chargers, and some felt the team needed more offense. They had a solid running game with the likes of Barry Foster and Byron "Bam" Morris, but Foster fell out of favor and was traded, and the team looked to develop more of a downfield passing game. Enter Stewart.

The funny part was, there was no question about who was going to be the starting quarterback entering 1995. Neil O'Donnell was entrenched as the man under center, and veteran Mike Tomczak was the backup. Stewart's role at best was going to be as

Quarterback Kordell Stewart had several ups and downs during his time with the Steelers. His best season was in 1997, when he threw for 3,000-plus yards and 21 touchdowns.

a backup or third-string quarterback. Coach Bill Cowher, however, started to notice Stewart's ability in training camp and early in the season playing the scout team, and started to toy with the idea of using him as a wide receiver as the team struggled to a 3–4 start. On October 29 at home against the Jaguars, Stewart saw the field as a wide receiver, starting the career of "Slash," and taking the NFL by storm.

Within weeks he was a main player in the Steelers' offense and had the magazine and television features that go along with such fame. He ran plays as a wideout, running back, quarterback, and even punted once against the Bills in a playoff game. That season he ended the year with 14 catches for 235 yards and one score. He also ran in a touchdown and threw another one.

Quarterbacking was always in the back of Stewart's mind, though, and time after time he said that was his goal. He finally got his chance to be a starting quarterback in 1997, and he shined. The team started slow, going 2–2, but then he started to find his stride, and the team began winning games.

By the time it was over, Stewart ended the year throwing for a little more than 3,000 yards, 21 touchdowns, and 17 interceptions, and rushing for 11 TDs. He was one of the most dangerous players in the league, and he led the club to the AFC Championship Game. That's where things started to go south for Stewart—in the eventual 24–21 loss to Denver, he threw three picks and lost two fumbles.

His career went downhill in 1998, and he was pulled late in the year for Tomczak. He threw 18 picks and 11 touchdowns, and was just not the same player as the year before. His confidence was shaken, and it took him until midway through the 2000 season to get it back. He started that year as the backup to Kent Graham, but by Week 7 was back under center.

He was the quarterback in the team's final game at Three Rivers Stadium in a win over the Redskins, and by 2001 he was ready to start fresh as the team moved into Heinz Field. He and the club made a run for the title that year, going 13–3. Stewart again was a big fan favorite, but as the team got into the postseason, he slumped. After a win over the Ravens, the club fell against a heavy underdog in the New England Patriots, and Stewart threw three picks in a 24–17 defeat. Many put a lot of blame on his performance, despite special teams allowing two direct scores on a punt return and a blocked field goal.

Just like that, it was over. The following year Stewart started the Steelers' first three games, but he wasn't the same. By Week 4 he was pulled for Tommy Maddox, who never lost the starting job to Stewart for the rest of that season.

The next year Stewart found himself in Chicago, and then his career wrapped up without much fanfare in Baltimore. To say that Stewart's NFL career and his career in Pittsburgh were up and down would be putting it mildly.

72 Roethlisberger's Record Day vs. Green Bay

The 2009 season was on a downward spiral when the team returned home for a December meeting with the Green Bay Packers. The club had lost five straight, which had for all purposes put them out of the playoff race, erasing any hopes of them repeating as Super Bowl champions. Still, at 6–7 the team had pride and the outside shot of the postseason to play for, but no one could have predicted the history that was about to be made by quarterback Ben Roethlisberger and the Steelers' offense this Sunday afternoon.

Roethlisberger had already had a solid season despite the team being under .500. He had thrown 19 touchdowns and 11 interceptions, and had four games of more than 300 yards, even a game of 417 yards in a win over the Browns in October at Heinz Field. This day would turn out to be his best, though, and one of the best in NFL history.

Green Bay entered the game at 9–4 and were playoff contenders in the NFC. They had a former Steelers coordinator running their defense in Dom Capers, and an up-and-coming offense led by quarterback Aaron Rodgers. All this made for what turned out to be the most memorable game of the 2009 NFL regular season.

Roethlisberger and the offense, which had managed just two field goals the week before in an embarrassing 10–6 loss to the lowly Browns in Cleveland, struck on their first offensive play from scrimmage. Roethlisberger took a perfect play-action and threw deep for rookie wideout Mike Wallace, who waited for the pass and pulled it in for a 60-yard score. It started a back-and-forth that was both fun and frustrating to watch.

The Packers came back with an 83-yard touchdown from Rodgers to wideout Greg Jennings to tie the score. But Pittsburgh closed out the quarter up 14–7 after running back Rashard Mendenhall went in from two yards out. The teams traded scores in the second quarter, with Roethlisberger throwing his second touchdown, this time to running back Mewelde Moore from 10 yards out. At the half, the Steelers led 21–14, and Big Ben had already thrown for 223 yards and two touchdowns for a QB rating of 140.2.

And the best was yet to come.

The third quarter saw the Steelers get a field goal from Jeff Reed to go up 24–14, and then after a Packers touchdown, Reed kicked another to make it 27–21. But just as the Steelers' defense had done way too often in 2009, they allowed Green Bay to get back into the game with Rodgers leading the team on a four-play, 62-yard drive to score with 7:49 left to make it 28–27.

Roethlisberger and the wideouts who had made big plays all day continued to pile up yards, as the Steelers went on a quick 44-yard drive to set up a 43-yard Reed field goal with 3:58 left to give the Steelers a 30–28 lead. It was at that point that coach Mike Tomlin made a rather curious decision. With the lead, he went for an onside kick, and cornerback Ike Taylor illegally touched the ball, giving it to the Packers at the Steelers' 39.

Rodgers marched Green Bay right down the field, and with a third-and-14 from the Steelers' 24, he hit James Jones with a perfect pass that covered 24 yards for a touchdown to make it 34–30 with 2:12 left. The Pack then got the two-point conversion to make it 36–30. It would be up to Roethlisberger and his offense to pull out one more offensive miracle to save any hope of a possible playoff appearance and a winning season.

Roethlisberger and the team started the drive at their 14 and began throwing right away, as expected. They had the Packers' help, with Green Bay committing a hold on the first play to put the ball at the 19. After a four-yard sack, Roethlisberger found tight end Heath Miller for seven yards, and then on fourth down got a pass to Santonio Holmes for 32 yards to the Packers' 46 with 1:14 left.

The game could have been over two plays later when Roethlisberger was picked off, but illegal contact was called on the play, giving the Steelers a first down. A couple plays later it was third-and-15 from the Steelers' 44, and Miller made a spectacular catch, giving the team a first down at the Green Bay 36 with 32 seconds left.

After a three-yard sack, another 15-yard gain to Miller, and two incomplete passes, the team was down to their last play with :03 left and the ball on the Packers' 19. That's when the quarterback and his favorite rookie wideout made the play of the season. Roethlisberger scrambled, then threw deep left to the end zone, and Wallace, who already had one touchdown, made a great catch with Josh Bell right on him in coverage. The play looked almost like the Santonio Holmes catch in Super Bowl XLIII, with Wallace's toes coming down just in bounds as he fell to the ground with the ball cradled in his arms.

After some nervous moments in the replay booth, the play was confirmed as a touchdown, and after Reed's extra point, the Steelers walked away with a one-point win, 37–36. Roethlisberger's numbers were historic: 29-for-46 for 503 yards with three touchdowns. It was the first time a Steelers quarterback had ever thrown for more than 500 yards in a game, and he became just the 10th QB since 1950 to throw for 500 or more yards in a game.

While the Steelers' season ended two weeks later, the day that Roethlisberger had will go down as the best any Steelers quarterback has ever had.

73 Burying the Browns 12 Straight Times

The Steelers and the Browns have waged some bitter battles over the years, with the Steelers having the advantage over their archrival. The teams even had to face not seeing each other for a while when Browns owner Art Modell relocated the franchise to Baltimore, opening up another rivalry between the Steelers and the Baltimore Ravens.

The Browns rivalry has always seemed to go in spurts. In the 1970s, as the Steelers were putting Lombardi Trophies in their front offices, they beat up the Browns on a regular basis. Then in the 1980s, as the Browns had their runs at the Super Bowl with players like Bernie Kosar, they exacted some revenge by beating the Steelers six straight times in the '86, '87, and '88 seasons.

After that, things got back to normal, and then the Browns left after the 1995 season. The Cleveland Browns retuned in 1999 to play the Steelers on opening night at Browns Stadium. And the Steelers left laughing, winning with ease 43–0.

The Browns did beat the Steelers in the 1999 rematch and again the following season in Cleveland. But then something happened after the Browns beat Pittsburgh at Heinz Field in October 2003—they simply forgot how to beat the Steelers.

From their second meeting in Cleveland in November 2003 until a freezing night in Cleveland in December 2009, the Steelers won every single game. They beat Cleveland just about every single way—shootouts, low-scoring games, warm games, cold games, whatever. The Browns and their fans lost 12 straight to the Steelers, and Pittsburgh enjoyed each and every one of them.

Ben Roethlisberger won his first 10 against the Browns, and players like Hines Ward, Willie Parker, and others usually put

The End of the Streak

The Steelers' domination of the Browns ended on Thursday, December 10, 2009, on a freezing night in Cleveland at Browns Stadium. Many felt the Steelers would have no problem making short work of the 1–11 Browns, and they would be able to break their four-game losing streak. Instead, Cleveland outplayed the Steelers, not making mistakes as they usually did and using the versatile Josh Cribbs to stun the Steelers 13–6. The night was cold and windy, and it looked like the Steelers were frozen in Lake Erie, playing their worst game in quite a long time against the Browns, who celebrated like they had won the Super Bowl.

up huge numbers against Cleveland. On a Thursday night in December 2006, Parker ran for 223 yards as the Steelers won 27–7. During the 2007 season Roethlisberger threw for four touchdowns on opening day and then threw for two more and ran for one in the rematch in November.

In the 12-game winning streak, the Steelers outscored the Browns 330–142, a staggering average of beating Cleveland by a score of 28–12. They also shut out the Browns twice in that stretch, including a 41–0 shutout on Christmas Eve of the 2005 Super Bowl season.

Then again, dominating the Browns should not come as all that much of a shock to the Steelers or their fans. The Browns have only made the playoffs once since their return in 1999 (Pittsburgh beat them 36–33 in that 2002 season), and they also have had just one other winning season. In 2007 they went 10–6 and missed the playoffs due to a late-season loss to the Bengals.

With this official 12-game winning streak in the rivalry, it would have been more shocking if the Steelers would not have been able to dominate a Cleveland franchise that seemed to have problems beating just about anyone during their first decade back.

74 Kevin Greene

He seemed more suited for pro wrestling (something he actually did at a point in his career) than the gridiron, and even though he only played three seasons in the Steel City, linebacker Kevin Greene made quite an impact with the city and with Steelers fans. Greene was a premiere 3-4 outside linebacker in the NFL, pounding offensive linemen and making life tough for opposing quarterbacks on a weekly basis.

Greene posted 160 career sacks playing for four different NFL franchises. He started his career in Los Angeles for the Rams, then after eight seasons and a lot of sacks, he came to Pittsburgh. The already established linebacker signed a three-year, $5.35 million deal to help out the Steelers' defense that had already been growing into one of the league's best.

He came to the club prior to the 1993 season and joined Greg Lloyd, quickly becoming part of a vicious 1-2 punch at the outside linebacker spot. He and Lloyd made pacts in the huddle to "meet at the quarterback," making it a race to see which outside linebacker got there first. Greene played on pure emotion, pushing aside linemen and making it a goal to put quarterbacks on their backs as many times as possible each week.

In his first season with the Steelers, the linebacker put up 12.5 sacks as the Steelers went 9–7 and were a wild-card team in the AFC. In '94 the defense got even better, unleashing terror on offenses with their nickname "Blitzburg." Greene and the club established a team record with 55 sacks, and he led the team and the league with 14, while Lloyd joined the fun with 10. Greene also forced a fumble and had three fumble recoveries.

The team missed the Super Bowl by one game, and the following year made it their goal to erase that letdown by getting to the big game. Greene again was a main cog in the defense with nine sacks, a pick, and two forced fumbles. The Steelers turned up the heat in the playoffs, topping Buffalo and Indianapolis before falling to Dallas in Super Bowl XXX.

Greene was a Pro Bowl linebacker in both the 1994 and 1995 seasons with the Steelers and was a first-team All-Pro choice in '94. The club lost Greene in the off-season to the Carolina Panthers, who paid him $2 million for a two-year deal. While his time with the Steelers was short, many fans bonded with the linebacker, wearing his No. 91 jersey on Sundays at Three Rivers Stadium and on the road as well.

Intense during the season, Greene was just as intense in the off-season. He completed ROTC while at Auburn and was commissioned a second lieutenant in the Alabama Army Reserve. During one of his off-seasons, he graduated from the RC-1-86 Armor Officer Basic Course in Fort Knox, Kentucky. As a captain in a 16-year career in the Army Reserve, Greene served his military commitments during the off-season after he chased quarterbacks during the season.

After Pittsburgh, Greene played one season with the Panthers, one season with the San Francisco 49ers, and then finished his career in Carolina. Greene did have another connection with the Steelers—in 2008 he and another former Steelers outside linebacker, Jason Gildon, served internships for the team as assistant linebackers coaches during training camp.

Now Greene shares his knowledge with linebackers in Green Bay. In January 2009 he was hired as the Packers' outside linebackers coach. He coached against the Steelers in Super Bowl XLV in Dallas, and earned that elusive ring as a coach with the likes of Clay Matthews Jr. at his side.

75 Top Five Steelers Nicknames

Throughout the years the Steelers have had a number of colorful characters who have littered the roster, sideline, and elsewhere. With that, here are some memorable nicknames that have been given to them over the decades.

1. Art "the Chief" Rooney

No one figure in Steelers history holds as much reverence as Arthur Joseph Rooney Sr., which is why the original owner of the club tops our list with his nickname—"the Chief." Rooney was the founding owner of the Steelers, this after he won enough money in horse racing to buy a franchise entrance fee in the NFL so Pittsburgh could have a team. He endured years upon years of losing, only to have one of the greatest runs as an owner in any sport in team history—four Super Bowls in six seasons. He passed away in August 1988, but make no mistake, without the Chief the Steelers would have never existed.

2. "Mean" Joe Greene

The Steelers' first-round draft choice (fourth overall) in the 1969 draft, "Mean" Joe Greene became the most dominant defensive lineman in the NFL during the Steelers' glory years of the 1970s. The Hall of Fame defensive tackle amassed 78.5 sacks along with 10 Pro Bowl selections and four Super Bowl titles with the famed Steel Curtain. Greene spent most of his career battling his way out of double and triple teams and still was the best player on the field just about every Sunday. He also took home the NFL Defensive Player of the Year award in 1972 and 1974. Add the famous Coke commercial to the list, and "Mean" Joe Greene never failed to live up to his name.

3. Chuck "Chaz the Emperor" Noll

The coaching mastermind behind four Super Bowl titles in the 1970s, Noll remains the only coach in NFL history to snag four Lombardi Trophies. He was a master when it came to drafting players, and his picks of players like Joe Greene, Terry Bradshaw, Jack Lambert, and Franco Harris showed just how good "Chaz the Emperor" was. Noll's nickname was given to him by legendary Steelers announcer Myron Cope, but it's a name that the Hall of Fame coach more than deserved.

4. Bill "the Chin" Cowher

Maybe the most famous chin in all of the NFL, Bill Cowher used that chin to his advantage, gaining more air time over the years than some of the players on the team. "The Chin" could not be stopped, as Cowher took the Steelers to eight division titles, 10 postseason playoff berths, 21 playoff games, six AFC Championship Games, and two Super Bowl appearances. You always knew when things were not going the Steelers' way, as that famous chin would shoot out further and further, usually followed by a form of spit that would come out during those yell-fests. There was no mistaking "the Chin," as Cowher roamed the Steelers sideline for 15 seasons.

5. Jerome "the Bus" Bettis

The Steelers' imposing running back battered teams from 1996 to 2005, ending his Hall of Fame career with a Lombardi Trophy in his hometown of Detroit. His nickname came during his time at Notre Dame, and of course, who else but Cope picked up on the name during his first season with the Steelers? To say that fans loved the name was an understatement. They brought cardboard cut-outs of buses to the game with them, showing their respect for the big back. Bettis jerseys are still a popular item among Steelers faithful today.

76 Beating the Birds Three Times in 2008

Physical. That's about the only way you can describe the rivalry between the Pittsburgh Steelers and the Baltimore Ravens. In 2008 that rivalry took on a whole new meaning when the teams met three times for just the second time ever, with the conference's biggest prize at stake in their third and final meeting.

These two teams simply do not like each other very much. Sure, there's a level of respect, but as Mike Tomlin says—it doesn't mean it gives you a warm fuzzy feeling about one another. For the 2008 season, there were not many good feelings about any player on either side.

The first meeting at Heinz Field came in Week 4 on a Monday night, September 29. The Steelers were coming off their first loss of the year, a 15–6 setback in Philadelphia which saw quarterback Ben Roethlisberger suffer eight sacks, and the team nine overall, when you add the one that backup Byron Leftwich took. They came into Monday night somewhat beat up.

The Ravens were an upstart unit, going 2–0 with a bye in the first three weeks of the season. They had a new coach, John Harbaugh, and a rookie quarterback, Joe Flacco. They came out the more aggressive unit in that first meeting, building a 13–3 lead at the half. The Steelers left the field an unhappy bunch, failing to get to Flacco much and struggling on offense, to say the least.

The Steelers' locker room was an interesting place to be at half-time, as Roethlisberger took the lead, telling his offensive unit that they were embarrassing themselves, which was obvious because they were booed off their home field. It lit a fire. In the third quarter they went to a hurry-up style on offense, and Roethlisberger hit wideout Santonio Holmes for a 38-yard score to make it 13–10 Baltimore.

Dominating Division Rivals in the Postseason

The Steelers are perfect in the postseason against their divisional rivals, never losing their game, going 9–0 against Cleveland, Cincinnati, Baltimore, and the old Houston Oilers. They topped the Ravens in the 2008 AFC Championship Game, topped Cincinnati in the 2005 AFC wild card game, and overcame Cleveland in the 2002 AFC wild card game after trailing by double digits in the second half.

They had two memorable AFC Championship Games against the Oilers in the 1978 and '79 seasons, winning the '78 title game easily 34–5, and then winning 27–13 the next season en route to their fourth Super Bowl. While they beat the Oilers and Ravens three times in the postseason, they also have topped the Browns twice, Baltimore twice, and the Bengals once.

It took the team a whopping 15 seconds to take the lead when a James Harrison hit on Flacco popped the ball out, and LaMarr Woodley picked it up to go seven yards for a score to make it 17–13 Steelers. The game went back and forth to the end, and after a late Ravens score with 4:02, left the two rivals went to overtime with the score 20–20.

The Steelers had already been without running back Willie Parker, and rookie back Rashard Mendenhall had busted his shoulder early in the third quarter on a hit by Ray Lewis. That left Mewelde Moore to carry the load. Moore did just that, hauling in a short pass over the middle from Roethlisberger and going 24 yards to the Ravens' 31 on third-and-8. It set up win No. 1, as Jeff Reed hit a 46-yard field goal to give the team a 23–20 win.

Eleven weeks later the stage was set for the rematch in Baltimore, this time with a lot more on a line. The Ravens were 9–4, and the Steelers 10–3. A Steelers win would clinch the AFC North and a first-round bye. A loss, and the Ravens would pull the teams even. Again, it would be a memorable battle that left fans wanting more.

The battle between the top two defenses in football played out as expected. Only one touchdown was scored, and even that didn't come without a cloud of controversy. The game saw the Ravens lead 9–6 with the Steelers backed up to their 8-yard line with 3:36 left. Leave it to Roethlisberger, who pulled out big plays all season, as he led them down the field, hitting pass after pass, avoiding the Ravens' rush.

The big play was a 24-yard pitch and catch from Roethlisberger to Nate Washington, who took it to the Ravens' 14. He then hit Hines Ward for 10 yards to the Ravens' 4. Three plays later, the quarterback known for making things happen when nothing should, rolled to his right and threw a shot to the end zone, where Holmes was standing just inside the goal line.

The first ruling was that even though Holmes' feet were in the end zone, he was down at the 1-yard line. Then, after a long look in the replay booth, the refs ruled that the ball broke the plane for a Steelers touchdown, giving them a 13–9 lead following the extra point with 43 seconds left.

One William Gay interception later on a desperation pass from Flacco, and the Steelers were AFC North division champs. Not only that, they had secured the all-important first-round bye in the AFC.

The two teams had one more go-around, this time with even more on the line. The Steelers beat San Diego in the divisional round the day after the Ravens upset the Titans in Tennessee, setting up a third and final meeting, with a trip to Super Bowl XLIII on the line.

The January 18 battle at Heinz Field took place in the evening, and the temps were in the teens, setting up a bitter-cold battle for survival. "Probably the most physical game in the history of football" is how Troy Polamalu described the game to NFL Films during the Steelers' Super Bowl edition of *America's Game*.

Again, it was going to be whoever played more physical, and on this day, it was again the Steelers. The Black and Gold dominated early, building a lead with two Reed field goals. Then the big play of the game took place. Roethlisberger, again scrambling, threw long for Holmes, who made a catch in the middle of the field, then raced the final 47 yards for a score to make it 13–0 about a minute into the second quarter.

The Ravens did not go quietly, though. They battled back, and by the time the Ravens scored with 9:29 left, the Steelers' 13-point lead was down to two at 16–14. Baltimore was able to stop the Steelers on their next possession, and then got the ball at their own 14 with 6:50 left. They got a first down, but then faced a huge third-and-13 from their own 29.

Flacco went back to pass and, looking for Derrick Mason, was hit by Harrison, as the ball was thrown. Polamalu made the stabbing pick, and then did what he always does, cut back. By the time he was done, he was pointing up to the stands to his young son as he ran though the end zone. The score made it 23–14 and ended the Ravens' final threat.

The win cemented not only the Steelers' trip to their seventh title game, but also made it official that the Steelers-Ravens battles forever would go down as some of the hardest-hitting in NFL history.

77 Don't Mess with the Terrible Towel

If there is one thing that seems to drive Steelers Nation to the edge, it's when an opponent decides to take it upon themselves to desecrate the almighty Terrible Towel. The towel is a symbol of Steeler Nation, and when it comes to the faithful who wave it every week at Heinz Field and on the road at opposing stadiums, it becomes a part of the team more than anyone could ever think. That's why the few times over the years that a player and/or team decides to stomp on the towel, it becomes big-time news in Pittsburgh.

There have been two very memorable times over the past 15 seasons that opposing players have decided to take it upon themselves to stomp on the towel, and both times that decision has come back to haunt them. The first time was back in the 1994 AFC playoffs when the Steelers hosted their archrival, the Cleveland Browns. The Steelers had already topped the Browns twice during the regular season, but Cleveland continued to say over and over that they were the better football team.

The Steelers dominated the football game, coming out fast and beating up the Browns all day with a 29–9 win that put them in the AFC Championship Game the following week. The motivation to beat up the Browns was high, but was taken to another level when Browns running back Earnest Byner made his way to the Steelers' half of the field during pregame warmups and stomped on the Terrible Towel.

"We were coming out twirling the towels, getting us and the crowd pumped up," Steelers defensive lineman Ray Seals explained to *Cleveland Plain Dealer* reporter Dennis Manoloff the day of the beating. "Then [Steelers fellow defensive lineman Brenston] Buckner drops one of his towels, and Byner comes over and stomps it in the ground. That right there brought what they got on them. Half our guys saw that, and we were like: 'That was wrong.' You see stuff like that in college, but not in the pros. I don't know what he was thinking."

"I can't believe he came on our side of the field during our introductions and did that," Buckner said to Manoloff. "He just added more fuel to my fire and got my team even more fired up. We were plenty fired up anyway."

All the trash-talking by the Browns during the week already had the Black and Gold seeing red as they took the field at home that day, and it seemed like Byner's miscalculated move only further

It's Cold Out There

There's been quite a few cold-weather games in Steelers history, but the coldest game on record was December 10, 1977, in Cincinnati, when the temperature at kickoff was just 2 degrees. The Steelers lost 17–10 that day. The coldest recorded game in Pittsburgh was December 17, 1989, as the Steelers beat New England 28–10. The temp at kickoff was 5 degrees. It was only 11 degrees when the Steelers lost to New England 41–27 in the AFC Championship Game on January 23, 2005.

pushed the team over the edge. The Browns never stood a chance, and it started with a dumb move by the Browns' running back.

Incident No. 2 was a lot more recent, and it indirectly seemed to put a curse on a team that felt like they had the inside track to playing in Super Bowl XLIII. The Tennessee Titans had steamrolled through the NFL in 2008, and many felt they were the team that would represent the AFC in the Super Bowl. The Steelers were in their way in Week 16, only to be beaten by Tennessee 31–14 in a game that cemented the Titans even more as the AFC conference favorite heading into the postseason.

The Titans, though, made a critical mistake near the end of their blowout win, as two of their key players, linebacker Keith Bulluck and running back LenDale White got hold of a couple of Terrible Towels. The two, more so White than Bulluck, took it upon themselves to first mock blowing their noses into the towels, then stomping them into the mud on the sideline at LP Field in Tennessee.

For the week after that win, the Titans defended what they did, and it seemed like a rematch would only be the right way to settle things, even though that game would again be at LP Field and this time would be for the AFC Championship. Well, the Steelers held up their end of the bargain in winning their divisional playoff game over the San Diego Chargers, but for the Titans—that was another story.

Tennessee was upset at home by the AFC wild-card Baltimore Ravens. The smashmouth Ravens and Titans waged war, but in the end, a 43-yard field goal by Matt Stover would give the Ravens a 13–10 win and a game against the Steelers for the AFC title. Many say that the Titans only cursed themselves that day against the Steelers, and while it wasn't Pittsburgh that actually knocked the Titans out of the playoffs, some say it was the power of the famed Terrible Towel that did.

78. Cowher-Donahoe Can't See Eye to Eye

The world of the NFL is business first, and sometimes, as in business and in life, people don't get along. Such was the case with the Steelers after a couple of subpar seasons in 1998 and 1999, when the team stumbled to 7–9 and 6–10 finishes. It was the first time in the Bill Cowher era that the coach was unable to get his team to the playoffs, and some whispers began to get louder about Cowher "losing his team" and his message no longer getting through to his players.

Never mind the fact that the Steelers seemed gutted year after year in free agency. It started with losing quarterback Neil O'Donnell after the Super Bowl in 1995 and then seemed to go from there, losing players like linebackers Chad Brown and Kevin Greene, wide receivers Yancey Thigpen and Andre Hastings, and many more. Teams seemed to target Steelers free agents—good or bad. Why? Because they usually thrived in the Steelers' system and in high-profile games.

Most Steelers free agents fizzled out once they went elsewhere, but losing them really hurt the Black and Gold. While they usually had players waiting in the wings to take their place, it was tough to replace Pro Bowl players and others who fit their system year after year. Not to mention there were some players that the Steelers felt would be playmakers who simply never panned out.

That led to the two struggling seasons for Cowher and the organization, which was also undone by an underlying battle behind the scenes between Cowher and Tom Donahoe, the director of football operations. The pair had combined to help the Steelers recreate the 1970s magic upon Cowher's arrival, making the playoffs each season from 1992 to 1997. But things began to deteriorate between them. Cowher wanted more power over decisions, while Donahoe felt he should maintain his huge say in picking the players, despite the two setback seasons. The two butted heads behind the scenes, and in the end, it was going to be something that could not move forward unless one of them left the organization. Both told Dan Rooney they would step down, and a decision was going to have to come from him. It would not be an easy one. Would it be Cowher who would be dismissed, a coach who came in for legendary Chuck Noll and led the team to six straight playoff appearances and a Super Bowl following the 1995 season? Or Donahoe, whose savvy led the team to pick some outstanding players in the draft and never got carried away in free agency, but chose some great complements to the squad.

At the end the day, Rooney knew that the wrong decision could set the team back years. After some back and forth, Rooney decided that finding a good coach was tougher than replacing Donahoe, and the Steelers owner accepted his resignation. Cowher had won the power struggle, and Donahoe was replaced by former Detroit Lions advance scout and local product Kevin Colbert. Donahoe landed in Buffalo in 2001, taking over the day-to-day operations for owner Ralph Wilson. The Bills' owner wanted to step aside from all the general manager responsibilities, and chose Donahoe to take his place. Donahoe's tenure in Buffalo further cemented Rooney's decision. He was fired after the 2005 season, when Buffalo went 31–49 in five regular seasons under his care without a single playoff appearance.

Everyone knows how it ended for Cowher. After Donahoe left, the coach went 72–39 in seven regular seasons with the Steelers, and 7–3 in four playoff seasons, including a Super Bowl win over Seattle. Rooney's decision was a win for the Steelers, and one that has benefited the club ever since.

79 Jason Gildon

Looking like a chiseled bodybuilder as much as an outside linebacker, Jason Gildon's 10-year career with the Steelers was filled with big plays and plenty of sacks. Playing with the team from 1994 to 2003, Gildon remains the Steelers' all-time leader in sacks with 77, and also put up plenty of tackles with 383 solo to go along with 128 assists. He also had 11 fumble recoveries with three touchdowns.

When Gildon's career began, he was a demon on special teams for Bill Cowher during the team's stellar seasons of 1994 and 1995. Those two teams made two AFC Championship Games and in '95 competed in Super Bowl XXX against Dallas. Gildon could be seen making plays almost every week on special teams.

Finally in 1996 he got his shot and took advantage of it. He took outside linebacker Greg Lloyd's spot when Lloyd went down with a torn knee ligament in the season opener against the Jaguars. Gildon stepped right in, and the team didn't miss a beat. He compiled seven sacks in his first season as a starter.

The following season he and Lloyd made a solid 1-2 punch on the outside, as the team went 11–5 and made it to the AFC Championship Game before losing to the Denver Broncos. Gildon had five sacks and recorded his first defensive touchdown. His biggest play of the season came in the postseason, though, when after Mike Vrabel stripped Pats quarterback Drew Bledsoe in a 7–6 game in the final minutes, Gildon pounced on the ball, saving the win.

By 1998 Lloyd had moved on, and Gildon was the leader on defense with his attitude as well as his play. He was physical and made sure that when he got to the quarterback, he would take him down. Gildon was doing his part, the problem was the rest of the team struggled under Cowher in his first year as coach.

In '98 the team went 7–9, and while Gildon had his best season as a pro with 11 sacks and a recovered fumble, the team missed the postseason. Much was the same the season after, as the team went 6–10 while Gildon shined, putting up 8.5 sacks with 57 total tackles.

The team started to turn around in 2000, and Gildon's career rose to another level. He put up 13.5 sacks, a touchdown, and 75 tackles. He helped the team go 9–7 and had a partner to help him out in Joey Porter, who put up 10.5 sacks of his own. Gildon made the Pro Bowl in 2000, and he and the team were ready for another run at the AFC title in 2001.

That year he was the leader of the defense, and the team had its best regular season since 1978, winning 13 games. Gildon compiled 12 sacks with an interception and a pair of fumble recoveries, one of which went for a touchdown. Porter had the brash attitude while Gildon simply went about his business, sacking quarterbacks and helping the team win games.

The club's goal of a Super Bowl berth fell one game short, as they lost to the Patriots in the AFC Championship Game. The following season they were again a playoff team, with Gildon making the Pro Bowl with nine sacks and 66 tackles. His final season with the Steelers was 2003, and despite the team not making the postseason, Gildon reached his final major milestone with the Steelers, putting up six sacks to reach 77, which made him the all-time team leader. The historic sack came on November 9 against the Arizona Cardinals, when his third-quarter sack of Jeff Blake broke L.C.

Greenwood's record. The sack also helped the team break its five-game losing streak, winning 28–15.

Gildon moved on to the Bills the next season but was released two weeks into training camp. He signed with the Jacksonville Jaguars midway through the season and was back to his old ways, collecting three sacks, including one against the Steelers and Ben Roethlisberger on December 5 in a Steelers 17–16 win.

80 Turkey Day Coin Flip Fiasco in Detroit

The 1998 season seemed to have promise for the Black and Gold, as they jumped out to a 2–0 record after wins over the Ravens and Bears. Then after a Monday night win over Brett Favre and the Packers in Week 10, the team was 6–3 and seemed right in the thick of things in the AFC. Enter Phil Luckett and the famous "coin flip fiasco" in Detroit three weeks later.

The Steelers were facing the Lions in the Silverdome to play what for them was a rare Thanksgiving Day game, only their third in team history. Pittsburgh seemed to have things in order, leading 13–3 after wide receiver Will Blackwell caught a deflected pass off the hands of running back Jerome Bettis from quarterback Kordell Stewart and took it 24 yards for the first touchdown of the game to give the Steelers a 10-point lead.

At that point, the team had bottled up Lions Hall of Fame running back Barry Sanders (he ended the game with 33 yards on 20 carries) and had limited Lions quarterback Charlie Batch. All looked well, but then, just like that, things went haywire. Detroit got a 51-yard field goal from Jason Hanson, then in the fourth quarter went on a six-play, 80-yard drive that saw Batch hit two big pass plays and ended with him hitting Herman Moore with a 21-yard score to tie the game at 13–13.

The Lions took a 16–13 lead after a Steelers fumble by Blackwell on the following kickoff, and the momentum totally shifted. The Steelers and Stewart would not be denied, though, and they went on a 15-play drive that covered 74 yards. With one second left in regulation, Norm Johnson booted a 25-yard field goal to tie the game and send it into overtime.

That's when one of the biggest gaffe's in NFL history haunted the Steelers and the rest of their season. Steelers captains came to the field, and it was decided that Jerome Bettis would make the coin flip call. Referee Luckett showed both sides of the coin to the teams and went to throw it in the air. Bettis called tails, and the coin came up tails, meaning the Steelers should have had their choice to get the ball first in overtime.

The problem was, Luckett said that Bettis said heads, and quickly asked the Lions what they chose, and they wisely took the ball. An irate Bettis looked stunned as he pleaded his case to Luckett while more than 78,000 fans in the Silverdome could not understand why the Lions were being given their choice of getting to kick or receive.

Seven plays and 41 yards later, Hanson marched on the field and was true from 42 yards, wrapping up a bizarre end to the last time the Steelers played on Thanksgiving. Luckett still claims that he heard Bettis utter, "Heads-tails," and he went with the first thing he heard out of Bettis' mouth—heads.

The future Hall of Fame back says differently, that he clearly said, "Tails." The loss put the Steelers into a severe tailspin, as it not only dropped them to 7–5, but they never won another game in the 1998 season, ending the season 7–9 and out of the playoffs. If nothing else, it changed the way the NFL handles overtime—now the player making the coin toss must declare heads or tails before the coin is ever flipped—all this thanks to the memorable "heads-tails" call that Bettis made on Thanksgiving 1998.

81 The Curse of the 1983 Draft

The Steelers' philosophy of building with defense first worked well back in the 1960s and '70s as the team built a dynasty with players like Joe Greene, L.C. Greenwood, Mel Blount, Jack Lambert, and others. The dynasty of the 1970s, though, faded away as players got older, and after the team's fourth Super Bowl in January 1980, it was time to rebuild. With it, the team again felt like defense was the way to go. It led to one of the most controversial decisions the team ever made in the 1983 NFL Draft.

The club had already undergone a couple of down years in the early '80s, and there was a chance in '83 to pick a high-profile player to revamp the roster. The quarterback position was one that was discussed quite a bit in the front office. Terry Bradshaw was nearing the end of his career with an elbow that would only allow him to play one game in the '83 season. The club had Cliff Stoudt and Mark Malone. Yet sitting in the draft was a local quarterback named Dan Marino, a player the team seemed to like.

Pittsburgh-native Marino played his high school ball at Central Catholic High School and went to the University of Pitt. Despite a subpar senior season there, many felt Marino would be a first-round pick, and more than one felt that the Steelers would take him and groom him, as the their quarterback of the future.

Noll wanted to continue his previous success by building with defense first. So with the 21st pick, instead of taking Marino right from their own backyard, Noll and the club took Texas Tech defensive tackle Gabe Rivera, a player Noll felt would anchor the defensive line like Greene did years before. It simply didn't happen.

Marino went six picks later to the Miami Dolphins and coach Don Shula. He went down as one of the greatest quarterbacks in

NFL history. He set passing records and led the Dolphins over the Steelers in the 1984 AFC Championship Game in Miami before losing to the 49ers in the Super Bowl that season.

As for Rivera, it's one of the true tragedies in Steelers history. "Senior Sack," as his nickname stated, was an All-American out of Texas Tech and was in the team's starting lineup right away. He had just started to finally show some spark before an accident caused his NFL career to end.

Rivera was the driver on October 20, 1983, in a car accident that left him paralyzed. He was thrown out the back window, and his spine shattered. "I remember the doctors didn't know my [shoulder blade] was broken in half until a few days later, when I finally could talk again," Rivera said. "I asked them, 'Why does it hurt there?' and they realized it was broken."

He suffered severe spinal cord damage and needed a wheelchair just for mobility. After months of physical therapy, he moved to Forth Worth, Texas, and despite the fact he only played in six games as a Steeler, the organization paid his full year salary and made sure he had health care.

It was a sad end to a career that could have flourished. Rivera has had to have numerous surgeries since the 1983 accident, and it seemed to keep the Steelers in somewhat of a tailspin through the '80s, as they made the conference title game just once in the decade and were disposed by Marino, the player they passed on for Rivera.

82 Santonio Holmes

The legacy of Santonio Holmes' career for the Steelers had numerous highlights, but also ended with a surprise trade in the 2009 off-season after the team became fed up with his off-the-field issues. Holmes, a first-round pick, won a Super Bowl MVP and made one of the most memorable catches in Super Bowl history, grabbing the winning touchdown in the final seconds of Super Bowl XLIII against the Cardinals in the corner of the end zone.

But, at only at 26 years old, the club had seen enough after a lawsuit was filed against him for allegedly throwing a glass at a woman in Florida. It was the third such issue with Holmes, who also was suspended for a game in the 2008 season after being arrested for possession of marijuana. Those issues put the Steelers in the tough position of basically giving Holmes away, as on April 11, 2010, the team moved him to the New York Jets for a fifth-round pick.

While no longer a Steeler, Holmes still had great moments in black and gold. He shined in the 2008 NFL playoffs, scoring a touchdown in each of the three Steelers playoff wins, including the winning grab on the biggest stage of them all in Tampa. At 5'11", he had the size and the speed to be a game-changer, and had shown as a Steeler in four seasons he was worthy of being the club's first-round draft pick back in 2006.

The Steelers were looking for another big playmaker on offense following their Super Bowl win in 2005 over the Seahawks. They had lost Plaxico Burress to free agency after the AFC Championship loss in the 2004 season, and after the Super Bowl win they lost wide receiver Antwaan Randle El to the Redskins through free agency. Enter Holmes, who was leaving Ohio State early to enter the 2006 NFL Draft.

Holmes had a successful career with the Buckeyes, catching 245 passes for 2,295 yards and 25 touchdowns in three seasons. He also was a part of the Ohio State 2002 national championship team, though he redshirted that season with the Buckeyes. His 25 touchdowns ranked third all-time for Ohio State at the time.

The Steelers liked what they saw from Holmes and made a deal with the New York Giants to move up to the 25th overall pick to snag the receiver. He was the first wideout taken by Pittsburgh in the first round since they selected Burress in the 2000 draft. His rookie season had plenty of ups and downs, as he fumbled a number of times on kick and punt returns, but by the end of the year had settled in as a starter opposite Hines Ward.

His rookie season ended with one of the team's most memorable plays of the year. In the season finale at Cincinnati he pulled in a slant pass from Ben Roethlisberger in overtime and raced 67 yards for the winning score. It not only gave the Steelers the win to end the year at 8–8, but earned Bill Cowher a victory in his final game as coach of the Steelers and knocked the Bengals out of the postseason.

That '06 season ended with Holmes catching 49 passes for 824 yards and two touchdowns. The '07 season saw the arrival of Mike Tomlin and also a breakout season for Holmes, who caught 52 passes for 942 yards and eight touchdowns. He averaged an outstanding 18.1 yards per catch, tops in the NFL, and showed his big-play ability.

By 2008, the word was out about Holmes, and while his per-catch average went down to 14.9, he still set a career high with 55 grabs for 821 yards and five scores. It was the postseason that established him as a star, as against the Chargers he got the team back to 7–7 with a punt return for a score, then against the Ravens in the AFC Championship Game, he made a catch at midfield and twisted and turned his way for a 65-yard score that put the team up 13–0 in the second quarter in a game they would win 23–14.

Despite his rise as a top NFL wideout, the marijuana possession issue before the team's Week 8 game at home against the New York Giants hung over him, and Tomlin benched him for the contest. He then opened up about his issues as a youth, telling the media in Tampa at media day he had sold drugs in Belle Glade, Florida as a youth, and that playing football helped him turn his life around.

That turnaround turned into a dream come true at Super Bowl XLIII, as in the final Steelers drive he caught four passes for 71 yards, including a long one that put them in position to win the game. Then after the first pass Roethlisberger threw to him in the opposite corner of the end zone was incomplete, the quarterback went right back to him, and this time he made the catch to earn him the game's Most Valuable Player award.

He followed up his super end to 2008 with a solid 2009, catching a career-high 79 passes for 1,248 yards and five scores. Holmes could have been one of the most successful wideouts in the history of the franchise, but the team decided to set an example for players who cannot stay out of trouble, and cut his career in Pittsburgh short with the April 2010 trade to the Jets.

83 Experience Steelers History at the Hall of Fame

History surrounds you when you travel to the small town of Canton, Ohio, and the Pro Football Hall of Fame is alive with tons of great history from the NFL and the Pittsburgh Steelers. The Hall of Fame, which is open from 9:00 AM to 5:00 PM every day except Christmas, is a great trip for any Steelers fan, and a great trip in general to learn about the history of the game.

Located about two hours from Pittsburgh, the Pro Football Hall of Fame is worth every second of the visit. From the moment you walk into the gift shop that boasts tons of great NFL merchandise, there are signs of Steeler Nation everywhere. The Steelers have plenty to boast about in the Hall, with 22 busts of those in the organization, from founder Art Rooney to Jack Butler and Dermontti Dawson, who entered the Hall in 2012.

There are also lots of great Steelers artifacts from various events that have to be seen to be believed. Ever see the actual piece of turf where Franco Harris caught the Immaculate Reception? Yes, the Pro Football Hall of Fame has it. Hines Ward's jersey from when he made a catch against Cincinnati on September 27, 2009, to put him at 10,000 receiving yards in his career is also there.

How about the Steelers' Super Bowl cooler from their 27–23 dramatic win over Arizona in Super Bowl XLIII? Yep, the Hall of Fame has it on display. And another great piece of old-school Steelers is an official game program from the team's opening-day win over the rival Oakland Raiders on September 17, 1972, at Three Rivers Stadium. The cost of that program—a whopping $1.

The Pro Football Hall of Fame opened on September 7, 1963, and has since seen plenty of Steelers faithful as well as players come through the doors. The current price to enter the Hall is $18 for adults, $12 for children 14 and under, and $15 for seniors 62 and over. The Hall itself usually takes about two to three hours to visit, and aside from the busts of the Hall of Famers, there are plenty of other great areas to see while you are there.

The Gameday Theater is one of the best experiences at the Hall. Opening in 1995, the theater shows a film that highlights the league from the long days of training camp to the hoisting of the Lombardi Trophy at the Super Bowl. While at the theater, your seat actually turns around to show you a different screen as the season progresses. It's an amazing experience, and like a lot in the Hall, there are plenty of Steelers highlights embedded in the film that will excite Black and Gold fans.

There are areas of the Hall dedicated to all the teams in the NFL, even those that no longer exist. It also tells of the rich history of pro football, showing fans some of the earliest artifacts, from Jim Thorpe to Vince Lombardi. There is an area for fans to see the history of the teams, and the Steelers wall, encased with a large portrait of running back Jerome Bettis, has a rundown of the team's divisional titles, conference titles, and, of course, its six Super Bowl titles.

Being at the Pro Football Hall of Fame for enshrinement weekend is a spectacular event. The football world looks upon Canton for the weekend, and it's not unheard of to run into Steelers Hall of Famers at the Hall that weekend—some of them usually make their way to Canton to see that year's class be inducted into the Hall of Fame.

The Pro Football Hall of Fame weekend then concludes with the Hall of Fame Game, and the Steelers are 3–2 in the game, last winning in what was Mike Tomlin's first game as the team's coach back on August 5, 2007, topping the New Orleans Saints 20–7. You can get all the information you need for the Pro Football Hall of Fame at www.profootballhof.com. It's a trip that is well worth any Steelers fan's time and one that is unforgettable.

84 Steelers Get "Tebowed" in Playoff Loss to Denver

The 2011 Steelers season saw the team win 12 games, but two losses to the Ravens cost them the AFC North title. The team had issues down the stretch, and in a late-season win over the Browns, QB Ben Roethlisberger suffered an ankle injury that made a trip back to the Super Bowl seem like an impossibility.

The team was also without the services of running back Rashard Mendenhall, who was injured in the team's finale against the Browns. The team would have to rely on a gimpy Roethlisberger and backup running back Isaac Redman, who was going to get a majority of the work on the ground.

Many felt their first playoff game was going to be a win, despite being on the road, as the team traveled to play the Denver Broncos in Invesco Field at Mile High. The game, played on January 8,

2012, was going to be between the NFL's top-ranked defense and a QB in Tim Tebow who threw for just 60 yards with an interception in Denver's 7–3 loss to the Chiefs the previous week.

Tebow's plight as a NFL quarterback was one that had been the lead story on the news, and emotions were stirred whenever his name was mentioned. His games always seemed to have more eyes watching them anytime he came on the field to lead the offense. Tebow never seemed to get the job done the easy way, which is why many had become fans of his.

Tebow had also become the most outspoken NFL player when it came to his faith. He was seen on NFL Films singing hymns before games, and he led prayer circles after games at midfield. He was the All-American kid, a guy that many fans either couldn't stand or cheered on every play.

None of that was the Steelers' concern this day, and it was tough to find any national expert who didn't think the Steelers would walk out of Denver with a win. Many felt their defense was just too good, and that the Steelers offense would easily score enough points to take down Tebow and the Broncos.

The Steelers were near double-digit favorites for the game, and it looked for the first quarter as if the experts were right. They took a quick 6–0 lead on two field goals, with Tebow showing no early signs of being able to figure out the Steelers' top-ranked defense.

Then, just that fast, the game changed. Steelers veterans Casey Hampton and Brett Keisel both went down with injuries on the defensive line early in the game, and after losing the two linemen Pittsburgh was nowhere near as formidable as it was when it held Denver to 10 total yards on its first two possessions.

Tebow started to hit his stride, completing passes downfield, and the game turned into a nightmare for the Steelers and Steeler Nation, with Denver going on a scoring spree in the second quarter, amassing 20 points. To say that it was stunning was an understatement.

Down 20–6 at the half, it would be up to Roethlisberger, who would have to attack the Denver defense to get the Steelers back into the game. The team rallied and cut the score to 20–13 with a one-yard TD run from Mike Wallace, and then a Shaun Suisham 37-yard field goal with 9:59 to play closed it to 23–16.

LaMarr Woodley recovered a fumble, and the Steelers tied the game with 3:48 to play when Roethlisberger hit Jerricho Cotchery with a 31-yard touchdown. The two teams traded possessions, and it seemed the momentum was on the Steelers' side when the clock hit zero and the game headed into overtime.

Denver got the ball first, and with the new OT rules, the only way the Steelers could lose on the first possession was via a Broncos touchdown, something Tebow and Denver had not scored since the second quarter. Little did Pittsburgh know what was about to happen.

With the ball at the 20, Tebow dialed up a play action and hit Demaryius Thomas for an 80-yard touchdown pass. Ryan Mundy came up for help against the run, and Tebow threw a perfect pass to Thomas, who torched Ike Taylor for 204 yards on four catches that day.

Thomas hauled in a high pass at the Denver 38, stiff-armed Taylor, and then outraced Mundy to the end zone. Tebow knelt in his own end zone, pounding a fist in triumph before taking a victory lap in jubilation, ending the season for the Steelers.

Tebow threw for 316 yards on 10-for-21 passing. Roethlisberger was 22-for-40 for 289 yards with a touchdown and a pick. After the game the stunned Steelers said they hadn't underestimated Tebow or the Broncos offense. It sure didn't look that way watching the game.

The Broncos lost the following week, but it didn't lessen the hurt the Steelers felt after being knocked out of the postseason a year after playing for the sport's biggest prize.

85 Maddox and Vick 2003 Wild West Shootout at Heinz

The 2002 season was one of transition for the Steelers. The team had reached the AFC Championship Game the season before but fell short of its goal of playing in the Super Bowl after a 24–17 upset loss to the heavy underdog New England Patriots. The next season started slowly—the team fell to the champion Pats on a Monday night to start the year 30–14, then the following Sunday night were carved up 30–17 by Rich Gannon and the Raiders at home.

Part of the issue was the play at quarterback. Head coach Bill Cowher had lost confidence in starter Kordell Stewart, who had played so well a season before but was unable to duplicate that at the start of the '02 season. In Week 3 against Cleveland at home the team was stale again and trailed late 13–6. Cowher made a bold move, benching Stewart for former Arena League quarterback and former first-round bust Tommy Maddox, who, being the backup, was the apple of every fan's eye.

The move paid off. Maddox lead the team to a score to tie the game, then in overtime was able to put together a drive to lead the team to a much-needed 16–13 win. It was evident that the offense responded to whatever magic Maddox had, and talk quickly turned to how this former XFLer was tearing up the league.

The Steelers' season turned around. They went on a four-game winning streak to turn a 1–3 start into a 5–3 mark heading into an early November game at home against Michael Vick and the Atlanta Falcons. The crowd at Heinz Field was in for a show—Vick and Maddox lit up the Pittsburgh sky with footballs and points in a game that would go down as one of the most memorable in Steelers history.

The game didn't start out as a barn-burner. The Steelers led just 3–0 after the first quarter. That's when things quickly got going. First it was the Falcons with a score when Vick hit Shawn Jefferson with a 43-yard pass to make it 7–3 Falcons before two minutes had even passed in the second quarter. The Steelers came right back with Maddox hitting Plaxico Burress for 33 yards to make it 10–7. The fireworks had truly begun.

Maddox less than two minutes later had the ball again and found Hines Ward from five yards out to extend the Steelers' lead to 17–7 with 7:15 left in the half. That's how the first half would end, and things seemed to be headed in the Steelers' favor. The first-half numbers were staggering: the Steelers already had 15 first downs and 270 yards, with Maddox throwing for 188 yards and two scores.

Atlanta wouldn't go down easily, and Warrick Dunn put on a show in the second half. It started with him going for a score from 59 yards out to make it 17–14. But Maddox, playing the gunslinger, found Burress again, this time from 62 yards out to put the Steelers back out in front 23–14 after the extra point was blocked.

A Falcons field goal with 6:07 left in the third made it 23–17, and again here came Maddox and the Steelers' offense. Maddox led the team on a seven-play drive that covered 67 yards and found tight end Jerame Tuman for an 18-yard score. The two-point conversion was Maddox to Ward, and the Steelers' lead with 2:25 left in the quarter was up to 31–17.

Things really seemed to go the Steelers' way when Todd Peterson hit a 34-yard field goal to make it 34–17 with 12:34 left, but little did the Steelers faithful know that Michael Vick and company were about to put on an offensive show of their own. The Falcons' quarterback led the team on a quick 2:34 drive that ended with a short touchdown pass to make it 34–24. Five minutes later Vick put together a long 10-play drive to make it a seven-point game with 2:26 left after a 40-yard Jay Feely field goal.

Tommy Maddox hit for 28 completions and 473 yards with four touchdowns in a shootout with Michael Vick and the Atlanta Falcons in November 2002. The game ended in a 34–34 tie.

Pittsburgh's offense, which had been so good all day, went into a shell. Amos Zereoue gained seven yards on two runs, then on third down Maddox looked to Ward, but the ball was incomplete, and the team was forced to punt with 2:04 left as the Falcons wisely used their timeouts to save precious clock.

The punt was a good one at the Falcons 16, but Allen Rossum took it back to midfield as he weaved his way for a 34-yard return. Quickly Vick went to work against an already tired Steelers defense. He hit Jefferson for 20 yards, then found him again for 23 yards to the 7 with 1:33 left. It took just two more plays for the former first overall pick of the 2001 draft to go in from seven yards out to tie the game 34–34. Heinz Field was shell-shocked, to say the least.

After four quarters that seemed to go on forever, the game went to overtime. The Steelers had the first shot and drove to the Falcons' 30. With a chance to win the game, Peterson's 48-yard field-goal attempt was blocked, keeping the Falcons' chances alive. The Steelers' defense came alive, helped out by a 14-yard sack of Vick that killed any chances the Falcons had.

Pittsburgh's second drive chewed up more than five minutes of the clock but stalled as the team had a huge holding penalty on the Falcons' 26 that killed any chance they had of moving again into field-goal range. Four plays later, Cowher decided against trying a 50-yard field goal and played it safe—Josh Miller punted 22 yards to the Falcons' 11.

The defense held, and again the Steelers had the ball with 2:48 left in overtime. On the third play of the drive, Maddox was picked off at the Steelers' 44, giving the Falcons a chance to win the game. Atlanta drove to the Steelers' 37, where Feely's 56-yard field-goal attempt was blocked, giving Maddox and his receivers one shot at a Hail Mary with one second left.

From his own 49, Maddox fired the ball high toward the goal line, and Burress made a mid-air catch. He was knocked down right away, which was a problem considering he was down at the 1-yard line. The refs looked at the play to make sure Burress didn't by chance get in, and he didn't, ending the game in a 34–34 tie.

The game set all kinds of records on both sides. The Steelers had 30 first downs, 645 yards of offense, and Maddox hit for 28 completions and 473 yards with four touchdowns. Zereoue ran for 123 yards, and Burress set Steelers receiving records with nine catches for 253 yards and two scores.

The game is recalled by many as possibly the most entertaining in Heinz Field history, and most say it was "Touchdown" Tommy Maddox's best day as a pro.

The First NFL Tie

Since the NFL put into play one 15-minute overtime period for regular-season games in 1974, the Steelers have had just two ties, including the first official tie. That took place in Week 2 of the 1974 season, when the Steelers traveled to Denver and battled the Broncos to a 35–35 final score. The other tie was the wild affair between Tommy Maddox and Michael Vick in 2002.

86 Join a Steelers Fan Club

It is impossible to tell how many Steelers fans currently don the colors of the black and gold each week when the team takes the field. With two Super Bowl wins over the past few seasons, it's not a shock to see the fan base grow. The Steelers and their fans have always traveled well, and it's not a surprise to see more members of Steeler Nation in an opponent's stadium than hometown fans.

As Steeler Nation has grown, there has been an upswing in the amount of national Steelers fan clubs, and there's also a large amount of bars and restaurants that host Steelers parties each week, even in cities where wearing Steelers colors are not always welcome.

In northeast Ohio, for example, there are a couple local places to gather and watch Steelers games. One such place is called The Blue Moose in Parma. Watching Steelers fans, old and young, chomping on the establishment's wings and outshining Browns fans can be humorous. And Browns fans who venture in during a game day have to know that they'll clearly be outnumbered.

The *Pittsburgh Post-Gazette*'s Steeler Nation page has links for no less than 31 Steelers fan clubs across the country. Steelcity Mafia hosts one of the biggest Steelers fans bases in the country, and a visit to their web page will show current and older players such as James Harrison and Rocky Belier wearing their merchandise.

Steelheadz of Virginia is another big fan club that boasts a large membership as well as get-togethers among Steelers fans. Anywhere you look, there seems to be a state that has a Steelers fan club. From New Jersey to Hawaii, the Steelers continue to be a true nation of fans.

Below are just a few of the current Steelers fan clubs:

Steelers in Hoboken, New Jersey
SteelersNYC
Southern Steel Fan Club of North Texas
DC Steelers Nation
SteelCity Mafia
Hawaii Steelheads
SteelTown in Uptown Charlotte, North Carolina
Harolds Steelers Fan Club
Iron City Pittsburgh Club of South Florida
Northwest Steeler Nation
Steelheadz of Virginia
Steeler Nation in Mexico
Jacksonville Black and Gold
Bay Area Black and Gold Club
Steelers Fan Club of Maryland
Steelers UK
Steelers Ohio
Steelers World in Germany
Pittsburgh Steelers Club of Atlanta
Las Vegas Steelers
Kansas City Steelers Club
Connecticut Steelers
Philly Steelers
Steelers Fans of Minnesota
Indy Steelers
Black & Gold Brigade
Steel Triangle Fan Club (Raleigh)
Psycho Steelers Fans of Panama City, Florida
Central Florida Black & Gold
Tulsa Steelers Fanatics
Triad Steelers (North Carolina Piedmont)
Heart of Dixie Steelers Fan Club

The clubs have always had their say at both home and away games. The Steelers have long been known for their very loyal and vocal fan base, and just by the number of fan clubs you see above, you know that just about no matter where you live, you are not alone in your support of the Black and Gold.

So if you feel you are in an area of the country that does not support the Steelers like it should, or at least as much as you do, do yourself a favor, jump on the computer, and look up local Steelers fan clubs or even find a meeting spot for other loyal fans to sit back and enjoy the games. You just may be surprised.

87 Sandwich Mania Takes Over Pittsburgh

Football and food seem to go hand and hand in our culture. Whether it's die-hard fans grilling outside the stadium on a Sunday morning, or fans ordering food over the phone on game day, having food, and a lot of it, is a staple when watching your favorite NFL team do battle on the field.

In Pittsburgh, food and the Steelers are very much connected, and it starts with the chain of shops that make the food. In Steeler Country, if you have never had a Primanti Brothers sandwich while enjoying a Steelers triumph, you have truly been missing the boat.

The sandwich chain shops were started back in 1933 (that was the year the Steelers joined the NFL—coincidence?). Currently there are stores that sell the famous sandwiches in Pittsburgh and surrounding suburbs, as well as three in Fort Lauderdale, Florida.

So just what is a Primanti Brothers sandwich, and what makes it so special? Well, it basically is a sandwich as big as any you will ever see. Two thick pieces of Italian bread, one or more grilled meats, cole slaw with Italian dressing, tomato, cheese, and, to top it off, french fries.

There's really only one word to describe it when you get one of these delicious Steeler staples in your hands: *wow*. It's a sandwich with the sides on it, which was exactly the premise that founder Joe Primanti was going for when he started the sandwich shop during the Great Depression. It was a perfect sandwich for on-the-go truck drivers who wanted to eat their sandwich (and the sides) with one hand while driving.

Joe's brothers, Dick and Stanley, joined up with him a little later and the first shop was opened on Smallman and 18th streets in the Strip District. The sandwiches have grown into an institution among Steeler faithful, and the stores are packed on game day with fans, and also late at night; it's the perfect food to eat after taking in a few beverages at your favorite watering hole.

The most popular Primanti Brothers sandwich is the cheesesteak, but there's a ton of different options to choose from, and the restaurants even offer cheeseburgers, pizza, and wings for those who, for whatever reason, can't seem to inhale an entire sandwich. The sandwich shops can be found not only in various Pittsburgh locations but also at Heinz Field as well, making it even easier for fans to enjoy their favorite variety of sandwich.

The sandwich spot has not been a secret for a long time, as national shows like *Man vs. Food* on the Travel Channel have filmed there, and even Jon Stewart talked about the sandwich on *The Daily Show*. The shops are a huge stop for tourists, as they not only have great food but also provide a great Steel City atmosphere.

Fans of the Pirates can find the sandwiches at PNC Park, where ESPN.com called it the number one concession on the menu. There's a certain comfort about going to a game and being able to enjoy your favorite Primanti Brothers sandwich; it's a mouthwatering experience that is a must for folks visiting Pittsburgh, or for that special game-day experience on Steeler Sundays.

88 Cowher Shines on Monday Night

The Steelers' players through the years have always enjoyed the stage of the big game. After all, they are 6–1 in seven Super Bowls and have risen to the occasion when the spotlight is on. For Bill Cowher, his coaching career always seemed in the spotlight, and the team *seemed to rise up for their coach when they had the Monday Night Football* lights on them.

The final game of the week has always had tons of eyes upon it. Everyone around the league—players, coaches, fans, and all the rest made *Monday Night Football* a tradition. Now it seems that the spotlight has turned a bit to Sunday night football on NBC, but Monday night remains a big part of fans' and players' viewing habits, even now that the game has moved over to ESPN.

When Cowher took over the team in 1992, something seemed to happen to the team when it came to playing under the lights. Sure, they had won plenty of games on Monday night under Chuck Noll (15–14 in 29 Monday night games), but nothing like under Cowher.

It started with an innocent 20–0 pounding of the hapless Cincinnati Bengals on October 19, 1992. From there, the team became the heavyweight champs of Monday night for some time. They went 6–0 in Cowher's first three seasons on Monday night, including two wins over the Buffalo Bills and three wins in their 9–7 1993 wild-card season.

The team finally fell on Monday night in the heat of Miami on September 18, 1995. The 9:00 PM kickoff didn't take away from the stifling heat in Miami, where it was 91 degrees, and the Steelers melted under the Dolphins 23–10. Despite that, they went on another four-game winning streak under Cowher on Monday night, taking his record to 10–1 with wins over the Browns, Bills, Chiefs, and Dolphins before they fell again in the spotlight in Jacksonville 30–21 on September 22, 1997.

It was that game in which Cowher almost pulled off a major coaching no-no—slugging a player. Yes, as the Steelers were looking to kick what would have been a winning field goal as time expired, Norm Johnson's kick was blocked. Chris Hudson of the Jags picked it up, and as he went down the sideline for a score to seal the win, Cowher looked as if he was going to lunge and throw a punch. He pulled back, lucky for him, and allowed Hudson to dance into the end zone to finish off the nine-point win.

Despite that loss, the Steelers and Cowher remained very good on Monday night over the years. He finished his 15-year coaching career with the Steelers 18–9 on Monday night, going an amazing 11–0 at home.

The Steelers were about as good as any team in football on Monday night on their home turf, outscoring the opposition 262–98 in those wins, an average final score of 23.8–8.9. While Mike Tomlin has already had success with his Steelers teams on the Monday night stage—going 4–0 in his first two seasons as head coach—it was a well-known fact that Cowher and his teams always got up for the prime-time spotlight.

89 "Renegade" Fires Up the Fans

If you have ever been to Heinz Field for a Steelers game, you no doubt have heard the stadium rock to a classic tune that, depending on your age, you may be familiar with. The song is played once per game (unless there is dire need), and the opposing teams usually lose their hearing once it fills up the stadium speakers and gets the Steelers and their fans in a frenzy.

The song is "Renegade" by Styx, a 1978 release that has gained more popularity thanks to Steeler Nation than anyone could have imagined. It's a huge part of the atmosphere at Heinz Field and a fan favorite that has become the theme song that fires up the defense and the crowd.

How did a song off a 32-year-old album become a hit to more than 65,000 fans every time the Steelers need a lift? Pretty much the way anything becomes popular—luck. Legend has it that the song was brought up to Steelers TV executive Rick Fairbend about two months before Heinz Field opened. At the time, a marketing assistant named Mike Marchinsky suggested the song be played at games. Marchinsky said he thought the song would sound cool at games after hearing it on a Styx's greatest hits album.

"It's a perfect song for Pittsburgh," Fairbend told NFL Films. "It's classic rock, it's what our crowd embodies." The song starts slow, builds up, and eventually hits the crowd with pounding lyrics about an outlaw who has been captured and is saying his sorrys and good-byes before he is hung from the gallows.

The song really took form in the Steelers' 2002 playoff game against the Browns at Heniz Field. Trailing 24–7 in the third quarter, the song played and got the crowd pumped up. The team started a frantic comeback, and the song got its encore when the Steelers went up 36–33 with less than a minute left. The team won by three, and the song has been in stadium circulation ever since.

Fairbend says that the team itself has called from the bench to have the song played, but they only throw it up there at the right times. You always know when the song is about to be played—the scoreboard goes totally blank. It's at that point the crowd knows it's time to get ready. "Renegade" is about to hit.

"The crowd, the offense, everyone on the entire sideline just gets so excited for it," Ben Roethlisberger said about the song. "I get goose bumps just thinking about it." Even the head coach approves of the song's impact on the team and crowd. "I like it, it gets our crowd up, and I think it brings the best out in us," Mike Tomlin said.

"Renegade" is now the staple of the team. It has started to get played at high school games and even in weddings, all thanks to an interesting idea by a marketing assistant who one day got a greatest hits CD and an idea. And now it's the song Steeler Nation is known by.

90 Public Enemy No. 1: Tom Brady

Throughout the course of Steelers history, there have been teams that have put a dagger into the hearts of the Steelers and their fans—teams like the 1994 Chargers that topped Pittsburgh in the AFC Championship Game or the 1995 Dallas Cowboys who overcame the Steelers in Super Bowl XXX.

A backup quarterback named Cody Carlson once took over for an injured Warren Moon in 1990 and on the final day of the regular season torched the Steelers to knock them out of the playoffs. Worse, it came in front of a national audience on Sunday night football.

With that said, no one player seems to have more disdain for Steeler Nation than Patriots future Hall of Fame quarterback Tom Brady. He has given the Steelers nightmares and basically has been responsible for keeping them out of not one but two Super Bowls under Bill Cowher. He also has recorded a couple of huge regular-season wins, against teams led by both Cowher and Mike Tomlin.

To say that Brady is everything that the Steelers fans dislike is an understatement. He's handsome, married to a model, and has graced the cover of *GQ* magazine. Yuck. If there's anything that Steelers fans hate, it's a guy who not only seems to have it all on the field, but off of it as well. You can't deny Brady's success, though. He's a sure first-ballot Hall of Famer and a guy who has broken plenty of hearts in Steeler Nation.

Brady stepped into the role of the quarterback Steelers fan love to hate in the 2001 season when he started for the underdog Pats in the AFC Championship Game against Kordell Stewart and the 13–3 Steelers. He didn't have a great impact in the upset win, but he did go 12-for-18 for 115 yards before he left the game with a knee injury and was relieved by Drew Bledsoe. New England ended the Steelers' season 24–17 mostly thanks to a blocked field goal for a score and a punt return for a score. Even so, the stage was set for Steelers fans to loathe Brady the following week when he hoisted the Lombardi Trophy after beating the St. Louis Rams 20–17 in New Orleans.

The Steelers and Patriots next met on opening night the following season. But while the Steelers might have had revenge on their minds, they were once again put to sleep by Brady, who threw for 294 yards and three scores for a 30–14 final score.

It took a bewitching holiday two years later for the Steelers to finally stop Brady. On Halloween 2004 rookie quarterback Ben Roethlisberger and the team halted the Pats' 21-game winning streak, winning 34–20 to go 15–1 in the regular season. But the Steelers weren't clear of Brady for good—he'd still find a way to break the fans' hearts yet that season. In one of the toughest playoff losses in Steelers history, Brady and New England returned to Heinz Field on January 23 and soundly beat Pittsburgh in the AFC Championship Game 41–27. Brady was on fire all day, hitting on 14-of-21 passes for 207 yards and two touchdowns to go along with a QB rating of 130.5. It was a long hard day for Cowher and the Steelers, and yet another day that Brady celebrated at the Steelers' expense. Maybe the toughest part was the fact that the night before, Brady was getting intravenous treatment as he ran a temperature of 103 degrees.

The following season he once again came into Pittsburgh and rolled the Steelers for 372 yards, going 31-of-41 and helping the Pats to a 23–20 win in Week 3. About the only saving grace was that New England was knocked out of the playoffs by the Broncos. The following day the Steelers topped the No. 1–seed Colts in the playoffs to earn the right to travel to Denver, where they beat the Broncos and eventually progressed to their fifth Super Bowl victory.

The final Brady win over the Steelers came in Week 14 of 2007, the Patriots' undefeated regular season. Upset by a guarantee by Steelers safety Anthony Madison that the Steelers would win, Brady gouged the team, going 32-of-46 for 399 yards and four touchdowns as New England won 34–13. It was the first time that Mike Tomlin felt the wrath of Brady against a Steelers defense, and the quarterback made it look rather easy.

At the end of the day, the numbers and record Brady has put up against the Steelers cannot be denied. He owns a lifetime 6–2 mark against them, throwing for 2,207 yards with 14 touchdowns and only five interceptions. Maybe one day in a big game the Steelers will have the last laugh, but for now, Brady remains Public Enemy No. 1 on the list of players Steelers fans love to hate.

91 Take In a Road Game with the Rest of Steeler Nation

Living in Cleveland all my life, I have been lucky enough to see plenty of Steelers-Browns games at the old Cleveland Stadium before becoming a member of the media in 1994. From there, I was able to attend games at Three Rivers, then Heinz Field, and I continued to see Steelers-Browns games in Cleveland, but from a totally different view. With that said, there has always been a simple fact that has amazed me about Steelers fans, and that simply is how many of them travel to see their team's games.

When the Steelers were not very good in the late 1980s, and even before Bill Cowher stepped in for Chuck Noll, the fans were passionate, but it didn't seem like they traveled with the club like they do now. Sure, there would be a smattering of fans in Cleveland Stadium and elsewhere, but Steelers fans seemed a bit reserved.

Once the club had a mini-rebirth in 1992, the floodgates for fans to invade stadiums all over America seemed to open. So as a

"Gerela's Gorillas"

Another colorful character of the Steelers' 1970s title teams was that of kicker Roy Gerela, who joined the Steelers in 1971 after playing with Houston for two years. Gerela kicked for the team from 1971 to 1978, and became an unlikely fan favorite. He got so popular with the Steelers' Ukrainian following, they started a fan club called "Gerela's Gorillas." A fan even came to the game dressed in a gorilla suit to cheer the kicker on. Gerela won three rings with the Steelers and went on to become an assistant coach at his alma mater, New Mexico State. He still ranks third on the Steelers' all-time scoring list behind Gary Anderson and current kicker Jeff Reed.

fan, if you have never had the pleasure of joining Steeler Nation on the road, do yourself a favor and find a way to get there as soon as you can.

Sure, it will take some effort, but this is the Black and Gold we're talking about. There's no better feeling than seeing a Steelers celebration in an opposing stadium. Usually you have to beware of a couple of things, which of course includes the belittling before the game from home-team fans, and if the Steelers happen to lose, you had better get ready for some real razzing as you leave the stadium.

The other thing about taking in a road game is your overall attitude. Remember, you are on enemy turf, and these people don't like you much, so being at least a little gracious is almost a must if you don't want to be swinging fists. If you go into an opposing stadium giving attitude to home fans, you're likely not only going to not be liked, you're going to end up having to defend yourself— it's just human nature.

I recall a Browns-Steelers game in 1993 at Cleveland Stadium. As a fan with my father (who is a Browns fan), I had my face painted half black and half yellow, was wearing my Merril Hoge jersey, and was ready to cheer on my team to win. Well, let's just say that my mouth got a little too loud for the fans' liking, nothing vulgar, just flat out cheering, and by the fourth quarter, it was dear old dad stepping in to protect his young. It's an experience you simply have to be careful of. Oh, and the Steelers lost 28–23 after Eric Metcalf's second punt return for a score, which made matters worse.

So be ready to be loud, but also be smart. If you're going to an opposing stadium where the team is not very good, you usually can get away with more, but at a place where the team is in the division, like Baltimore, or fighting for a playoff spot, things could easily get tense based on how things play out.

Back in 2005 when the team was in the playoffs, their first game was in Cincinnati, and of course the upper corner my seat was in had plenty of other Steelers fans, but things did get very tense. Even more so when Carson Palmer's knee was shredded by Kimo von Oelhoffen early in the game. Bengals fans felt it was their day, and they didn't want to hear it from Steelers fans after their franchise quarterback had just been knocked out. So again, be gracious when you show up at opposing stadiums.

As far as finding tickets, there are places like eBay and StubHub that have tickets for every game, but be prepared to pay. Fans of other teams are not dumb, and they know that in some cases they can almost pay for their season tickets if they just sell their tickets to that one Steelers game. Fans of the Black and Gold simply are willing to pay, so be prepared to pay a hefty price to see the Steelers on the road.

Places like Jacksonville have Steelers fan clubs, so if you're going to a place like that, look it up beforehand to see if there are any events. Also look into buying a white Steelers road jersey, you want to make sure you look the part. It shouldn't be tough to find other Steelers fans in opposing stadiums—all you have to look for is yellow towels.

"You know, I'll be honest with you, it was kind of surprising there were a lot of Steelers fans in the crowd," former Redskins coach Jim Zorn said after a Steelers Monday night win in D.C. in 2008. "It reminded me of the Super Bowl in '05 when they were giving out those yellow towels and stuff like that. I don't think it affected us any, but it was unusual to see so many yellow towels."

Make your presence known, Steeler Nation, and do it on the road, where sometimes it means the most.

92 1989 Season Opens with Historic Loss

While there have been some memorable games in the Steelers-Browns rivalry, one game that Steelers fans would love to forget was the opening day massacre laid on the club by the Browns in 1989. The Steelers were coming off a 5–11 season in 1988, and while there wasn't much expected of the 1989 team, the young club under the control of coach Chuck Noll was hoping to get off to a fast start that season.

Needless to say, opening day at Three Rivers Stadium against the Browns was a way to do it, but not only didn't it happen, the team also was beaten from pillar to post that afternoon.

The matchup took place on September 10 and was a late-afternoon start on the opening-day slate. The game also had some intrigue—former Steelers defensive coordinator Bud Carson, who led the team on defense in the great days of the Steel Curtain, was the new head coach of the Browns. You could see after the game just how much it pained Carson to have beaten his close friend Noll and the Steelers so badly.

Needless to say, nothing went right for the Steelers on this gray day at home. The club committed eight turnovers, as new Steelers running back Tim Worley, a first-round pick that April, lost three fumbles in his first start. The fumbles led Cleveland to a 17–0 lead in the first quarter, and it was more than over at halftime as the

Steelers Use Blowout as Motivation to Get Revenge

The Steelers' 1989 season recovered two weeks after the awful 51–0 defeat by the Browns, as they beat Minnesota at home and got things turned around. The rematch with the Browns took place in Cleveland on October 15, and the club got a measure of revenge, beating Cleveland 17–7 to move to 3–3 on the season.

The Steelers had to start Todd Blackledge at quarterback for an injured Bubby Brister, and he wasn't exactly stellar, hitting on just 32 percent of his passes. The Browns gave the game away, committing seven turnovers as the Steelers picked off Bernie Kosar four times. The Steelers built a 10–0 lead, then after Cleveland drew close at 10–7 in the fourth quarter, the Steelers put the game away when Dwight Stone returned the ensuing kickoff deep into Browns territory, and a Warren Williams score closed the win for the gritty Steelers.

Browns led 30–0. Worley's first fumble at the Steelers' 5 was recovered by Browns linebacker Clay Matthews for a quick touchdown.

Bubby Brister, the starting quarterback for the Steelers on that fateful day, also didn't play well, struggling just like the rest of the team. The quarterback was 10-for-22 for 84 yards and three picks. One pick tipped off the hands of fullback Merril Hoge and was returned for a score by Browns linebacker David Grayson. The linebacker had a career day, scoring on a 28-yard fumble return and then a 14-yard interception return, as well.

The stats for the game were mind-boggling. The Browns had 19 first downs to just five for the Steelers. Cleveland had 357 yards to just 53 for Pittsburgh. Cleveland also dominated the time of possession, holding the ball for 40:50 to just 19:10 for the Black and Gold. The Steelers crossed midfield only once, and Brister was sacked five times.

"It was the worst I've ever seen as a coach," Noll said after the game. In a statement of the obvious, Tunch Ilkin maybe said it best: "We stunk today." Brister, who was never one to mince words, took the loss maybe harder than some of his teammates. "You saw it, I saw it. Everybody saw it," he said. "We looked like [expletive]. Every time we tried something, it turned into a disaster."

Brister was out to prove that he was a quality NFL quarterback, and the game did little to prove that he was a quarterback on the rise in the NFL. He did rebound to have a better season and a career that spanned a couple of teams and a Super Bowl title with Denver, but opening day 1989 was a bitter memory.

The headline in the following morning's *Pittsburgh Post-Gazette* said it all: "51–0—Steelers Bomb in Opener as Browns Waltz to Win." The loss is the worst in franchise history, and it erased the prior worst defeat, a 54–7 loss to the Green Bay Packers in 1941.

While the season started with that setback and a defeat the following week (41–10 against the Bengals), Noll got things turned around by Week 3, and the club went 9–7, making the second round of the playoffs before losing to eventual AFC champion Denver.

93 Black and Gold on the Web

In this day and age of fansites and blogs that cover just about anything you can want in the world, the Pittsburgh Steelers have their share of sites dedicated to every facet of the team. Of course, like any NFL team, the Steelers have their own official site, which is simply www.steelers.com. The site is one of the better ones of the NFL teams, with fantastic coverage of Steelers news, as well as a lot of multimedia information. They also post a lot of the team's official press releases and have info on tickets and other Steelers-related events. Longtime Steelers writers Bob Labriola and Teresa Varley do an amazing job with the site and with stories.

The Steelers Official Newspaper

The Steelers' official newspaper, *Steelers Digest*, has been published for the past 25 years and is read by Steelers fans worldwide. The publication is sent out 24 times a year, once a week during the preseason and regular season, and once a month in the off-season. While the Web is a great place for breaking Steelers news, *Steelers Digest* does an excellent job of commentary and in-depth coverage of the club.

As far as fan sites go, I am little biased toward my own Steelers site—www.steelersgab.com. It's my passion and was a dream to always be able to write about the team that I love, and when my partner and I started our network in August 2006, right away I thought about doing a site dedicated to the Steelers. That dream came true when we expanded our network in June 2007, and needless to say it's been a great ride since. Steelers Gab has always been a great place to hear what fans think, as well, and even after the toughest losses, fans are always ready to speak up on the Black and Gold.

SB Nation's Steelers site is www.behindthesteelcurtain.com. The site is huge and also has a solid following of Steelers fans. They also have the partnership of Yahoo! Sports behind them, which gives them even more of a following. The site also has plenty of quality Steelers info, such as a roster, stats, and some great commentary.

Steel Curtain Rising (www.steelcurtainrising.blogspot.com) is a solid site that's been around since 2008. It is filled with solid commentary and good news items that Steelers fans should visit every day or two. The site doesn't have a ton of bells and whistles, but some of the commentary and stories are very interesting and well-written.

Another very good site run by the Fansided network is Nice Pick Cowher (www.nicepickcowher.com). They have a lot of up-to-date Steelers news, along with solid commentary about the team and coverage of other teams around the NFL.

Steelers Today (www.steelerstoday.com) has a lot of Steelers news and does a nice job covering the team from all the big news to the roster moves and whatnot. Joey Porter's Pit Bulls (www.joeyporterspitbulls.blogspot.com) goes back to November 2006 and does a good job on commentary and news on the Steelers. It also covers the Pirates and Penguins, as well, to give Pittsburgh fans a lot to choose from.

A couple Steelers players have their own websites as well, including quarterback Ben Roethlisberger, who has a site at www.BigBen7.com with some news as well as the goings on of the franchise quarterback. Linebacker Lawrence Timmons blogs at his own site, located at www.timmons94.com. He writes there on a regular basis on the team and his personal on-field experiences.

So when it comes to covering the Steelers, the Web has you covered. Whatever style of coverage you want, you are sure to find it all over the net. Take some time and visit these sites and become a part of the Steelers on the Web. It's a great way to get in on the action and be even more a part of Steeler Nation.

94 The First Game in 1933

Ever wonder where it all started? Well, the Steelers were not always the Steelers (like a lot of you already know), but they started back in 1933 as the Pirates, a group of local college players who played at Forbes Field. The club in those days was not even owned by Art Rooney, but was under the ownership of Gregory Taylor, who hailed from Lewis Center, Ohio. The first time the Steelers took the field in '33 was on September 20, and it was against a much more experienced and better club, the New York Giants.

The Pirates were coached by Jap Douds, who would only serve with the team for one season. The first game saw what was by all accounts a surprising crowd of about 25,000 fans on hand. The *Pittsburgh Post-Gazette* reported that the crowd at the team's first game "grew enthused at times but a long succession of timeouts and injuries dragged the play along and many grew impatient."

Of course the Pirates not putting up many points and being outplayed by the much more advanced and experienced Giants team may also have led to the crowd not being all that enthused about the pro game. They were used to cheering for the college game, which dominated the football landscape at the time.

"We have boys just out of college who are strong and fast and imbued with confidence and the desire to win," Douds said in the *Post-Gazette* the day before the game. "Along with these we have some experienced play in Tony Holm, Elmer Schwartz, and Bucky Moore. True, we are new to the game, but we are confident of holding our own even with the powerful Giants as opposition in the first game."

Well, the Giants were not exactly ready to allow the Pirates to have a party at their expense in the first game. The Giants, or the "Gridiron Goliaths" as the *Post-Gazette* called them the day after that game, won with 16 fourth-quarter points. The Pirates kept the game close for the first three quarters, but the Giants pulled away in the end.

The only points that the Pirates scored in their first game came on a rather unlikely play—a safety. It took place in the third quarter to make it a 7–2 game. John Oehler, a center from Purdue, blocked a punt that rolled into the end zone, an automatic safety in those days, for the only Pirates points of the night.

The Pirates walked away from the game with a defeat, but actually must have taken quite a bit out of it, since the following week they defeated the Chicago Cardinals 14–13 at home at Forbes Field. The team wrapped up its first season of pro football with a mark of 3–6–2, and Douds was replaced after the season by Luby DiMelio, who coached just one season, in 1934, as the team went 2–10.

The Pirates' jerseys looked oddly like that of a prison uniform. Yes, it was black and yellow, much like today, but that is about as far as it went. The jersey was yellow with black stripes on it. Much like hockey uniforms at the time, the Pirates had the Pittsburgh city crest on it. That changed three seasons later. These uniforms were worn again by the team in 1994 as throwbacks. Players donned the '33 uniforms in a home win over the Colts and an overtime loss in Arizona that season.

95 How the Steelers' Logo Came to Be

It's a logo that gives great pride to the team and their city, and for the Steelers, it's the only true logo they have ever known. Many people draw it, wear it, and some even tattoo it on their bodies, but a lot of people don't know the true history of the Steelers' logo and where it even came from. The logo began with the club back in 1962, when Republic Steel, based out of Cleveland, Ohio, of all places, suggested the Steelers adopt the logo for their team.

The logo includes the word "Steelers" on the left in the middle, and is surrounded by three asteroids, or hypocycloids of four cusps. The first meaning of those three asteroids, the yellow, red, and blue were: "Steel lightens your work, brightens your leisure, and widens your world." It was changed later on to represent the things that go into making steel—yellow for coal, red for iron ore, and blue for scrap steel.

The addition of the logo on the side of the Steelers' helmet didn't exactly come all that easily. In the 1950s the players wore their numbers on their helmets, while other teams in the league began to come up with popular logos. Then finally the club got the suggestion about the Steel logo, and it was officially added in 1962. The actual Steelmark logo had only the word "Steel" on it, and then in 1963 the team added the last three letters to spell out "Steelers" after a petition to AISI, who took over the logo from U.S. Steel.

One interesting thing about the Steelers' logo is the fact they are the only team of the 32 current NFL teams that wear their logo on just one side of the helmet. Of course there is only one other team in the league without a true logo whatsoever, the rival Browns, so really out of the other 31 teams with logos, the Steelers are the only one with a single logo on the right side.

That odd fact started in 1962, when Art Rooney told equipment manager Jack Hart to put the logo on just one side of the helmet. The owner wanted to see how the logo would look on the then-gold helmets the players wore, so Hart tested it on only one side. The logo looked stunning, and the team had its best season, going 9–5. When they played their first postseason game, they changed from gold to black helmets, and from there the look stuck.

Over the years the team has undergone some different uniform designs, but mostly they have stayed with black jerseys for home games and white jerseys for road games. With that said, the logo of the three asteroids has never changed, which is why when the team wears their throwback uniforms, they never need to do much with their helmets, unless they go back to the gold helmets, which has been done a few times.

At the end of the day, a suggestion from Republic Steel, a petition from the team to add a couple of letters, and a test to see how it would look on just one side of the helmets all combine to explain why the Steelers' famous logo is as it is today.

96 The 1976 Season

After winning back-to-back Super Bowls, the Steelers eyed another title in 1976. While they didn't accomplish their goal of a third straight title, what they got was a season that some say was the Steelers' best in terms of the way they dominated the NFL. The club started the year with a stunning 31–28 loss to their biggest rivals—the Oakland Raiders. The Steelers had built a lead, only to let it slip away to the team they had beaten in the previous two AFC Championship Games.

A 31–14 home win at Cleveland was followed by three straight losses, which put the team at 1–4, and it looked as if they were going to simply play out the season. They didn't lose again for two and a half months, making it to the final step before their third straight Super Bowl.

What took place was the best performance a team defense had ever seen. After quarterback Terry Bradshaw was driven into the turf by Joe "Turkey" Jones of the Cleveland Browns during the team's final regular-season loss, 18–16 in Week 5, the defense took it upon themselves to dominate the rest of the way. And what a job they did.

Starting with a 23–6 win the following week with Bradshaw out, the Steelers' defense, led by Joe Greene and the Steel Curtain, began a streak that was legendary. They scored five shutouts in the final eight weeks of the regular season, including three in a row in Weeks 7, 8, and 9, beating the Giants, Chargers, and Chiefs. They allowed the Dolphins a field goal in Week 10, then felt a letdown when they let the Oilers score two offensive touchdowns and a field goal in a 32–16 win in Week 11.

Weeks 12 and 13 saw the team dominate the Tampa Bay Buccaneers and Oilers, scoring shutouts of 42–0 and then 21–0 to end the season at 10–4. The defense allowed 22 points in the final eight weeks of the regular season, an average of 2.75 points per game. It's a mark that simply will never be broken—with the offenses the way they are today, a team scoring five shutouts in eight games is next to impossible.

The offense had its moments too, as Bradshaw came back from injury to throw for 10 touchdowns and 1,177 yards, but the running game was really the key to the offense's success. Both Franco Harris and Rocky Bleier rushed for more than 1,000 yards: Harris went for 1,128 yards and 14 touchdowns, Bleier for 1,036 yards and five scores.

The team steamrolled the Baltimore Colts 40–14 in the first playoff game in Baltimore, but the win came with a severe price. The Steelers lost both Harris and Bleier to injury, and without them the team simply couldn't stand up to their archrival the following week in the AFC Championship Game in Oakland.

With a measure of revenge on their minds for the past two AFC Championship Game losses, the Raiders exercised some demons against the beat-up Steelers, winning 24–7. The team was down to one healthy running back, Reggie Harrison, who simply wasn't Harris or Bleier. Many still consider the '76 Steelers the greatest Steelers team, and one with the best defense ever to take the field.

The team continued to play at a high level in 1977 and finally got back to the dance in the 1978 and 1979 seasons. The defense continued to play well, but by the time the Steelers made the next two Super Bowls, the offense had matured into a big-play unit, complete with Hall of Fame quarterback Bradshaw, Harris, and wideouts John Stallworth and Lynn Swann.

97 Antonio Brown

Throughout the course of Steelers history, the franchise has had a number of great wide receivers. From Hall of Famers John Stallworth to Lynn Swann, to more recent stars like Louis Lipps and Hines Ward, the team has always had great pass catchers.

The 2010 NFL Draft saw the Steelers look to add depth to their wideout corps, and with it came the drafting of a player not many knew much about—Central Michigan's Antonio Brown. Drafted in the sixth round, just making the team wasn't a sure thing for Brown, but after a training camp in which he shined, Brown quickly made his impact on a Steelers team ready to make another run at a title.

Brown grew up in Miami, but not exactly in the Miami you see on television; his was a part of Miami that was overrun with drugs and gangs. He had to learn how to survive, so leaving college early and trying to make an NFL squad was nothing compared to the way that Brown had grown up on the tough streets of Miami.

He turned to football and discovered early he was very good at it. He played quarterback in high school, and tried his talent at wide receiver at a local All-Star game. Then he decided to move away from Miami and head up north, set to try to make the Central Michigan squad as a walk-on.

Brown wound up as the best player for the Chippewas, finding his niche as a great punt and kick returner. He was named as a first-team All-American by *The Sporting News* as a punt returner in both 2008 and 2009. In his junior season, Brown turned the corner as a receiver, catching 110 passes for 1,198 yards with nine scores.

He decided that after losing his coach and quarterback at Central Michigan, it was in his best interest to move on to try his

Fourth-and-3 in AFC Title Game Frustrates Green

While Eric Green always felt he was open enough to catch a pass, no play that didn't come his way frustrated him more than the final Steelers offensive play in the 1994 AFC Championship Game loss to the San Diego Chargers.

With the Steelers down 17–13 at the San Diego 3-yard line on fourth down, a pass-play was called where quarterback Neil O'Donnell would have a couple of options once he dropped back. The quarterback took a couple steps back once he took the snap, and instead of looking to Green or another one of his possible receivers, O'Donnell threw a quick-hitter to running back Barry Foster, which was knocked down incomplete. Green was distraught as he felt he was open in the end zone and that the quarterback didn't look for him. The play would be the last in a Steelers uniform for Green, as well as for Foster.

hand in the NFL. He sat through six long rounds, but finally after watching 194 players get selected, Brown got the call from the Steelers and an opportunity to join their squad.

While it might have been a dream come true, it was not an easy path for Brown, as he faced plenty of competition to even step on the field. The first time he touched the ball as a pro, versus the Titans in Tennessee, he took the opening kickoff 89 yards for a score, but that was the highlight of his first half of his rookie season.

Brown was inactive for seven of the Steelers' first 11 games. When he did play, he didn't have that big of an impact, catching just 16 passes in the regular season, though 14 of them came in the final five games. He was starting to catch on, and little did Steelers fans know that the play that would define the postseason run of 2010 would directly involve Brown.

It took place in the AFC divisional playoff game against the hated Ravens, a game in which the Steelers struggled early and found themselves down 21–7 at halftime. They fought back and tied the game at 24–24 and faced a critical third-and-19 with 2:07 left to play. Brown lined up wide and raced past Lardarius Webb, pulling in a 58-yard pass against his helmet.

The catch set up a two-yard Rashard Mendenhall touchdown that eventually won the Steelers the game 31–24. Brown played in the next two playoff games, including the Steelers' Super Bowl XLV loss to the Green Bay Packers.

He stepped up in 2011, and while he wasn't a starter at the beginning of the season, halfway through he took over, and once he did, it didn't take him long to quickly become a star. He was voted MVP by fellow Steelers players that season, pulling in 69 catches with 1,108 yards and two touchdowns. He also averaged just over 27 yards per kickoff return and 10 yards per punt return.

Brown was voted to the Pro Bowl and seemed to also have a place in the hearts of Steelers fans. Always flashing a big smile, he became a huge fan favorite for his play on the field and his outgoing personality, often talking to fans on Twitter and telling them to always remember: "chest up, eyes up."

The 2012 season was a frustrating one for Brown, as an ankle injury against the Giants in November forced him to miss three games, and by season's end he caught 66 passes for 787 yards with five touchdowns. He was taken off kickoff returns, but did return 27 punts for 183 yards, close to seven yards per return.

Moving forward, Brown has already spoken about being the leader of the Steelers wideout corps and teaching the young players of the Steelers the ways to do things. If he tackles being a leader like the way he has everything else, there's no question Brown will continue to be a huge success.

98 "Coach Dad," Dick LeBeau

"Dick LeBeau is arguably the best ever to coach defense." Those are the words of former Eagles quarterback and current NFL analyst

Dick LeBeau came to the Steelers in 1992 and served as defensive coordinator from 1995 to 1997. He returned to Pittsburgh in 2004. The Steelers have won two Super Bowls with LeBeau running the defense.

Ron Jaworski when it comes to longtime Steelers defensive coordinator Dick LeBeau. And he's right. LeBeau, who has had two tours of duty with the Steelers, is considered a defensive genius, and for all the right reasons. He has had a successful NFL career both as a player and a coach, and in August 2010 was honored for his legacy with induction into the Pro Football Hall of Fame.

LeBeau's playing career saw him play his college ball for the legendary Woody Hayes at Ohio State, then move on to star in the defensive backfield for 14 seasons with the Detroit Lions. He had a solid NFL career, putting up 62 career picks with the Lions for 762 yards and three touchdowns. He was also a three-time Pro Bowl selection.

The coaching legacy of LeBeau started in 1973 as an assistant with the Philadelphia Eagles. He moved on to the Green Bay Packers in 1976 and then joined the Cincinnati Bengals in 1980. He started in Cincy as their defensive backs coach and then became their defensive coordinator in 1984. He had a big impact on the Bengals' defense and helped them win three AFC Central Division titles in 1981, 1988, and 1990, and they won the AFC twice, in '81 and '88.

His first stint with the Steelers started in 1992 as the team's secondary coach. He helped some of the Steelers' stars such as Carnell Lake and Rod Woodson become even better, and after Dom Capers left the team, LeBeau was named the club's defensive coordinator in 1995. In his first year at the position, LeBeau helped the defense make it to the Super Bowl, and their defense did their part in almost upsetting the Cowboys in Super Bowl XXX.

LeBeau moved back to the Bengals in 1997, and within a few seasons his zone blitz scheme that he has mastered took form. By 2000 he took over as the head man for the Bengals and was their head coach for three seasons before being let go after the 2002 season. He then went on to be an assistant with the Buffalo Bills before going back to the Steelers in 2004.

It is this second go-around with the Steelers that has finally put LeBeau on the map and given the Hall of Famer the credit he deserves. His defenses, led by the zone blitz and fire zone, have wreaked havoc on opposing offenses. The Steelers have won two Super Bowls with LeBeau running the defense again, and he has made countless stars of players using his system.

He also was able to make the transition from one head coach to another. When Bill Cowher stepped down after 2006, LeBeau stuck around for new coach Mike Tomlin. It paid off with a huge 2008 and LeBeau running one of the best Steelers defenses ever. They led the NFL in total yards allowed (237.2 per game), against the pass (156.9), and in points allowed per contest with just 13.9.

The defense was a big reason for the team's sixth Super Bowl win over Arizona in February 2009, and LeBeau was the mastermind behind it. Despite now being in his seventies, LeBeau shows no signs of slowing down—this after more than 50 years in the NFL. His players refer to him as "Coach Dad," and he's been a huge reason behind the success of the Steelers' defense in the years he's been in the Steel City.

99 Gary Anderson

When it comes to kickers, it's a thankless job. The good ones are much more recognized now than in years past. When you talk about great Steelers kickers, the one name that has to come to mind first is longtime kicker Gary Anderson. He kicked for the Steelers from 1982 to 1994, and while most football fans remember him for one missed kick in 1998 with the Minnesota Vikings, his career with the Steelers was one that saw him always at or near the top when it came to the game's best kickers.

Born in 1959 in South Africa, Anderson's father was an Irish-born Protestant pastor and a former professional soccer player. Gary looked to follow in his dad's footsteps and play in Europe, but it was a twist of fate that saw him eventually playing American football.

Anderson was practicing soccer on a high school field in Pennsylvania, kicking field goals with a rugby ball. The school's high school football coach, Charles Chiccino, saw him kicking and got Anderson tryouts for four colleges, including Syracuse, where Anderson landed.

The kicker was promised a spot on the football and soccer teams, and he played both for two seasons before finally deciding to play just football in 1980. He was drafted by the Buffalo Bills after graduation in the 1982 NFL Draft, but the seventh-round pick was cut before the season. It took just a few days for the Steelers to pick up Anderson, starting a 13-year career that saw him become an unlikely fan favorite.

The one-bar face mask kicker wearing No. 1 on his jersey always got cheers from the Steelers faithful when he took the field. He was 5'11", 193 pounds, and never was known for having the strongest leg but was always clutch when needed. He led the AFC

Anderson Shares Longest Field-Goal Record

While many felt that Gary Anderson never had the strongest leg, he proved otherwise on November 25, 1984, when he set the Steelers' franchise record with a 55-yard field goal at Three Rivers Stadium against the San Diego Chargers. Anderson had a 53-yard field goal against the Colts in 1984, and has three 52-yard field goals to his credit as well. Former Steelers kicker Kris Brown also has a 55-yard field goal on his résumé, that coming in the 2001 season at Arrowhead Stadium against the Kansas City Chiefs. Brown tried a franchise-record 44 field goals in that 13–3 season.

in scoring in both 1984 and '85, and was a Pro Bowl kicker in the '85 season. Even with that, he seemed to get better with age, though he did have some rather unimpressive seasons in 1986 (21-for-32 on field goals) and 1991 (23-for-33).

In 1992, when Bill Cowher took over as coach, Anderson was 28-for-36 on field goals, 77.8 percent. The '93 season was his best in black and gold—he went an amazing 93.3 percent on field goals, hitting on 28-of-30 as the team went 9–7 and was a wild-card team in the AFC. As the team reached the AFC Championship Game in 1994, Anderson again was good, hitting on 24-of-29 field goals and going 32-for-32 in extra points.

He played two seasons in Philadelphia, but it was one season in Minnesota that fans still remember Anderson for. That year was 1998, and the high-flying Vikings went 15–1 while Anderson hit an unreal 35-of-35 field goals and 59-for-59 extra points. With a chance to take his team to the Super Bowl, Anderson missed the biggest field goal of his life in the NFC Championship Game. It was a 38-yard field goal that he pushed wide left with the team up seven with just over two minutes to go that opened the door for Atlanta to tie and later win the game.

It was a kick that would haunt Anderson the remainder of his career, but not one that should take away his career with the Steelers, which sees him at the top of the list for points scored in the history of the franchise with 1,343. He has numerous other records with the Steelers, and fans still recall his smooth kicking form and one-bar face mask that made him a favorite in Pittsburgh for 13 seasons.

100 Keys to a Great Tailgate at Heinz Field

Those who do it every home week of the football season call it an art form. Some do it just a few times a season simply to get ready for a game. Whatever the case may be, if you have ever had the chance, tailgating at Heinz Field the day of a Steelers game is a football fan's rite of passage.

While fans in Kansas City, Green Bay, and even Cleveland feel they have the patent on tailgating, there are some serious fans who put that theory to the test in Pittsburgh come football season. Fans begin to fire up grills right when they are allowed in most of the lots around Heinz Field, which is five hours before kickoff.

Various Steelers fan clubs use home games to get together to tailgate, and usually can be found around the Gold parking lots, which are tough to get passes for but are the best tailgate lots around Heinz Field. Those lots always seem to have the best activity, and the ones that people target for the best gatherings.

As far as not getting into those Gold lots, there is quite a bit of parking elsewhere that is still close enough to the stadium to enjoy. Unreserved cash lots are both north and east of the Gold lots and usually end up being $20 to $30 a space. Most of those lots also welcome tailgaters, but you have to make sure of that before the coals get met with fire early on a Sunday morning.

Tailgating is most importantly about preparation. In order to have a successful tailgate at Heinz Field, or any stadium to see the

Steely McBeam

Yes, he wasn't exactly the most beloved mascot in the history of the NFL, but the Steelers did unveil an official mascot called "Steely McBeam" as part of their 75th anniversary. The mascot's name was selected from a pool of more than 70,000 suggestions from fans. He didn't catch on right away, as Steelers message boards on the Internet and columnists seemed to despise "Steely." Those who didn't like him even started a petition to stop him from being the team's mascot. Today, though, he is a little more accepted and can be seen at all Steelers home games at Heinz Field.

Steelers, you have to have the right stuff, and that starts with the food. Yes, a tailgate can be a disaster if you don't have the right food on hand. A couple types of meat usually is the most important product you have to provide if you really want to impress your guests: ground meat for hamburgers; hot dogs or another type of sausage; and the always popular wild-card meats, like steaks, pork, ribs, or otherwise. Screw up the meat portion of a tailgate at Heinz

Field, and your day can quickly go downhill no matter how well the Steelers play.

Bread to go along with the meat is another important ingredient. If you're planning on having those hot dogs encased with a bun, you'd better make sure you bring that along as well. Then there are the snacks that accompany the tailgate that usually start the event as the meat and other possible foods get heated up.

Chips, cheese and crackers, cookies, and small elements won't ruin a meal but can enhance it and usually are needed to get things started. Make sure that you make a complete list of what you will have on hand and that the foods all make sense. It's also helpful to go out of your way to grab it the day before.

Then there is the grill and the fire. A fire torch of some sort or matches along with lighter fluid are things you will need to make sure this tailgate goes the right way. Also make sure you do the right thing and clean the grill before you throw your meat on it.

Also make sure that everyone in your party knows where your tailgate is. As stated above, a lot of out-of-town groups like to come in and have their tailgates as close to Heinz Field as possible, but sometimes with the most popular lots sold out, it's simply not possible. That's why you need to get there as early as you can and have people's phone numbers on hand to let them know where you will be.

A proper tailgate is a great way to get your NFL Sunday at Heinz Field started. Even if you do it just once in your life, do yourself the favor and go all out and tailgate at Heinz Field for an experience you will never forget.

Acknowledgments

I dedicate this book first and foremost to my Lord and Savior, Jesus Christ. For without Him, none of this would be possible. To my mom and dad, who have stood by me over the years and supported me in anything that I do. I love you both more than words, and thank you for your support in my love for the Steelers, this despite it not always being easy. You took me to training camp and games in Pittsburgh and allowed me always to watch my team, even when it conflicted with Browns games. Thank you!

To my wonderful wife, Shanna, and second family, who always seem to understand when a game or sporting event pulls me away from family events. To my three older brothers, John, Russell, and Mike, who, despite being Browns fans, have always been in my corner, as well. To the rest of my wonderful family and friends who have been there with a kind word over the years, I love you all dearly.

And to my church family at the Cleveland Baptist Church, more so to Pastor Kevin Folger, Pete Folger, Ron Van Kirk, Jack Beaver, Jeremy Cron, Doug Schweitzer, and my friends in the radio room. I appreciate your encouragement and keeping me grounded over the years during this incredible ride.

To my many friends in the media who have been so great to know over the years, Tony Rizzo, Jeff Sack, Dennis Manoloff, Tim Alcorn, Jenna Homrock, Bruce Drennan, Lindsey Foltin, and all the rest. You guys make being part of this industry a blast every-day. To my business partner and good friend, Sujeet Patel. And to Steeler Nation—the best fan base in sports—I hope you enjoy the book with all the great and even some not-so-great memories through the greatest franchise in sports.

Selected Bibliography

Books

Freedman, Lew. *Pittsburgh Steelers: The Complete Illustrated History.* Minneapolis, MN: MVP Books, 2009.

Mendelson, Abby. *The Pittsburgh Steelers, Revised and Updated: The Complete History.* Lanham, MD: Taylor Trade Publishing, 2005.

Ross, Alan. *Steelers Glory: For the Love of Bradshaw, Big Ben and the Bus.* Nashville, TN: Cumberland House, 2006.

Websites

answers.com
behindthesteelcurtain.com
coachdungy.com
ESPN.com
fanhuddle.com
hillboys.com
igosteelers.com
ironcitybrewingcompany.com
kdka.com
mcmillenandwife.com
merrilhoge.com
nfl.com
nfl.fanhouse.com
pabook.libraries.psu.edu
packers.com
pittsburghlive.com
PittsburghSteelers.co.uk
profootballhof.com
Pro-Football-Reference.com

Periodicals

Atlanta Journal Constitution
New York Times
Pittsburgh Post-Gazette
Pro Football Weekly
Sporting News
Sports Illustrated
Time
USA Today
profootballresearchers.org
rockybleier.com
sercc.com
sportsecyclopedia.com
SteelerGridiron.com
Steelers.com
thestate.com
wqed.org
YahooSports.com